# Manifestations:
## True Stories Of
## Bringing The Imagined
## Into Reality

Foreword By Kyra Schaefer

As You Wish Publishing, LLC

Connect@asyouwishpublishing.com

602-592-1141

ISBN-13: 978-1-951131-90-6

Library of Congress Control Number: 2019914077

Compiled by Kyra Schaefer

Edited by Todd Schaefer and Karen Oschmann

Printed in the United States of America.

Nothing in this book or any affiliations with this book is a substitute for medical or psychological help. If you are needing help please seek it.

As You Wish Publishing is committed to making a difference beyond the words you are about to read. Once we reached 101 author registrations we donated $500 to MillionLittle a 501c3 committed to helping traumatized children heal through creativity. An additional $40 was donated by individual authors to help with the cause.

Dedication

To those who wish to co-create a fuller, more profound life experience.

# Table of Contents

# Foreword
## By Kyra Schaefer

Manifestation is all around us. All the things you are currently experiencing were born from a place in you that said one of two things, "I don't want this anymore." And "I would love more of this, please."

It seems pretty straight forward. I want something, and I get it by thinking about it which seems easy enough. There is so much more to it than that. In the following pages, you will learn what it takes to become a master manifestor. The real people sharing their stories in this book are just like you. They knew life could be better and trusted; they could have what they desired. To get to the point where we can have a positive expectation fulfilled, is a process of growth, allowing, trust and patience. The authors of this book are here to show you anything is possible. From miraculous healing, allowing in financial abundance, romantic relationships and more, you get to journey with them and learn what they have done to let in more of what they want so you can as well. If you have this book in your hands, it's a good bet you have already accepted your manifestation quest and are on your way to allowing in more love, kindness and abundance.

**The best way to use this book:**

I recommend reading through the table of contents and flipping to the page that resonates the most with your current situation. You may find insights and wisdom from an author that you haven't read before. You may also find a connection with an author as you learn you are never alone in this world.

I also recommend that you hold the book between your hands and ask a question, such as: "What is the message I need to most hear in my present situation?" Let the book open to any page. You may find the answer comes quickly from the writing in this book.

Your creation abilities may improve as you read these stories and gain insight. Some of the stories may hold wisdom and secrets for your explore for yourself. You get to decide how you would like to experience this work. We hope that you will get what you need and expand with more positivity and gain new awareness along the way.

**What this book isn't:**

The articles in this book are not for those looking to get warm, fuzzy, and cuddly feelings. The articles are from real, genuine, and down-to-earth people. They don't sugarcoat the reality of their experiences. At the same time, they are unapologetic in their approach to taking the leaps in their lives that were necessary for their growth and development. I applaud the wit and bravery, the raw vulnerability and the integrity of the authors in this book. This is real life, my friends. It's hard, it's authentic, and there are unimagined gifts that reside here.

When we take the leap toward manifesting more of what we desire in our lives it's not always easy. In many ways, it may seem impossible. If you have reached for this book, there is something here for you.

You may like to join our Facebook group and find daily manifestations guidance at:
www.facebook.com/groups/manifestationscreations

# Do You Believe In Magic?
# By Rollie Allaire

That's an interesting question. I believe. Not in the "wave your magic wand" kind of magic, but "I can make things happen in my life" kind of magic.

Several years ago, I discovered I was Métis. What I learned from my Aboriginal beliefs was the energy of Moon Medicine. Over the years, I've learned from many inspiring people, like an elder who taught me to "take what I need and leave the rest." Over the years, I've taken what has resonated and left what hasn't. I urge you to do the same.

Did you know that Grandmother Moon revolves around Mother Earth in about 28-29 days? And that Aboriginal peoples refer to the menstrual cycle as *moon time*? There's a strong connection between the Moon and menstruation, as well as mood. This has been known for years, but it's been ignored until recently.

When menses is entered, it's referred to as a *dark period*. Reflection is inward, and this is the New Moon. This is when female bodies cleanse and clear in preparation for the intention of giving birth. Two weeks later, the body ovulates and prepares for pregnancy at a Full Moon.

This is a lot like manifesting to the Moon's energy. At the New Moon, we set intentions for what we want in our lives, and by the Full Moon, we're nurturing our life to seed it, or we're birthing it, much like the Moon's cycle.

Each month, the Moon rotates the Earth. The sky's dark as Grandmother Moon reflects inward at the New Moon. This is a time to take stock—when the Moon and the Sun are on the same side of Mother Earth. To Earth, it looks like the dark side of the Moon is facing us.

Historically, women took this time away from everyone, as it represents the menstrual cycle. It's a time to retreat and regain strength to start again, to "reboot intensely." Visualize filling yourself up to recharge under this New Moon, and purge all unwanted thoughts and excess "junk."

As Grandmother Moon makes her appearance, we see only a sliver as she moves into the Waxing Crescent. This is the time when the sun moves closer to the moon and begins to lighten up. A crescent appears until it grows into a First Quarter Moon.

This is the time for setting intentions, hopes, and wishes—for laying the mental groundwork on projects, developing intentions, writing checks to the universe, or burying your crystals. After recharging under the newness of Grandmother Moon, your desires are ready to be planted.

By the time she reaches the First Quarter, we're now taking action. A week after the New Moon, we're now executing our plan, as Grandmother Moon reveals more of herself.

This is when obstacles appear, and we begin to feel resistance. The time for rest and setting your intentions are over, and it's time to work harder than ever. Things will be thrown, and you may need to make decisions on the spot. Stay calm and be flexible. Make decisions that will bring you closer to your desired outcome. Keep focused on your desires.

Write yourself a daily to-do list or keep a journal to track everything you are doing to move through this resistance. As you complete each task, cross it off.

The Moon continues to grow as she moves into the Waxing Gibbous phase. It's easily seen during the day, because a large portion of it is illuminated. This is the time when we're making adjustments, refining, and editing our goals.

Grandmother Moon illuminates into a Full Moon when the Moon and Sun are on opposite sides of Mother Earth and appear fully to us. They are also in different zodiac signs. At this time, we fight to balance between the two extremes. This heightens tension, creating high emotions. It's important to not get emotionally attached to anything during this time.

New opportunities may appear, or you may see results from your hard work. This is the time to reap the benefits of the seeds of intention that you sowed at the New Moon. Be open to receiving these.

Grandmother Moon becomes less illuminated as she moves towards the Last Quarter into another New Moon in the Waning Gibbous phase.

Now you should feel the benefits of your recent hard work. You should see an abundance of the "crops," even if it's only small outcomes to the intentions you set. This is a good time to give to those around you—feel the love.

From the Full Moon, the Moon wanes (becomes smaller) into the Gibbous Moon, and then becomes the Last Quarter, making our way back to another New Moon.

As the Moon decreases, it's important now to be ready to let go. As we live life, things like being hurt, broken, and anger surface. This is when we release our anger and let go of grudges.

Purging rituals are extremely important to allow new intentions to become present. This is where the saying "get rid of the old to make room for the new" comes from.

Now there is only a sliver of Grandmother Moon lit up and decreasing as it moves towards the New Moon in this final phase. Waning Crescent phase is the time to surrender, rest, and recuperate. You've now gone through an entire cycle—things have come and gone—willingly or not.

You'll be preparing to set new intentions with the new cycle, but not during this Moon. Simply relax and surrender to the universe.

All of this happens by connecting with that inner-self we all have inside. We have our true life's purpose. We have the power within to tap into those areas in our life where we want to see magic happen in our lives.

*"Be the change you wish to see in the world." ~ Gandhi*

When we connect from within and work with the magic in the world, this quote becomes increasingly true.

# I Got The Job...Or Did I?
# By Linda Ballesteros

Have you ever had a job that made you dread Monday morning?

Maybe you have had a narcissistic boss who took credit for your ideas and only looked for opportunities to advance their career.

I am not sure what came first, the narcissistic boss, or my thirst for change. All I know is that at the end of the day, I had to make some changes, but I didn't know where to start.

I had recently begun reading Florence Scovel Shinn's books, *Your Word is your Wand, The Game of Life and How to Play It,* and *The Power of the Spoken Word*, where I was introduced to affirmations.

What could it hurt to try Shinn's philosophy?

The worse that could happen was—nothing.

The first step was to create a series of affirmations stating that I already have what I want. I wasn't sure how that was going to influence the situation, but I said I would give it a try, so here we go.

I created about five or six affirmations, which I wrote on index cards and kept in my car to read at every opportunity, especially during my long daily commutes. Several were so totally opposite of my current situation that they almost got stuck in my throat. Like, "I have the best boss." How can I possibly say this out loud multiple times a day when I don't believe it?

Within a few days, I noticed less and less resistance and found that the affirmations flowed with ease when I spoke them. Saying them upon getting into the car, at red lights, in gridlock traffic, and before getting out of the car now became part of my routine and part of the game. The dread of walking into the building became less prevalent, and I began to feel lighter.

One morning as I scrolled the internal job postings, which I did every morning, there was a position that jumped off the screen almost as if it were highlighted. I felt an excitement even though this was not an area in which I had any experience. The position was in a division that had recently relocated to Texas from New York. Before I knew what happened, I had applied for it.

The rest of the day, I noticed "mind bugs" or self-doubt popping up.

"These people are from New York. I am sure they are so much smarter and more professional than me."

"What if I am not smart enough to do the job?"

"They are probably laughing at my submission right now."

Despite the negative thoughts, I continued saying the affirmations, which again, I found comforting and seemed to quiet the mental chatter.

Within a couple of days, I received a call from human resources (HR). They wanted to schedule an interview with the division manager over the posted position. This position was at another campus, so I would need to coordinate the interview after work. I certainly would not want my ego-driven boss to know that I was looking to leave his empire.

The interview was scheduled, and HR provided all the details. Again, the self-doubt I had prior reared its ugly head. You see, I was genuinely stepping outside my comfort zone because I was good at what I did. I was well-respected, not only by my peers, but also by local executives. Texas regional directors would reach out for my assistance on projects.

What am I doing?

Am I making a mistake?

It took a lot to quiet the voices this time, but by the time I arrived for my interview, I had a sense of *knowing* that this position was mine. When I walked through the front door of the beautiful brand-new building, it felt familiar. I knew exactly where to go and looked at the people on the elevator as if I had seen them before.

The interview went well, and when I got to my car, I called my husband and said, "I got the job!" Being an executive of large companies, he was surprised that they would offer me the position on the spot.

Oh, they haven't offered me the position. I just know that it is mine.

The next morning, the phone was ringing as I walked into my office. I was not surprised when it was HR. In a split second, I could see myself packing up my office and mapping a new route to work.

"Linda, I wanted to let you know that you did *not* get the job."

Wait—what did she say?

Before I could respond, she continued.

"However, they were so impressed with you and what you can bring to their team that they have created a position for you."

It worked!

I was so excited because, for the first time in my life, I felt that I was an active participant in the outcome of a situation. In that instant, I knew my days of feeling like a victim were over. This not only shifted my approach to challenges, but it changed my mindset forever.

Don't get me wrong.

This does not mean that my life has been Shangri-La since. It means that I discovered a power within that we are all born with, and I tapped into it to create a situation that was for my highest and best good.

If you have used affirmations with little or no success, I encourage you to revisit the exercise with deliberate intention and focus. Once you have created a set of affirmations to support what is best for you, use visualization to tap into the emotions of *having* it. Emotions act as the gas pedal when manifesting. The more emotions and feelings you put into your visualization, the quicker you will be on the receiving side of making your wishes come true.

Now, start manifesting!

# You Can Have Anything
## By Kim Balzan

I have always heard that you can have and do whatever you want in this world. It took me years to understand and wrap my head around this concept—it felt like 40 years of struggles.

Over the years, I have learned the power of manifesting and having burning desires that come to be right in front of my eyes! I will tell you that I had a little trouble accepting some of the things that I had manifested, because I was shocked when they arrived.

Today, I know and understand the power of gratefulness, of having joy in your heart. We need to take time to be truly grateful, even if only for being alive. All of us have so many things going on every day, and we keep running everywhere, not taking breaks. I know this because I have done it, and it didn't feel good! I now know to take that time to be grateful and to manifest what I want my life to be. Manifesting may not seem easy at first—it takes practice and patience.

By manifesting, I have created a successful holistic practice that is constantly growing, and my plan is going worldwide. I am living in the house of my dreams, and am married the man of my dreams. I am driving cars that I manifested down to the color I wanted. I could go on and on about so many things—some of them are funny. One was a steamer trunk for my clothes that I found abandoned in a parking lot, and to this day, I still use and love it!

The thing about manifesting is, you have to act as if you already have what you want. Now for me starting out, I would sometimes fake it because I couldn't believe it could be so easy. Of course, some things may take more time than others. You also have to pay attention because there will be times things you want are right in front of your face, but you are not aware or awake to your life.

So if you are wondering how to change your life and start getting what you want in every category, I will tell you what has worked for me and has helped so many of my clients.

I like using a vision board. This is something you can make easily, cutting out words and pictures that resonate with what you want your life to be. Once it is made, you need to put it somewhere that you will see it every day. So much so that, even when you can't see it, you can still imagine everything that is on it. I mean, you can be driving in your car and see in your mind everything that is on your board.

Put only what you absolutely love on this vision board, and also know that sometimes you will pull off a picture or two and replace them with something else that you love. When you look at this board, truly memorize what is on it.

Close your eyes and meditate, see yourself in the places you have on your board. Maybe it's Italy—see yourself looking at fields of sunflowers. Imagine you are walking down a cobblestone street. Say to yourself silently or aloud, "I love how the cobblestones feel on my feet as I walk. I love seeing and hearing people speaking Italian in the streets. I love the way the air smells at lunchtime with the scents of homemade pasta and pizza!" Act as if you are there, and it will seem, in your mind, that you *are* there. This is powerful manifesting. Thank the universe for all of your wonderful travels to Italy!

The power of our minds is incredible. If this is hard for you to understand, then look at it as daydreaming with a purpose.

Another tool that I use daily is working with crystals. Quartz crystal, in particular, is what is called *programmable*, meaning you can hold the crystal in your hand, and you may say, "When I hold you, it brings me peace and calmness," or, "I feel joy within in me instantly." Maybe you want it to help release fears you may have. Crystals are beautiful, and there are a lot to choose from. Today they are everywhere because they work and have been around for thousands of years. You can go to rock shops or even look on the Internet. When you find the perfect stone for you, find an intention that you can say to your stone.

I recently sold our last home, and I swear it was from manifesting and using crystals. I used a beautiful picture of our home, and I put special crystals wherever my hand was drawn to put them on this picture. I realized that it created something called a crystal grid.

A few years ago, I went to one of the largest gem and mineral shows. I had parked my car and started walking through numerous booths that were set up and tons of people. I felt drawn to start walking a totally different way than I had planned, and felt like I was on a mission! All of sudden, I walked into a tent and grabbed a huge crystal—it had to be about eight to ten inches long—and walked up to the man and said, "I think I want to buy this." The man laughed and said, "That is an extremely powerful crystal you picked out. It's a Lemurian crystal." I had no idea what it was, but I knew I had to have it. Know that when you are picking a crystal, it will probably draw you right to it! This crystal is special to me, and I use it all the time.

May you be blessed to know and believe that you can create the life that you want to live and experience!

# When The Soul Whispers
# By Kristi Blakeway

*"Listen to your heart and your intuition.*
*They know exactly what you want to become." ~ Steve Jobs*

We each have a little voice inside us—the voice that guides us, questions us, or stops us in our tracks. Sometimes it makes sense. Sometimes it doesn't—or at least we can't make sense of it at the time. I am a firm believer in trusting my gut even when it makes little sense to do so. There is a knowledge that exists below our conscious surface that often comes to us in a whisper.

A few times in my life, I have listened to this whisper, and I've been amazed at the unexplainable wisdom that comes from within. These moments are perplexing, as they defy reason, yet they are significant enough to convince me that our souls have a way of guiding us in the right direction. I have also had moments in my life where I have ignored intuition, and let logic rule, only to find myself steered off track. The older I get, the more I am convinced that true happiness comes from aligning my actions with the whispers of my soul.

**Voicemail for Jen**

I met my best friend, Jen, before the days of cell phones. We instantly formed the type of friendship that remains strong regardless of how often we connect. One evening, when Jen was pregnant with her first child, I had an intense gut feeling. I sensed Jen was about to go into labor. Wondering if I was right, I phoned her house and reached her voicemail. Knowing she had relatives in town, I suspected she might be out for dinner.

"Jen, it's me. I have a crazy feeling. You are going to have your baby tonight. It's a boy. He's going to be born at 9:18 p.m.!"

I hung up, knowing Jen would laugh at the ridiculousness of my message. Hours later, my phone rang. Jen's voice was a whisper—I assumed she didn't want to wake her houseguests.

"Friend, I had a baby. It's a boy, born at 9:18 p.m."

"Ya, right! You did not! Were you out for dinner?"

"Kristi—I am telling you I had a baby. It's a boy, born at 9:18 p.m."

"Jen—you listened to my message."

"What message?"

This continued for a few minutes while I waited for Jen to laugh, and she waited for me to celebrate. When her husband took the phone and confirmed their son's birth, it sunk in. Jen had a baby boy, and I had one of the first unexplainable moments where I had listened to my intuition.

## Lottery Ticket

My husband and my boys are big sports fans. During football season, they buy lottery tickets to bet on NFL football games. One afternoon, I told them I was going to bet too. They laughed and asked how I would know who to bet for, as I am the furthest thing from a sports fan. I laughed and told them I would trust my gut. I filled my ticket with 13 teams that had the most vowel sounds, such as the Philadelphia Eagles and the Cincinnati Bengals. The next day, we sat stunned, as I correctly predicted the first 12 wins.

The 13th game was scheduled for Monday night. We knew I wouldn't have a perfect ticket, as the first-place team was playing the last-place team, and I had chosen the underdog as they had more vowels. My family stared in disbelief while I jumped in amazement! I had a perfect ticket! We were about to win thousands of dollars! My husband sat me down and said, "I'm sorry. There was no chance your team was going to win. I thought I was helping. I changed your ticket." My ticket did win us a few hundred dollars, but the lesson was worth more. Occasionally, logic doesn't have all the answers. Sometimes, it's okay to trust your gut even when it makes absolutely no sense.

## Nanna

I had a beautiful connection with my grandmother, whom I called Nanna. We spent every summer together at our family cabin. One summer evening, while grocery shopping with my husband, I reached down to pick up a bottle of ketchup, and I froze. He asked what was wrong. I looked up and told him it was Nanna. I knew she was not okay. We called our family cabin to learn an ambulance had been called. Again, I can't explain how I knew, but I am glad I lived that moment. Nanna is no longer with us, but knowing our connection ran deeper than the explainable gives me the confidence to believe I can still connect with her on a spiritual level.

## Listening to Logic

Six years ago, my husband and I debated whether we should uproot our family from our quiet suburb and move closer to the city. We made a list of pros and cons, and the pro list was longer, so we decided to move. After settling in for a few months, I finally had the courage to ask my husband if he liked our new home as much as he expected. In seconds, he answered, "No!" Despite many plusses, it didn't feel like our home. On paper, our move had made sense, but we forgot to ask the crucial question: "What *felt* right for our family?" Once we asked this question, we knew what we had to do. Six months to the day after moving in, we moved back to our quiet suburb. Our realtor went on vacation with her extra income, and we settled into our new house, knowing in our hearts we were once again home.

We all have an inner voice—a compass that guides us to where we are meant to be. When we are brave enough to listen, and we align our hearts with our actions, we find exactly what we are looking for.

# Butterfly Dreams
# By Kristi Blakeway

*"What if I fail? Oh, my darling, what if you fly?"* ~ *Erin Hanson*

Books are magical. We can all think of our favorite story as a child or a book that inspired us, challenged us, or shifted our thinking. Books offer an escape, where readers can cuddle up, lose track of time, and feel like they are part of the story. For as long as I can remember, I have wanted to create that magic and write a book. I love the idea of spreading good in our world and wanted to write a book that could give back to those in need. Writing a book hung in limbo as a lifetime goal—one I imagined, but one I did not know how to achieve.

As a school principal, my life is busy. Spare moments are infrequent, and I have to be quite intentional in finding time to write. I started by creating a blog. Luckily, people other than my mom began to read and share my work, and I slowly gained confidence as a writer. I blogged about education and documented my students' experiences helping the homeless in Canada's poorest neighborhood. Blogging became my risk-free way to share my thoughts with the outside world. I realized that taking the time to write gave me the ability to organize my thoughts and determine what mattered most to me. Despite this, the thought of writing a book still seemed daunting. Who would my audience be? What would I write about? How would I find a publisher? I shifted my focus and spent time sharing stories through public speaking engagements. My book remained a distant dream.

As my life continued to run at a hectic pace as a mom, wife, and principal, I began to realize that writing actually helped me slow down. Writing soothed my soul and grounded me. I began to see writing as a gift of self-compassion, and I dreamed of the day I could combine my love of storytelling and writing. Despite this, my dream of a published book was still in the "one-day" column, and not something I imagined in the short term.

As I ignored my internal nudge, I noticed I was developing a strange habit. Each weekend, I would head to Costco under the premise that I was gathering our weekly groceries. Once inside, I would let my cart drift towards the book aisle. I would pretend to shop for books, but actually, I was imaging my book nestled neatly amongst the bestsellers. I was beginning to manifest my future.

In February of 2019, an ad popped into my Facebook feed advertising an International Women's Summit, hosted by Celebrate Your Life Events. A friend and I signed up, eager to hear inspiring speakers such as Elizabeth Gilbert, Glennon Doyle, and Cheryl Strayed. The event was magical, renewing, and uplifting. On the second day, I heard Zainab Selbi speak. Zainab spoke about her work helping women from war-torn countries. Years into her work, after meeting every typical measure of success, she realized she wasn't telling *her* story. She was inviting women around the world to be vulnerable and speak out, but she wasn't sharing her personal story. In this moment, I saw my book. Like Zainab, I had been writing about others for years, finding ways to help, but I wasn't weaving in my individual story. The word *weave* stuck in my mind, and I started to see chapters unfold right in front of me.

As ideas began to flow, I found a quiet corner in the hotel lobby and started to write logical ideas in sequential order. Unfamiliar with visualization, I focused on practical steps I would need to take. As I sat, concentrating on my list, I experienced one of the most powerful moments of my life. With no warning, I visualized a bright yellow butterfly rising up, floating right through my mind. I sat there, stunned. What had happened? Where did this image come from? What did this mean? The image was so vivid, I knew I was meant to experience it. It was a symbol of transformation.

I headed home, inspired by the conference, and ready to start writing. I knew I was on the right path. I set up my writing space, free of clutter, near our front window. I perched a ceramic yellow butterfly on my desk as a reminder of my call to write. It became my inspiration piece.

Two weeks into this journey, Kyra Schaefer, from As You Wish Publishing, popped up on the Celebrate Your Life Facebook page. She reached out to CYL guests and invited us to join her in her collaborative book, *Inspirations: 101 Uplifting Stories for Daily Happiness*. I signed up that day. Kyra and her husband, Todd, walked me through the journey of becoming a collaborative author, and helped me understand how a book goes from the idea phase to print.

By June of 2019, I took the leap and signed up with As You Wish Publishing to write my book. As I began to write, in my newly created space, I heard a tap on the window. As I looked up, the largest yellow butterfly I have ever seen circled through our front porch, danced in the sunlight, and returned to rest on our windowpane. I smiled, knowing it was meant to be.

In November of 2019, my book, *Beyond Hello*, was released. My dream came true, and my book now sells on Amazon and in local bookstores. With each book sold, a donation is made to buy a meal for someone living on the streets. My book may not be at Costco yet, but I will keep manifesting, and hoping my yellow butterfly guides me where I am meant to go. We each have the ability to listen to our hearts and turn the imagined into reality.

*"Just when the caterpillar thought the world was over, it became a butterfly." Barbara Haines Howett*

# Magic Happens In Circles
## By Gillian Campbell

Have you ever manifested something that you needed at the right time?

I still remember the moment my husband walked in the door, crying and holding a piece of paper, and said, "It's a brain tumor." I was at the dining room table with my two-year-old son, coloring, while my two-month-old baby girl was asleep in a wrap on my chest. Scott had recently returned home from his doctor's visit, where he received results from a CT scan. He had been experiencing what the doctors call sensory seizures. Scott explained this as being similar to sleeping on your arm for too long until it falls asleep and becomes tingly when you try to move it. The sensory seizures would start in one part of his body and travel all the way down to his toes. It was sometimes painful, but each time it happened, he was filled with worry and wonder. Doctors told him maybe it was a pinched nerve, or maybe it was something else. There was no urgency for them to dig deeper for the cause as it wasn't affecting Scott's functioning, so he lived with those seizures for nearly two years. They became more frequent until, finally, he found a doctor who made him an appointment for a CT scan. That day changed all of our days since.

I don't even remember how I made it through those first few years, but I do remember thinking I needed more support in my life—support that was different from any relationship I had previously held in my life. I sought it out, and what I found was exactly what I needed. I found a women's sharing circle, which was, essentially, a circle of healing, love, and support.

Between my postpartum depression and Scott's brain cancer diagnosis, we were putting one foot in front of the other. The fear was overwhelming. Fear of the future, fear of being a single parent, fear of my children not growing up with their dad or getting to know him, and fear of losing the love of my life. Once fear takes hold of your life, it can drag you to some extremely dark places.

I am grateful for my children during that time. As much as I struggled in those first few years of motherhood, I know now that my children were given to me to help me see the new, the curious, and the innocence in life even in dark times.

I vaguely recall how I found the circle. I believe it started with a conversation with a colleague about feeling drained of energy. We chatted about alternate ways of finding strength, and energy healing came up. I googled it and found someone. She was like a warm hug in everything she said. She emitted so much love, light, and acceptance for me, which I had not felt in a long time. After my first meeting with her, I could feel myself gaining the energy and confidence to move forward. She helped me to realize that I had the power to help myself. She led me to her sharing circle for women. Through this circle, I found the most beautiful and supportive strength in myself and in the circle. This was when I discovered that I had the power to create what I wanted in my life through my thoughts, actions, and perceptions. Magical things happen in circles.

Throughout history, women's circles have been a fundamental part of many societies to strengthen and support sharing, healing, and connection. Jean Shinoda Bolen, a Jungian analyst and activist, writes, "When women come together and make a commitment to each other to be in a circle with a spiritual center, they are creating a vessel of healing and transformation for themselves, and a vehicle for change in their world."

The tools used in our circle are applicable to my life, and I continue to use them on a daily basis to guide me through ups and downs. Intentions include living heart-first rather than head-first, giving myself love, respect, and boundaries, and practicing self-compassion. From this place of knowing, I can then give love, boundaries, and compassion to others in a much more authentic way.

I continually practice respecting myself enough to consistently give myself time for meditation and quiet time to reflect. I am reminded that there are cycles and rhythms of life (seasons, moon, growth), and I recognize that we also experience cycles and rhythms. Growth is a dance; there will be good days, and there will be bad days, but each good day gives me the strength to look at bad days with the lens of what I have learned since the last bad day. Every bad day or moment or situation will have a lesson in it. And finally, I remember to practice gratitude. Gratitude for all that life brings us: gratitude for the lessons, gratitude for the struggles, and gratitude for the successes. We are all human and will all have times of light and times of darkness in our lives. The perspective we take creates a space from which to respond to these challenges.

I now know that I manifested what came into my life: the love, the support, the healing, the journey, all of it. I decide on a daily basis what I am allowing into my life and what I am allowing to flow through me. It is with gratitude that I am on this journey in life. I am manifesting my life. My thoughts, my actions, my time, and my attention all contribute to where I am going and what life-lesson I will learn next. I will continue to grow and learn and manifest my hopes, desires, and dreams. While our family continues to navigate the challenges that come with cancer and cancer treatment, we continue to find gratitude in everyday life and having the opportunity to heal. Knowing that you have the power, what will you manifest?

# The Amazing Power Of The Heart
# By Janet Carroll RN

It's time.

**H**ave you noticed there are big changes going on in the world around us, as well as big changes going on deep within ourselves? Have you noticed these changes are the biggest, most daunting, and most stressful changes that we have ever encountered before? And, have you noticed that the old ways of surviving and thriving no longer work? We must now think differently and in new ways to be able to survive and to thrive.

Like me, we've all been taught that the brain is the most important and powerful organ in the body. Surprise! It's actually the heart! Who knew?

Did you know that if you can achieve a neurologic connection between the brain and the heart, you can shift into a *coherent* (harmonious and flowing) state? This is where the healing miracles of this unified connection take place physically, mentally, emotionally, and spiritually. The HeartMath Institute has been scientifically researching the heart for 30 years, and is now flourishing around the world. It has blown my socks off!

- Both the brain and the heart emit electro-magnetic energies:
  - The heart is 100 times more powerful electrically than the brain!
  - The heart is 5,000 times more powerful magnetically than the brain!
- The heart's feelings (gratitude, appreciation, compassion, love) will change your inner world.
  - For the first time, feelings are acknowledged as an essential component of healing.
- The heart is a sensory organ, has a "brain" consisting of 40,000 neurons called *sensory neurites*, is in constant

communication with the brain every minute of every day, and does most of the talking!

- The most powerful brain-heart connection, *coherence*, facilitates the merging of our physical, mental, emotional, and spiritual energies and is achieved with your heart-breath and concurrent feelings.
- On a daily basis, we live 5% of our day in our conscious patterns, and 95% in our sub-conscious patterns. This will take on new meaning later when I discuss what I learned about prayer and affirmations and how to make them powerful in this time of new ways of living.

## HeartMath Quick Coherence® Technique

"Coherence is the state when the heart, mind, and emotions are in energetic alignment and cooperation. It is a state that builds resiliency—personal energy is accumulated, not wasted—leaving more energy to manifest intentions and harmonious outcomes."
~ Dr. Rollin McCraty, Research Director, HeartMath Institute

Here is HeartMath's powerful (and basic) Quick Coherence® technique to connect your brain to your heart:

1. Gently and quietly, focus on your heart as you shift your awareness to your mid-chest.
2. Begin to breathe in and out slowly:
   a. Breathe *in* to a slow deep count of whatever rate feels best to you. (Ex: 1-2-3-4-5)
   b. Breathe *out* to a slow deep count equal to the length of your *in* breath. (Ex:1-2-3-4-5)
3. Now, imagine someone or something that brings the feelings of appreciation, gratitude, compassion, or love into your awareness.
4. Slowly and gently feel those feelings as you breathe *in* all the positive energy and fill your heart to a count that is comfortable for you. (Ex: 1-2-3-4-5.)

5. Slowly and gently breathe *out* at an equal rate to the *in* breath. Ex: 1-2-3-4-5
6. Repeat for 2-3 minutes.
7. Repeat at any time during your day to center, renew, and regenerate your body, mind, emotions, and spirit.

Please note: I have an "inner balance" device that records my heartbeat and lets me know to what degree I am in coherence.

## Affirmations and Prayers

"A thought that is imbued with the *power of emotion* produces the feeling that brings it to life. When this happens, we've created an affirmation as well as a prayer. Both are based in feeling, and more precisely, in feeling as if the outcome has already happened. Studies have shown that the clearer and more specific we are, the greater the opportunity for a successful result."
~ Gregg Braden, *The Spontaneous Healing of Belief*

It is through the emotional/feeling nature that affirmations and prayers are manifested. For example, most of us speak an affirmation or a prayer while in a conscious mental state, meaning that we are in our brain only. To powerfully manifest what we want, we must activate our feeling nature to gain access to the subconscious, where all our patterns of resistance lie. It is there that the affirmation/prayer and positive feelings can quickly change our patterns.

## Bottom Line

To catalyze a new level of power in manifesting your affirmations and prayers, do the HeartMath Quick Coherence® technique to achieve coherence and connect your brain to your heart. In that coherent state, imagine the affirmation/prayer and feel the feeling as though your desired outcome has already happened.

"The HeartMath technologies can help you calm your nervous system, manage your emotions, and quiet your thoughts. By learning a simple technique, you can stay in a calm, balanced place and function efficiently in the midst of change and fast-paced environments. The HeartMath technique Quick Coherence® includes focusing on the heart, changing your breathing pattern, and creating positive feeling. And by practicing with the Inner Balance or emWave2 technology, you can see the visual evidence of the body changing from stress mode into a calm and coherent mode. You can learn to quickly change your physiology and feel better physically, mentally, and emotionally."

~ www.HeartMath.org

# Tears Of Joy!
# By Melissa S. Casteel

W e've all had that moment—you feel a huge "A-ha," and your perspective, or your life, is completely changed. That's called a paradigm shift.

My intention here isn't to present information that you've already read. There is no new information. My intention is to present this information in a manner that could bring about a paradigm shift for you, an awareness you can create your greatest life!

The many times I watched (and thought I absorbed) the movie, *The Secret*, and felt face-to-face with Joe Vitale as he spoke the truth about creating our world—it never impacted me much. Then, while studying, I turned to the next chapter, and there it was:

"He thinks in secret, and it comes to pass:
Environment is but his looking-glass."~ James Allen, *As a Man Thinketh*

Wow! Immediately I saw myself with a beautiful hand mirror. I was looking at my face, the setting around me, my whole life—I did this! Whether good or not, whether I liked it or not, I am responsible!

I'm responsible? Well, my "manifestor" was obviously not working. Where was the house in the mountains I had visualized? And my successful coaching business, the slim body with the cute clothes, and the jet share program I desired? All these wonderful things I wanted, and nothing was manifesting! What was I doing wrong?

Now, don't get me wrong. I've had terrific manifesting experiences. I've manifested money for trips, jobs, and opportunities. I have created many things in my life, but I still want the house in the mountains and the slim body.

We've all had the experience of thinking about something—a cup of coffee, a few extra dollars, something wished for—and it simply shows up. Well, that goes the other way, too: something you don't want or you fear shows up in your life. Surely, I didn't create that. Yes, you did.

While looking for a definition that rang true for me, I ran across this at Vocabulary.com:

> "A *manifestation* is the public display of emotion or feeling, or something theoretical made real. Manifestation's origins are in religion and *spirituality*: If something *spiritual* becomes real, it is said to be a *manifestation*."

We manifest every day! Manifesting can be described as "making it real." You focus on a desire, meditate on it, visualize it, feel it, and you receive it and realize it. We are incredible beings of creation made of the same energy that creates universes! We can have, do, or be anything we choose or want.

In spring 2018, my husband, Tony, and I learned of an upcoming family reunion on South Padre Island, Texas. I have fond memories of going there as a young girl and didn't want to miss it. I know opportunities to see family members are limited, so I wanted to go! I said, "I want to take the whole family!" Tony said, "Sure," in an unconvincing tone, which meant we couldn't afford it. So, I tucked my sadness away, figuring the trip was a no go.

That afternoon, much to my amazement, a gift arrived from my father, in the form of a check, allowing us to pay for flights, a beautiful beach house, a rental car, and food! It was amazing! I was so excited and thrilled; I cried tears of joy!

I didn't realize what had happened until I saw that Tony was wide-eyed and flabbergasted at this turn of events! He stopped me dead in my tracks, grabbed me by my shoulders, and had me look at what I had manifested! Wow!

So, where does the seed of manifesting come from? The imagination. Absolutely everything is the product of someone's imagination. And that creation of the imagination grows in intensity and becomes manifested into reality.

Here are a few tips, ideas, and action steps you can use to create what you want:

First, take an inventory of what you are exposing yourself to. Do you watch television? How many hours per day are you dedicating to watching someone else living out their dream? How much time do you spend on social media? It would be nice if we could filter out the negative, but that isn't going to happen! Monitor your social media use. It can suck you in quickly. Also, consider the people you hang out with—are they building you up? If you don't leave them feeling better about yourself, reconsider the association. Keep in mind, you need to leave them better than you found them, too. That is a basic human responsibility.

Second, do you have a life script? Do you have a vision of where you want to be? What type of person do you want to be? Write that out. Create the perfect life for you, then record it on on your phone and listen to it frequently. Do you have a vision board? A vision board is a visual model of where you want to be. Create one and look at it daily.

There are only three steps to manifesting. Step one is asking, which we do all day, every day.

Step two is knowing the Universe always says yes.

Step three is receiving it or allowing it. That's where we can encounter a stumbling block, and we might think our manifestor is broken. It's not. There's nothing broken about you that you can't fix.

I use the term manifestor like it's a working piece of equipment that could wear out or break. You, as a physical being, are a marvelous manifestor, and you're busy every day manifesting your life, good or not. Make no mistake about it—you're creating your life on a daily basis. There is no manifestor equipment in you that can be broken. So, create the life of your dreams! Make the most of life!

I have learned that my manifestor needs the occasional polish—a review and renew that lights fires and creates the future I want as bright, beautiful, and bountiful! Create a life that brings you tears of joy!

# The Business Of Manifesting
# By Catherine Cates

I began my business 15 years ago, and it is still running, and it is profitable. I credit its success to manifesting. When my son was a toddler, I decided I wanted to own a business after having been in the corporate world for many years. My only requirement was to have a business that allowed me to work from home and provide the flexibility to be available to my young son.

That left questions for me to answer. What would my business be? What did I want to do? What could I offer? What am I capable of? And most importantly, how am I going to answer these questions?

We have been conditioned to ask who, what, where, when, why, and how. We don't need to. It's not our job to figure that out. When first letting go of the wheel to let source guide you, it's not always easy. It takes practice. Once you can let go of the questions and let source take over, it happens. I promise. It did for me and it will for you too.

Figuring it out with a book or talking to a career planner or forcing a business idea because it sounded good on paper didn't resonate with me. Instead, I went right to the source, literally, and asked for an idea.

Every day when my son napped, I meditated. Before meditating, I set my intention to inspire me with the "what" my business will be. Low and behold, one day that I'll never forget, I was walking through the Old Navy parking lot with my son and "bam," the inspiration hit! Just like that. That's frequently how it happens.

Answers and inspiration don't always come during meditation; they can come later, so always be on the look-out for them.

The Universe inspired me with the perfect business idea that married my needs and talents with a service that offered solutions to parents. In 2004, having an online business of that type was groundbreaking and translated into instant success. That was no coincidence because it was a divinely inspired business idea that I took inspired action to create.

Once my business was up and running, I followed my intuition daily to operate it. To figure out my next move, I stay connected to the divine. It is still running profitably today—mostly because I listen to my intuition. It is through our intuition that we communicate with the divine.

Following divine guidance by listening to our intuition, taking inspired action, and engaging our passion is a recipe for success. But it's not all of the story.

When we force, push, or second-guess is when our dreams don't always come true. Even if we want it, if we aren't aligned with inspired action, chances of it manifesting are smaller.

Manifesting uses the principles of the law of attraction, which states we must be a vibrational match to receive whatever we desire. Like attracts like. To be a vibrational match requires paying attention to your thoughts and keeping them positive, especially about what you desire. To bring in the energy of manifesting, beliefs must also be in alignment with what is desired.

Beliefs are extremely powerful and are critical to success in manifesting. They define our world, yet they have no meaning unless we give them meaning. For the best results, it is essential to cull out the ones that don't line up with our desires. Beliefs come in two types: limiting ("I can't do this!") or empowering ("Wow! I'm so excited to do this!"). Always take note of which types of beliefs you are harboring.

A classic book, yet still relevant, *Think and Grow Rich*, gives the perfect example of the importance of beliefs. The author, Napoleon Hill, interviewed 500 of the mega-wealthy of his day, such as the Rockefellers, Carnegies, and Vanderbilts, to discover their secret for creating wealth. The common denominator for all the tycoons was their belief in themselves, not their skill sets or intelligence, although certainly, those factored in. As a result, he coined the notable phrase that still stands today, "You must believe to achieve." I often add to it, "that which you are willing to receive."

One reason I was able to manifest so seamlessly is that I never once questioned if this was the right thing for me to do. I had no doubts or resistance. My beliefs were empowering, not limiting, which propelled me to run with it. I was confident in this decision because it was divinely inspired, and I could feel the resonance in it. It felt right. When you can feel that, there is no reason to doubt.

Letting go of doubt, fear, and anxiety will open a space to allow you to stand in your true divine power. In that space, you are connected to your intuition, and you know this is right for you. Having that certainty, act on the divine inspiration. That is when the magic, the manifesting happens.

We are all divine beings that have the ability to manifest anything we desire. We do it every day and don't realize it. Remember that parking spot up front you wanted and got? That's manifesting. Remember that coupon or discount code you wanted, and suddenly someone offered it to you? That's manifesting.

If you don't know you manifested or how you did it, it's hard to repeat it. Now is the time for us to remember that we can manifest and how to do it.

Step into your power. Know that you are a divine creator. Meditate to feel into that. Talk to the divine. Once you have this level of awareness, manifesting happens with ease. Troublesome thoughts float out of your mind, effortlessly. Belief systems that no longer resonate fall by the wayside. A calm, peaceful knowing overtakes you, and you feel connected. In this connection, you have wisdom and knowing. From this, take inspired action.

# Oh Lord, Won't You Buy Me a Mercedes Benz
# By AJ Cavanagh

When I was a child, my dad would say I could pull rabbits out of hats. It was his way of saying I could swiftly manifest the things that brought me joy. Most kids do. They usually don't have any thoughts opposite to what they want, unlike most adults. "Of course, you got that," he would say, or "What are the chances of him finding that?" Was it all good luck, the innocence of childhood, or a simple matter of timing and synchronicity?

In 1992 I moved out of home, and out of the country, to live and work in Canada. I had a steady job, a decent apartment, and an old Mazda that got me from A to B. I had made myself a new life and was fascinated by how thoughts turned into things.

I remember being out with my friend, Beverly, when a line from a Janice Joplin song, sprang to mind: "I've worked hard all my life, oh Lord, won't you buy me a Mercedes-Benz?" We laughed, and right then, I decided to offer the universe a challenge: "If the law of attraction is real, then I want a Mercedes-Benz," I said out loud. We both chuckled and sang the song's familiar verse satirically. But I was serious! Asking for a Mercedes-Benz was the most unlikely thing I could request. My menial salary made the challenge a good one—I knew I couldn't afford it then, or anytime soon!

We laughed it off, but the idea stuck. From then on, every time I was out in my old Mazda, I pretended I was driving a Benz. I imagined the experience of sitting in large leather seats and the joy of coasting down the highway. The fun part in my asking was it did not come from lack or longing—it came from a belief that an abundant universe would provide. I loved allowing myself to "play-big" by wishing for something as grand as a Mercedes-Benz, and I imagined it existed somewhere and was already mine.

I decided not to worry about *how* I was going to get it and focus instead on the experience of owning one. Another few months went by, and I was still driving my used Mazda, and then the magic started. One afternoon, for a few seconds, I felt as if I actually *was* driving a Mercedes-Benz! The steering wheel seemed much larger, and the car, spacious. I remember thinking, "I genuinely *do* feel this," but a few seconds later, the sensation was gone.

Then disaster struck, or so it seemed. One Saturday morning, I turned the ignition, and nothing happened. Not even a click. Beverly sent over her mechanic. "I'll have to tow it back to the shop," he said, "I can't see why it won't start."

The next day he called, "Your car is ready to be picked up. It started today, no problems." Great! I arrived at his shop soon after, and to my astonishment, saw my old Mazda parked beside no less than five Mercedes-Benz cars! I laughed and said, "I'm amazed you have all these. It's been a dream of mine to own one." And he then told me a precious little story. His shop was around the corner from a popular Chinese restaurant, whose owner had a liking—no, a compulsion—for Mercedes-Benz. "I'm working on these for the owner who collects them. If you want one, I can sell you this." He pointed to an older dark-blue classic, with a caramel-leather interior. "He signed it over to me last week as payment, but it's taking up space here in the lot. You can have it for $2,100. That's how much I've put into it." It seemed the law of attraction had brought me a Mercedes-Benz after all!

And that's when my manifesting revved into top gear. I needed $2,100 in less than a week, and was able to sell my Mazda for the original price I paid for it almost two years earlier, which *coincidentally* was $2,100. From then on, there was no doubting the law of attraction, for it had delivered!

I loved that car and enjoyed telling others the story of how it came to me when my time-worn Mazda mysteriously wouldn't start. A few years later, I moved back to Australia for a new opportunity, and had to sell the beloved Benz!

Back in Australia, my Dad let me use his car until I could find a car for myself. I thought, "I wonder if I could do it again," and then let the idea go as perhaps pushing my luck. But I was astonished to see, only a few days later, a Mercedes-Benz for sale in our neighborhood. And you know what? It was the same make, model, year and color, inside and out, as the Mercedes I had left back in Vancouver! I rushed home and told my parents excitedly, "You'll never guess…" and my Dad replied, "There he goes, pulling rabbits out of hats again!" The price was right, and in a week, it was mine!

Had I discovered some kind of golden goose or magic genie? No, but what I had found was that everything has a vibrational frequency. By focusing my thoughts, I was able to match them to the frequency of the car of my dreams—twice! I never worried about how it would come or what others had to say, as this would create the opposite frequency of what I wanted to attract.

Our ability to manifest is not only a spiritual way of getting the physical things we want, but an opportunity to consciously shift our everyday thoughts to higher vibrations. The result is that we then naturally attract the circumstances and things that bring us joy.

# The Mundane Moments Of Manifesting
# By J.M. Clarke

**M**anifesting is getting annoying. Everywhere you turn, social media seems to be talking about money, lifestyle, and speaking to large crowds in amphitheaters. I'm not so sure about that. I mean, sure, follow your passions and put no limits on where you can go, but my moments of manifesting have been fairly mundane.

Manifesting, in its most simple form, is creating the narrative that is most aligned with your best instincts—the self that operates from a place of love. It is that moment when your mind is able to witness your emotion and behave according to your highest self regardless of the intensity of your feeling. It is consciously choosing to reach for the better moment—the better life.

I have a black marble countertop rimmed by a silver metal trim. Above the dishwasher on the left side are two distinct dents. They tell a story. My second son was still a baby and giving me all sorts of trouble. He was not the easy child I felt I was promised by the universe. My first son had proven to be a challenging baby, and it had taken me a long time even to consider having another. I tried for a second only after I experienced a quiet promise in my soul that this one would help resolve some of the difficulty of my first experience. This promise felt like a farce as I stood trying to load the dishwasher. Parenthood had become my biggest challenge to date, and my normally competent self was feeling lost, frustrated, and disappointed. Like so many moms, my hopes for motherhood were not being met in reality. In a moment of pure unraveled despondency, I came undone, and, with a heavy metal spoon in my hand, I directed all my rage onto my undeserving countertop.

At least once a week, I notice the grooves that are prone to gathering grime. It is a countertop scar that leads me back to how I clawed my way out of that narrative. It was several years before I came to a place of understanding how to manifest a different reality. It started with practicing mindfulness. I started to witness my reactions instead of living them. That helped, but it wasn't the silver bullet. I then started to explore this idea of manifestation. I was not drawn to the material expressions of this concept. Obviously, I wanted lovely things and wonderful experiences, but beyond that, I desired a deep sense of peace and connection within my home. So how do I manifest that?

I started by visualizing it. I imagined what it felt like, smelled like, looked like to be a contented mother. Then I started speaking it. I started using only positive language both to and about my children. I stopped complaining and replaying the negative moments. I didn't gripe to my friends about the issues with my kids in the same way. If I did speak about it, it was to find a solution. I started to carve out the narrative I wanted. This didn't change immediately, nor was it always effective. However, the moment I started speaking and visualizing a different experience, it started to happen. Now, I still have many "unmanifested" moments; however, my reality has started to match the narrative I desire.

This ignited the possibilities for me. If I could manifest a different reality in this most mundane yet challenging part of my life, what else could I do? Could I play with this? Have a little more fun? Create more? Be more? I think, yes.

But here is the key—I had to get extremely clear on what my values were and where my hang-ups were. I started to do the work around some negative thought patterns and responses. I started to recognize what my highest self felt like. I got much quicker at recognizing whether I was acting out of love or fear (or any of fear's offspring: anxiety, insecurity, doubt, selfishness). I got ruthless with myself and called out my inconsistencies.

The relentless pursuit of love in all its forms is the springboard to turn hope into reality. I am developing my capacity to operate from love. As I get better at doing this, the world around me is starting to change. I am witnessing my best life peeking out frequently. As this happens, my outer story starts to reflect my inner visualization. I am surrounded by love, care, peace, and humor. I practice manifesting this as I fall asleep. I imagine how I respond, how I love, how I rest my ego, how I protect my energy from the assaults of the day. However, it is not a magic show, and I am faced with the challenge and choice of living this way moment by moment. The reality that I am bending the world around me to meet my desire for my life is exhilarating.

If the image of manifesting brings to mind vacations, mansions, and money, I may not be the woman to talk to. However, if you are inspired to transform your life from the inside out, start thinking about how to change your story in the mundane moments when you want to attack countertops. For me, that is where the manifestation magic truly happens.

# A Non Woo Woo Approach To Manifesting
## By Janice Dau

**W**hat does an accountant know about manifesting? Isn't manifesting considered the realm of the "woo-woo" intuitive?

Not always. Because I'm an accountant/mystic, you can guess that I've taken a logical approach to my journey. It has been humorous, profound, and illuminating. I have read many books about manifesting, each with a different approach from Abraham Hicks to Deepak Chopra to Oprah Winfrey. People make it sound so easy.

As an accountant, I like order. Perhaps there is a recipe for manifesting? To one cup of passion, add three clicks of your heels. Do the ingredients have to follow a specific order? Fifteen minutes of "I am" presence meditation followed by grounding and visualization? Surely there is a flow chart I can follow?

Manifesting is about energy and your thoughts (which are also energy). So, let's learn about energy.

Let's start with your body and narrow our focus. Internally, we have organs, like your heart, then heart tissues, and heart cells. Cells are comprised of protein molecules. Those molecules are made up of atoms and subatomic particles. Let's imagine the atom's nucleus would be the size of a tomato seed. The electrons that travel around the nucleus are smaller still, about the size of a grain of salt. Imagine these salt grains traveling in orbits around a football field with the tomato seed in the center.

That then leaves around 99.99999% empty space. The physicist Nassim Haramein states ". . . it turns out that what we call reality is mostly space with a little bit of a jiggle—a little vibratory fluctuation or, as described in quantum theory, a waveform generating what we call atomic structure." What a wonderful thing to imagine: getting smaller and smaller and feeling and visualizing all of that space.

This space is not a void, but rather a unified field or the field of potential energy. Using this kind of visualization from large to subatomic particles can help you feel more connected to the energy. You are a wizard commanding the energy of the universe!

Imagine this soup of energy as a field of possibility. The quantum field is a blank canvas waiting for your command. So, what is the paint? How do I create a picture? With beliefs and actions!

You create with your thoughts: if you believe it, it is true. Think about that for a minute. If you believe in a thought, then it is true—for you. This is because your brain will continue to find things that reinforce your beliefs. You discount examples that do not align with your beliefs/biases. If you believe you aren't worthy (for whatever reason), you will find evidence that supports that belief.

Because our subconscious brain is one million times faster than our conscious brain, be aware of the programming/thoughts you carry in your mind. Close to 70% of our thoughts are negative in the form of fear, protection, and survival. These automatic negative thoughts, or ANTS, come in a variety of nefarious forms. It is helpful to be familiar with the five different types so you can know when they occur and try to eliminate them.

Like your body, your thoughts and beliefs are matter in the form of vibrations. In the way that music is vibration that we can hear, think of your vibration as your singular song. Your beliefs are vibrations that originate from your brain, a transmitter of electromagnetic pulses. This is where your brain comes into the picture as it holds the beliefs and thought patterns of each person.

Through habit, we often run the same programs in our brains. At some point, you may think that you don't like where you are, what you are doing, and so on. You want to manifest a new way of being. How do you do that? When you change your vibration, you change your perception and reality. Through your desire to change, you become aware of your ingrained beliefs and destructive ANTS.

Remember to love yourself, even when recognizing that some of your beliefs may be limiting or self-destructive. Realizing that your beliefs have gotten you this far is a great place to start. Also, knowing that you are ready to let go of limiting beliefs in favor of more expansive, coherent, and connected beliefs is an excellent first step.

Finally, as you are working on your beliefs, you need to take action. You cannot merely sit back and believe, hoping your dreams will come true. Waiting for something to materialize is not manifesting. Also, if you are in a state of anticipation, the universe will keep delaying because that is the energy you are drawing to you.

Every fiber of your being must be aligned with your desire. Your actions must also align with this goal. If not, stop the action, as it is not bringing your aspirations any closer. Along the way, make sure you see the humor, be humble, and know you always have a choice. In other words, rather than react, choose a response that reinforces your heart's desire.

In summary, the logical mystic's guide to manifestation requires that you must first be aware of the potential energy around you. Be cognizant of your beliefs and biases as they create your reality. They might keep you from seeing the beauty that is right in front of you. Next, know that life is about the journey. If you want to manifest X, and then start waiting for X to appear, you are missing the point. It's what you do in the moment that matters, especially if you are grateful for all that you have. Finally, have fun. Be kind to yourself. Use your imagination. Stop being so serious. When you are too emotionally attached to the outcome, it is difficult to manifest. It works best if you are emotionally neutral, or even amused by the potential ways you can achieve your goal. Now go have some fun!

# Manifesting Better Relationships
## By Janice Dau

S ince manifesting is about bringing in more of what you want, there are tools that I have found to be immensely helpful in my quest to improve my relationship with my family. These tools can work with kids, partners, and co-workers—folks I refer to as beloveds. These tools are like broad-spectrum antibiotics. They cover a lot of situations and relationships. My go-to tools are healthy boundaries, recognizing patterns, do-overs, and time outs. Also, always remember to laugh and have fun. Nothing changes the energy like a good chuckle.

The first tool is creating healthy boundaries. There are several benefits to having clear boundaries around what your responsibility is and what the other person's responsibility is. The first benefit is that you gain clarity about who you are. When you decide which situations are comfortable and which ones drain you, you learn about your wants and needs. When you keep your energy, you have additional energy to do the things you love rather than the things you think you should be doing. This is important if you work with the law of attraction. Author and inspirational speaker, Esther Hicks, says that your only job is to be clear about that with which you resonate. This makes the universe's job much easier.

The second benefit of having clear boundaries is that I can be respectful of other people's boundaries. When I learned I was smothering my beloved with my energy by thinking I was keeping her safe, I realized that I was keeping her from her path and the things that would help her grow. In essence, I was saying, "I don't trust you to make the right decisions." Holy cow, that is not what I wanted my beloved to think! By respecting her boundaries, I was telling her that I trusted her to make decisions for herself.

Setting boundaries accomplishes two things: it encourages you to acknowledge other people's ability to choose as sovereign beings, and it allows you to keep your vital energy available for the people and things you value and cherish. Also, you have clarity surrounding what your responsibility is and what you need to leave alone. You aren't imposing your energy, in the form of advice, feedback, or action, on the situations that aren't yours, so you ultimately have more energy for yourself.

A corollary of having boundaries is, "I can do it *for* my beloved." Turns out, this denies your beloved a chance to grow and become resilient. However, as parents, even for adult children, you want to ease their way, so you think, "Doing this isn't a big deal for me, so I'll do it for them." This may not be as helpful as you would think.

You've probably heard the story about a man who tried to help a butterfly out of its cocoon by slitting the cocoon open. The butterfly that emerged had small, unformed wings, and died soon after. It needed the struggle out of the cocoon to force the fluid into its wings to stretch and open them so that the butterfly could fly. By trying to shortcut the process, the man had instead doomed the creature. Perhaps you may be shortcutting your beloveds of the process of struggle that results in resilience and confidence.

The next tool is recognizing the pattern of behavior that starts the downward spiral of interpersonal conflict. In *The Dance of Anger: A Woman's Guide to Changing the Patterns of Intimate Relationships*, Harriet Lerner speaks of how our reactions can become a dance. In an argument, person A reacts one way, then person B reacts to A, and then A reacts to B. This can be seen as a dance where you step here, and I step there. Pretty soon, we are in a dance of anger, where the thing that was the first trigger is completely forgotten, as we are now far down the road. Your dance has become so ingrained that you hardly notice you are doing it, but then it feels familiar because you have done it so many times.

Once you see this pattern, there are options.

When you see the spiral beginning, or if you need some time to observe your emotions, I love calling for a time out. Yes, time outs for adults. What a wonderful thing to pause and go into my room, before I say anything I'll regret. Assuming the situation is safe, I'll say, "I need a time out now. I'll be back in 15 minutes." The first time it was shocking to my beloved, but now it is part of our way of interacting. Time outs are great for regrouping and doing things to take care of myself, like grounding. Ask yourself, "Is this truly what I want to say? What am I drawing to me?"

Then, once you have regrouped, you can ask for a do-over. In golf speak, this is called a mulligan. It means that you get to go back and reset, trying again. I have said, "I don't know how we got here, but can we do this over? I'd like to be a better person." In life, asking for a do-over may take the other person off guard. Also, it shows that you recognize your role in how things may be going south and that you want your interaction to be less emotionally charged. Do-overs disrupt the dance.

I have found that do-overs are effective in that it gives everyone a chance to reset. How many times have we reacted with words we didn't mean? Perhaps we weren't paying attention. Either way, do-overs are a great way to reset and restart the conversation.

You'll notice that none of these tools talk about changing the other person. As you know, you can only change yourself. By having clear boundaries, recognizing behavior patterns, taking time outs, and allowing do-overs, you can attract more of the relationships that you want to have in your life.

# Finding Our True North
## By Dr. Saida Désilets

Nothing was going right. The more I pushed, the less happened. And I was on the fast-track to getting sick. Then I remembered: What I desire desires me.

What I desire desires me? Not if I'm switched off and stressed! That's hardly magnetic.

I learned early in my life that it was my ability to relax, soften, and allow that would magnetize what I desired far faster than trying to willfully go for what I wanted. That tended to shut me down and tighten both my body and my awareness.

This was when I made the conscious choice to go against my obsessive tendencies to keep pushing, and stopped everything I was doing. Instead, I switched off all my devices and went to the beach. The beaches in Greece are some of the most beautiful in the world. They are raw, wild, and exquisitely breathtaking.

As I slid into the silky Mediterranean sea, I was aware of how all the pushing had me unable to feel my body, never mind be able to tune into what truly mattered to me.

Suddenly, ripples of pleasure moved through me like the rising pulses of a sweet and unexpected orgasm. I let this exquisite sensation expand by focusing all my attention on the sensations of the water on my skin, while absorbing the azure beauty I was immersed in.

I slid into the sea further, deeper, until I had to float. This is where I completely let go and reminded myself that nature is my best teacher, and now it was time to listen to her.

Slowly, my inner ocean started to move, my heart relaxed, yet passionate. And I painfully realized, "I'm only being used ten percent of what I could be!"

So, in the quiet of my being, I spoke strongly, with the ecstatic joy of knowing that by voicing what mattered, I would experience it as living truth: "Use all of me! I'm all in. Send me the right people, the resources and opportunities, and use 100 percent of my genius!" I felt a wave move strongly through my being and outwardly radiate until I couldn't tell the difference between myself and the world around me.

Suddenly, I was no longer overwhelmed or scared. Suddenly, I felt as though every cell of my being was vibrating with existential confidence: I had touched my true nature and purpose.

After a few additional moments of stillness, I felt the urge to move, and I swam until I couldn't swim anymore. Finding my cozy setup on the rocky beach, I lay down to absorb the escalating excitement of what was already moving toward me!

When I finally reached for my phone, there was a message from a close friend who decided to include me on a dream project, which would require 100 percent of my genius to be a part of it! And then another opportunity came, a chance to bring the genius of my work to South Africa, a place I feel is like a soul home for me.

And to make things especially poignant, over the next week, I was offered three additional incredible opportunities!

Manifestation is the result of being in the right relationship with our desire. Desire isn't what we have been taught to believe it is. Rather than the source of humanity's suffering, desire is like an ambivalent force of nature that impacts every single one of us. It's such an intense (and intimate) force that it's nearly impossible to ignore.

The problem isn't desire itself. The problem is when the ideals, expectations, and mandates of others shape our desire. Now we're going for something that's a little left of center, something that will fail to hit its mark.

So what to do with our deep yearning? We pay attention. We must become aware of the things that light us up, and not only name them, but start to say yes to those crucial hints that pop up day in and day out. And then, we must dare.

It is through audaciously standing for what deeply matters to us that we break free of the influence of hijacked desires and finally allow our true desire to take its place as our true north. From there, we begin to engage in an intimate and profoundly gorgeous relationship with life itself.

It's at this point, we start to recognize that manifestation is not the act of making something happen, but the profound experience of co-creating with the mystery of life itself.

An invitation into co-creating with desire:

Step 1 - Curiosity:

When things are not flowing, when we ache for something to emerge, when we know there's more to this than what we currently know, it's a call to grow quiet and be curious! Pay attention to the presence of enthusiasm as it signals that we are being touched by something greater than ourselves. Name it and follow that.

Step 2 - Acceptance:

When you sense a desire that is deeply touching you, say yes. Especially if you cannot fathom how it will come to be, let yourself feel the tenderness of vulnerability and whisper your yes in the privacy of your inner heart. Your yes is a signal that you are willing to receive the inspiration and co-create with it.

Step 3 - Dare:

Daring is needed here because often, true desires don't conform to the ideals around us. Things will have to change, and at times radically! Being daring to stand for what you desire will support you in moving through self-doubt. Remember, we are all descendants of those who dared.

We are meant to live extraordinary lives. Every single one of us has a unique gift and unique life path and all we need to succeed is to begin to recognize that we are not alone, that life is "doing us," and to follow the bread crumbs that show up. And when something we ached for arrives, we say, "More of that, please!"

# Sparkling Sunshine Spectacles
# By Katie Elliott

**P**erception is everything! When I changed my perception of myself, others, and the world around me, *my* life changed. I realized that my reality was determined by how I perceived and interpreted life. My perception depends on which set of spectacles (glasses) I choose to wear. Glasses represent the invisible filter through which I see the world. Life's positive or negative experiences will likely determine which pair I *choose* to slide on my nose for the day. I have worn numerous frames throughout my life. They vary in color, size, and shape. I have an array of frames from which I can choose at any given moment. If I want to start my day over, I can pick another pair to wear.

If I begin the day with positive thoughts, I have an optimistic outlook. When I open my eyes in the morning, I look around and make a gratitude list for everything I have. I pray and meditate before I get out of bed. I look at myself in the mirror and smile ear to ear. I give myself a kiss and a big hug. I have set the stage for a great day. Which glasses will I choose to wear today? The bright pink ones seem to fit my mood. I walk outside and say hello to everyone. It's amazing the crazy looks I get from some people, but most will smile back. Everyone I see has the same freedom to choose whichever set of glasses they want to wear. Which glasses are you wearing now?

As a young child, I decided to wear a pair of *warrior* glasses. They were flaming red frames with yellow flashing lightning bolts. No one could see them, as they were invisible, but they could surely feel the heat from them. I chose this pair to avoid being hurt or rejected by others. I wore these glasses every day because I didn't know I had any other options. I didn't want anyone close enough to peek into my little soul and see the *real* me. As I rode my bicycle around town, I stuck my tongue out at strangers, neighbors, and even friends before they could say hello. My game in life was *I'll get you before you get me.* I didn't even know I was wearing the glasses. I couldn't seem to help myself. All I wanted was to be loved and accepted. Seeing life through warrior lenses prevented the manifestation of the things I wanted and needed.

The time came when I desperately wanted to find a new pair of glasses. My outlook and attitude needed an adjustment. I wanted to see things from a different perspective. I searched high and low until I found a pair that fit me perfectly. The frames were baby blue covered in little angel wings. I refer to them as my *inspirational* glasses. They felt light and looked heavenly, yet they were titanium. I knew it was going to be a challenging journey. I had to do some tough work to become the person I could see in my minds-eye. I desperately wanted to find the path others had traveled that led them out of the darkness and into the sunlight. Deep within, I discovered tremendous strength that I didn't know I had. The challenges were many, but the blessings were bountiful.

Today I choose to wear a pair of *sparkling sunshine spectacles,* dipped in rainbow glitter and bursting with rays of sunshine. When I look through these magical lenses, everything looks brighter. I can easily see the good in the world. Acceptance is now my friend. I'm able to live life on life's terms. I get energized and motivated to try things that used to scare me. I am authentic and share the real me without feeling fear. I'm an eternal optimist looking for the silver lining in all situations. I believe the world is full of wonderful people doing their best. I give grace to others, as I have also received grace. I smile at everyone, hoping to brighten their day. I try to be a bright light for others in the darkness. I want to be an inspiration for those who are struggling. I hope to spread sunshine wherever I go and leave a trail of sparkling glitter behind.

I am grateful for all of the glasses I have worn throughout my life. Each pair taught me lessons that I might not have learned any other way. My warrior spectacles protected me as long as I needed them.

I was given a second chance at life when I found my inspirational baby blue frames. The sparkling sunshine glasses have brought me so much happiness. They are my favorite pair to date. I am excited about all of the glasses I will get to wear in the future. I am thinking they will be mother of pearl frames.

Go find the spectacles that could change the way you see the world. Happy hunting!

# Silence On A Harley Can Be Deafening
## By Kathryn Eriksen

I twitched as the sharp needle pierced my skin and dove into the vein on the back of my hand. As the lab tech gave me a look, I took a deep breath and tried to relax.

"This is the time it will be positive," I told myself as the red stream of my life filled the tube. The mantra continued to run through my brain until she released the rubber band around my bicep.

It was over.

A war waged inside my head as I left the fertility office and drove back to our small town.

"You are wasting so much money!" cried the voice of fear. "You've already gone through this process two times, and it hasn't worked."

My calm voice answered after a moment, waiting for her turn. "It's worth this last try. Who knows, it might work!"

Fear was having none of it. "Some women aren't meant to have babies. Maybe you're one of them."

"We don't know that! Just because it hasn't worked before doesn't mean it didn't work this time."

Fear tried one last salvo. "This isn't how you are supposed to make babies!"

That last comment was always the one that made me cringe. Nature was in charge of when conception happened. Science controlling what is nature's province always seemed wrong to me. It's almost as if I had forgotten that God was even part of this process.

A sharp reminder was about to be delivered.

"I'm sorry." A long pause. "You're not pregnant."

The voice on the other end of the phone was kind and sincere, but no amount of kindness could change the awful fact that I was incapable of conceiving a child.

Grief, loss, and pain became my constant companions. Fear had a field day reminding me of the loss of a long-cherished dream. Calm couldn't do much, other than to be there.

I couldn't seem to find my way out of the tunnel of despair. It wasn't until my dear husband proposed a crazy idea that I felt slightly more myself.

"Let's go to Sturgis!" His enthusiasm made his eyes shine, and his face glow.

"Where is Sturgis? And why in the world would we want to go there?"

"It's in North Dakota—near the Badlands."

"That answers the 'where' question. But why would we want to go?"

He paused and leaned across the table to be sure he had my attention. "You know that Bob and Donna bought a Harley, and they love it?"

At the mention of the motorcycle, strong feelings rose from the depth of my being. "You know how I feel about motorcycles, especially since we're trying..."

I couldn't finish the sentence. It hurt too much. But then I realized that now, with the last treatment a bust, we didn't have to hold back from doing whatever we wanted to.

Silence descended on our kitchen table as I contemplated the possibilities. It might be a great distraction for me, and we would go on a big adventure. The stories we could tell our nephews would be amazing!

"Let's do it!"

That one decision that seemed so impulsive turned out to be the turning point of our story. Sitting on the back of a rumbling, hot, motorcycle with no opportunity to talk (this was before Bluetooth headset communication) gave me plenty of time to think.

It was almost a forced journey into silence. I had only my thoughts, fears, doubts, and hopes to keep me company. After several mind-numbing hours of looking at the brown West Texas landscape, even my mind became still.

And that is when it happened.

I heard a voice inside my head ask me a simple question. I had been running away from answering this question because I was so focused on the goal of pregnancy. I never took the time to look at my motivation behind the goal.

And now, sitting on the back of that motorcycle, my husband driving us to the Badlands, I had to face the truth behind my actions.

I was treating the entire process like a puzzle that I had to solve. I had placed science and all of its wonders at the top of my pedestal, never turning to God except in my despair. My ego was running the show, and the results spoke for themselves.

The question I heard so clearly that day was: "Do you want to get pregnant or be a mom?"

I had firmly planted my feet in the quicksand of "wanting," the ego's playground. Wanting never goes far, because it is designed to keep us stagnant and stationary. When you focus on wanting, it is like standing outside a beautiful window display, nose pressed against the glass, coveting the object inside but never receiving it.

Being, on the other hand, is a radically different energy. When you are being, you create from the inside and believe that it, or something better, will show up on the outside.

Wanting is ego. Being is love. It's that simple.

I had made the classic manifestation mistake! Wanting became my mantra, my identity. As long as I stayed in wanting, I could play the victim. People would feel sorry for me, even as they bounced their baby on their knee and silently thought to themselves, "Thank goodness that didn't happen to me!"

I forgave myself somewhere between Amarillo and the New Mexico border and surrendered to Love. I concentrated on being a great mom and imagined us holding our sweet baby girl. Joy and happiness became my companions, as natural as breathing.

The darkness of my despair could no longer exist in the light of Love.

At the next rest stop, I pulled my husband aside and asked him a simple question. "What do you think about adoption?"

He smiled and nodded. "That feels right. Let's check it out when we get back!"

Nine months later, we were thrilled to hold our daughter. That was 21 years ago, and she is my greatest manifestation story.

# Manifestation Through Faith
## By Rina Escalante

**B**elieving in something is called faith. Some people believe in the Universe, synchronicity, Buddha, Allah, or a myriad of many other things. Who's to say what is right or wrong? Believing in something is what is important.

*We all have our individual way of manifesting positive things for ourselves.*

I was a pretty sickly child. The inside of hospitals was commonplace for me here in the U.S. and when we'd go visit family in El Salvador. Although my body was weak, my spirit was always strong and still is to this day. I believe our spirit is what carries us through our lives. I never gave up then, nor do I give up now with all the hardship life has handed me.

*Our spirit will manifest anything we ask it to bring forth into our lives—be patient and kind to yourself.*

When my daughters were two and a half and nine months old, respectively, I had to have my gallbladder removed. My papi was worried because I was so young to have a possible precarious surgery. As they were rolling me into surgery, he had a fearful look in his eyes, and I knew what he was thinking. I told him not to worry, that God knew I had two daughters and He wouldn't take me away from them. I had put forth my known belief and refused to have any negative thoughts about my outcome.

When I started to come out of anesthesia, I felt my eyelashes fluttering and I heard my husband at the time say, "What about the tumor?" Although I was only semi-conscious, I knew I had gone in to have my gallbladder removed, but tumor? What was he talking about? So I did my best to speak and said, "Tumor? What tumor?" Then I heard, "Oh no! She's awake! Give her medication!" I once again slipped into an intoxicated slumber—I had awoken in the intensive care unit.

When the surgeon removed my gallbladder, it was most likely one day from bursting and causing sepsis. While I was under, the surgeon decided to "look around," and found a tumor on my liver the size of a man's fist, about to burst. Thankfully, the tumor turned out to be benign. Maybe my papi had a premonition? Prior to this major surgery, I refused to believe a negative outcome was possible.

*Always manifest positivity for any outcome, even if it may be fearful.*

I am a three-stroke survivor. In 2010, I had the first of three strokes. The first stroke was a hemorrhagic stroke in my cerebellum. I was taking a shower when I thought I was hit by a lightning bolt. I lost my ability to walk, speak, and control of my right arm, which meant I had lost the ability to write with my hand. Losing those abilities was a big personal hit, initially. That first day when the neurologist told me that I'd suffered a major stroke, I was in shock. The evening after the neurologist had given me this life-changing news, I simply prayed and thanked God for giving me my life. At that moment, I realized there had to be a reason for me to still be alive.

I remember asking my family to purchase a set of one-pound weights I could wrap around my hand. Since I was going to be in the hospital for ten days, I might as well start my rehab! I began exercising my wonky right arm, lifting it over my head and counting to ten. I outstretched my arm in front of me to the count of ten and repeated the exercises. I refused to believe that my arm was going to be lame because of the stroke. I was unable to walk and I had to go to speech therapy too. There was not one day that I did not practice at least one thing. If it wasn't my speech and comprehension, it was lifting my legs and learning how to swing my arms when I walked. I also had to relearn how to brush my teeth and all the menial daily tasks. I was desperate to cook again—my favorite thing to do. I began by directing my family, but I was driving them crazy by telling them what to do, step by step.

I eventually began chopping slowly and carefully measuring, but was only able to cook one pot at a time because I was unable to multitask. Luckily I had a treadmill at home, so I practiced walking slowly. Gaining skills and abilities became my job. I visualized myself doing *normal*, everyday things I used to do prior to the stroke. My "ride or die" girlfriend would take me out on bike rides to help me with my balance. I ended up having a bad bike accident that left me terribly bruised and scraped up, but it never deterred me from my long term goal of overall balance and a sense of normalcy.

*Always manifest your abilities and possibilities.*

The next year in 2011, I had eleven or more mini-strokes (precursors), and in 2012, I suffered the second stroke that has left me without my peripheral and depth perception vision. I can no longer drive and have to walk and take public transportation. *My legs are now my power and strength!*

In 2014 I suffered my third stroke. I actually died in my best friend's car as she was rushing me to the ER. This last stroke has affected my short term memory, but oddly, it has brought back vivid childhood memories, which I must admit, is both good and bad. Hey, I have my life!

1. Never give up and know recovery is everlasting

2. Manifest your spirit and strengths.

3. Enjoy life!

*What I can tell you about positive manifestation after experiencing life so far, is to always visualize where and what you want for yourself, because I believe you can make **anything possible.***

# Success Can Be Had After Brain Trauma
# By Rina Escalante

Since 2010, I've had three significant strokes and eleven or more Transient Ischemic Strokes, or mini-strokes, that have left me unable to do the type of work I love. I was instrumental in the creation of a leadership development management program. I eventually wrote a white paper about our successes and the recommendations for the follow-up program. The strokes left me feeling as if I was hit by a "reset" button. Each time these events happened, my continued weakened brain lost mass, and memories, vocabulary, and retention were either irretrievable or consumed by my first language, Spanish. According to my speech therapist, the brain resets itself to the first language the brain remembers. I have discovered that I can remember words in my mother tongue, then I search my mind endlessly, looking for the translated word in English. There are instances where it doesn't take me long, other times, it takes days or weeks to remember the word if at all. After these types of brain trauma events, I also began to suffer cerebral seizures, caused by emotional stress. It seemed as if my brain was becoming impuissant, and it was up to me to make it strong once again.

Healing is possible if you're willing to put in the work.

After I had the second stroke, I was not in a nurturing environment. Nor was I in an environment where healing would have been attainable or achievable. It became extremely adverse to my overall mental and physical health. Eventually, I was given sanctuary by a close friend who saw my need. He was so gracious and gave me his room, while he slept on the couch. He also cared for my beloved dog; he was so loving to us. It became extremely difficult for him in his living situation, so I called out for help, and my distress signal was answered. When I left, he made sure I had money because my situation was dire. There were many angels in the forms of dear friends that immediately rescued me out of a bad situation without judging or questioning me.

Always place your beliefs in forces greater than yourself.

Two days later, I was blessed to have been surrounded by mountains and the beauty of south Lake Tahoe for the beginning of my true healing and in the capable hands of one of my best friends, Tamara. She is a lifelong learner and had been a teacher. She taught me about morning juicing, going gluten-free (to my fierce resistance), and the importance of my overall diet for my healing. She began by taking me for walks in the beautiful, peaceful mountains with her puppy, Blitzen. It was so calming hearing and seeing the water flowing down the mountain and smelling the clean mountain air. She eventually worked us up to run down the mountain—I felt so powerful! Knowing that at one time I could not walk, to now I was running down a mountain swaying back and forth, avoiding rocks, stepping on boulders on my way down the hill, my breath heaving, feeling excited, accomplished, and alive! Going on those treks with Tamara, prepared me to eventually face one of the largest physical feats of my life up to that point. With members of her tribe, I conquered Mount Tallac, elevation 9,738 feet. I felt so alive when I peaked that mountain!

As the seasons changed, I learned how you need to prepare a property for winter during the fall season. I found great exercise during winter shoveling snow. I felt accomplished after seeing the nice clean rows, and my body felt strong. Using my mind and body was imperative to my healing. Being from northern California, we don't typically notice these changes, except for maybe closing the umbrellas, bringing in the pillows on the bench tables, and raking the falling leaves, other than that not much else, unless there was a bad storm.

Taking physical action, then making the connection, is necessary for brain trauma survivors.

After my necessary healing up on the mountain, I headed home to the Bay Area, where I felt familiar. I was blessed to have been offered a place to rest my head with another one of my friends I had known since we were in the eighth grade. We had become best friends through our illnesses. She has Multiple Sclerosis (MS), so she understands my disabilities and has experiences with the same types of specialists. I was in much need of specialist medical doctors, additional therapy, disability public transportation cards, and training on how to use public transportation for legally blind people. Thankfully, my friend Kathy was empathetic, and we called each other, the "other half of our brain." I think I may have had another two cerebral seizures when I was living with Kathy and her husband, Greg. Her husband was the one that identified my behavior prior to my having anxiety attacks. He taught me what to look for in my behavior and to find ways to calm myself down so I would avoid having a full-blown anxiety attack that could potentially send me to the hospital.

I have been stroke-free since 2014 and seizure-free since 2015. I have been blessed to have had such giving, kind, selfless, and loving people in my life. I must admit, the friends I write about here are not the only influential people that have crossed my path. Angels are real and surround us, whether you believe or not. They may be called something else in your belief system, but there are powers that are beyond our control.

Always be a kind, giving, and loving spirit. Be selfless, the kindness you give will one day return to you; believe that! Love with all your heart, it will show in your spirit. Never give up hope; you can accomplish anything you set your mind to do. You have the power within you!

# I Can't Stop Dancing
# By Corey Feist

There you are, standing in conversation. Maybe with a friend or in a crowd of people. You're talking about the unusually quick changes in the weather this year.

Then, and while you can't quite place it, you start to notice something in the distance. A sound—in your mind and more like a feeling. The sound begins to gain energy.

Your foot starts moving.

A rhythm takes form.

Now, you're talking about something exceptionally interesting you saw the other day on the internet. You feel your hips begin to move, almost by themselves. A pulse. A beat.

Your eyes close—only for a moment as you exhale, a release from somewhere deep inside.

The energy intensifies, and you notice that you're not the only one. People all around you are moving. Some only a little. Some completely immersed.

You're intimately aware of the beat now. A driving rhythm. A melody.

100 beats per minute. You're getting hooked.

110 beats per minute. You're committed.

128 beats per minute. You've arrived.

The ecstasy. The intimacy. The energy. Now it's everywhere, and the urge is to go until there is nothing left to give.

You look up to the corner of the room.

Barely visible over the top of an open laptop, is a man with headphones resting crookedly on his hat. His face is awash with colored lights emanating up from his dominion. His head, arms, shoulders, and hips are rocking to this beat like it's his partner. He moves as if this is his creation, as if this is his doing.

I'm the guy in the headphones. And it is my doing.

People generally don't dance out of nowhere, or for no reason. And it's more than because a good song is playing over the radio. Not to say that it doesn't happen. Now, did you start dancing, or did the music cause something within you that moved you to dance?

I was born with a low resistance to the power of music, so becoming a DJ wasn't much of a stretch, and I've been DJing now for over 25 years. However, it's only recently that I learned, when it comes to bringing the dance, I am a master of manifestation. People don't dance simply because there is music happening. If I don't create the space for dancing, all that's happening is that some dude with headphones is playing a soundtrack to whatever *that* is that people are doing.

When I looked, I discovered that what's happening is that *I* manifest an access for my audience to give over control from their minds to their bodies. I manifest an access to people's primitive instincts and to their individual self-expression. An access that supersedes their need to be separate and defended. And that's what I have been doing for over two decades.

How do I do that? It starts with manifesting the experience in myself. I don't go from zero to a hundred with a snap of my fingers, though if I could, that would be awesome. I start with an intention; a vision of how the night is going to go. If I give up that intention for a second, it's over. I usually have a small playlist of songs that I think people will respond to, and the rest is an organic creation that is generated between myself and my audience. And at its peak, the experience is nothing short of magical.

I think the key to manifesting major things that you want for yourself and your life starts with identifying the things you are already manifesting in life, and you *are* manifesting things in life. You may be manifesting powerful relationships, being a powerful resource that people come to, winning at pool, or amazing parking karma.

Identifying that I am a master of manifestation in enlivening dance floors everywhere, I saw that I could manifest anything I want in life and that it's not magic or accidental. I'm now producing and publishing my music. I am manifesting a career in music that I'd often held as impossible. It's not only possible, I'm doing it.

I remember hearing the concept of manifestation. It sounded super "new age-y" and a like bunch of crap that ponytailed hippies monetized for fame and fortune. It all sounded too easy, too good to be true, *woo-woo*, and ridiculously unrealistic. And from a certain perspective, that's not inaccurate. It's also a powerful phenomenon that happens every day around the world. I was convinced that people were being sold on some idea that, if they asked the universe for it, it would manifest. Like that visit to Santa at the mall.

Inside of this inquiry around manifestation, what I discovered is that to manifest what you want for yourself and your life has several steps. It is beyond a wish, but it's not a great deal more complicated than what I described above.

Declare what you want to manifest. Live from inside that intention, and the actions you will take to fulfill that intention will cause that thing, or condition, to manifest. Envision your goal. Act with intention. Manifest results.

Before, getting the dance floor going was simply something that happened—luck or a good day. Knowing I am the source frees me up in my songwriting. My actions are writing and releasing music, as I do from my DJ deck. I mix music from inside my intention to get people to give it up and move their body, by giving it up to move *my* body. And over time, the room, or the universe, joins me in that intention and, together, we achieve it. I now access a global dance floor, and it keeps growing.

There is no greater aphrodisiac or drug for me than when dance manifests around me. I can manifest anything I want. I know, because I've already been doing it.

# Are You A Branch On The Vine Of Manifestation
# By Beverly Fells-Jones

As I read the following passage today, it became easy to understand that we all have the gift of spirit within us:

"I am the vine; you are the branches. If you remain in me and I in you, you will bear much fruit; apart from me you can do nothing. If you remain in me and my words remain in you, *ask whatever you wish*, and it will be done for you." John 15:5-7 (NIV)

When we disconnect ourselves from the collective of humanity (the vine), we cannot bear the fruits of manifestation in a large or small way. Each of us is a branch on the vine. By choice, lack of knowledge, or by training, many disconnect.

Jose Silva, creator of the Silva UltraMind ESP System, described us and our spirits as drops of ocean water. No matter where we are, we are still ocean. A single drop, by itself, can do little. However, many drops of ocean water in succession, over a period of time, can erode a stone, or the billions of drops together pounding against the shore can make major changes to the shoreline. As a branch on the vine, we are able to produce wondrous things because we are using the collective energy of the creator.

When we are so driven or have a consuming desire that we want so badly, our human-thinking brain will find ways to make things happen. We define goals, create the step-by-step plan, and then put those strategies into place. We may produce, however, it could be with more difficulty than being part of the collective vine. In this world, we have many gurus who teach all of the steps for achieving our dreams, separate from the vine. I will agree that the numerous books in the business and self-help section give you strategies that can work.

Wouldn't it be nice if you could do it another way? Wouldn't it be nice if you could ask and know that an easier process will reveal itself? Wouldn't it be nice if achieving what you desire would be easy unless the vine believes you should be going in another direction? Fortunately, there is a way, and it is noted in the Bible in the fifteenth chapter of John and elsewhere:

> "If you remain in me and my words remain in you, ask whatever you wish, and it will be done for you." John 15:7 (NIV)

What does this have to do with manifesting? People who do their thinking at the *alpha brain wave* level (becoming one with the vine), where they use their intuitive and creative right brain hemisphere, get the information they need. Those who disconnect from the vine by doing it their way or without divine guidance may find a more difficult path. The alpha brain wave level is the ideal level to think— and the ideal level for decision making. Some people do it naturally; most don't. By practicing meditative prayer, you relax your body and slow your thoughts, which takes you into the realm of the creator.

When you go into meditative prayer, after you have identified, in detail, what you want to achieve and what it will feel, look, smell, sound or even taste like when you receive it:

1. Ask for what you want. What is the goal you want to achieve?
2. Once you ask, visualize it being completed and a phrase you will hear or say to indicate that it is done. One of my clients chose the phrase, "free at last" to indicate her request had been granted. Another chose, "Thank you, Jesus." Another visualized sleeping in her new home. Whatever you choose, "feel it real" when doing the visualization.
3. Be in gratitude. Tell the creator, "Thank you," because you have already received your request. It is sitting in an

alternate invisible universe (Heaven), and is looking for a way to manifest into your world.

After your prayer, be aware that, over time, you will receive all the answers you need to be successful. People will show up in your life as you need them, or you will be compelled to call or be somewhere to receive. If you are a business person, you still need to get your company created, get tax numbers, and any other legal documents necessary. If you are looking for a location, go into meditative prayer and ask for the best one. Visualize being in a location that is best for your business and that people are coming in droves through your doors to patronize you. The creator will send you the answers, and you will be walking in the knowledge that your leader is guiding you to the right decisions.

Sometimes the request comes in a way or package that is unexpected, or an alternative will show up. Trust that if the thing you ask for does not show up, one of three things has happened:

1. You asked, but were not clear.
2. You asked in the negative, and the negative showed up.
3. Something better is coming your way.

After using meditation consistently over several weeks, you will be able to close your eyes, quiet your thoughts, and be in a meditative state instantly. When there, you can ask your question and expect an answer. Do this whenever you are in a situation where you need to make a decision. Scripture says, "Ask whatever you wish." One time I was in the grocery store, and I asked if I should buy a certain item. The answer came back as no. I got home, and I had three of the item I was going to buy.

You are never wrong when you trust your intuition and learn to hear the voice of infinite intelligence.

> "According to your faith, let it be done to you."
> Matthew 9:29 (NIV)

And it is so!

# Ask And You Shall Receive
# By Kelly Fisher-Brubacher

I started teaching in 2001, and I loved my job right from the beginning. It took me a while to find my groove, but once I started teaching French, I knew I had found my niche. I happily taught for 13 years. I had a classroom to teach in, a great program, and for the most part, the students were having almost as much fun as I was.

Then our school closed and we amalgamated with another school and moved into a new building. We were crammed into this building, and there were no extra classrooms, so I traveled class to class, delivering my program from a cart. I did this for three years without a second thought.

I can't say for sure when the feeling started to settle in. It crept up on me and gradually became more obvious. It became harder and harder to get up and go to work each day. Something was weighing me down, and I couldn't put my finger on what it was. I felt restless, dissatisfied, and unhappy. I still loved the students—they were the highlight of my day—but there was a heaviness in me every single day I had to go to work, and I couldn't shake it.

I had a 30-minute drive to school each day. It was my time to get my head on straight for the day. Every day, I said the same words, "Please God. Please help me get through this day. Please help me to give a smile or a kind word where it is needed. Please give me the strength to be happy today." One day, however, my prayer was different. This day, I asked God for a different job. I asked Him to find me a job where I could be happy. I told Him that if it still had to be in teaching, that was fine, as long as I was happy.

A series of events began to unfold. First, I felt compelled to make a phone call. Our board has a yearly transfer meeting when principals can choose staff not based on their seniority. Teachers have to put their names on the transfer list at the beginning of the year. That year, I had been off for surgery when the forms went out, so I missed the deadline to get my name put on the list. I immediately felt a strong compulsion to phone the board office and plead my case, and when I did, they offered to put my name on the list!

The next day was the transfer meeting. Let me first say that it is incredibly difficult to get transferred within our board. Jobs simply don't open up. Yet one did, and I received a phone call and a job offer. I accepted it on the spot. I had to. I believed it was a gift straight from God. This had to be the job I had asked for.

I moved to the new school, and settled in, believing I had landed in a job that had been hand-picked for me. The first year was good. The students and I got off to a great start—I was happy, and so were they. By the middle of the second year, however, on my now 40-minute commute, I was praying myself to work again: "Please Lord. Please help me get through this day. Help me give a smile or a kind word where it is needed."

I knew I had to do something. One day on my way to work, I asked to be shown what the problem was. I asked for understanding and clarity. Suddenly, my entire career spanned my thoughts. I saw back to the time when I was over the moon happy with my job. What was different? The answers leaped out at me. I had a classroom back then. Now I am a prep teacher who goes from class to class, pushing a cart. I got to go on trips and coach sports back then. I got to interact with the students in a whole different way back then.

As the realization hit me, a list of important criteria flashed through my thoughts: I wanted a classroom, to have a homeroom of students that I get to greet every morning, to be closer to home, and to still teach French to the whole school. Hearing it aloud, it seemed ridiculous. It was asking to have the best of both worlds—be a prep teacher, but not be a prep teacher. Impossible.

When the postings came out, I looked through the list carefully. I didn't see any that fit my impossible criteria. Had it not been for a friend and colleague, I would have missed it altogether—junior grade with core French. I was unconvinced. She urged me to apply, telling me it was an amazing school. It got me thinking, so I asked others in my school. They sang the school's praises.

I called about the posting. It was a grade five/six classroom for part of the day. In the afternoon, it was core French with all the students. When I asked if the teacher would have a classroom, the secretary answered that, indeed the teacher would have not only one classroom, but two—one to teach French in, and the other for homeroom in the morning!

It has been an amazing journey back to loving my job. As I look back, I realize some things. I had to ask for help. I had to accept that maybe there were a few steps to take to reach my goal. I had to step out in faith—twice! I thought the first move was taking me to my dream job, but when that crumbled, I had to be willing to move again. Lastly, I had to listen—to the circumstances around me, and to the people who had been carefully placed around me to help me arrive at my destination.

# Ordinary Poor Girl – Overcoming
# Chaos and Trauma
# By Anne Foster Angelou

My early life involved poverty, violence, alcoholism, and mental illness. After I left home in 1963 at age 19 with my large, cheap trunk filled with dolls, books, clothing, and photos, most of my life has been a result of my individual choices. My first step of independence was bravely crossing the country from Tampa, Florida, to Seattle, Washington.

Born a British war orphan to an 18-year-old American widow in WWII in 1943, I was raised by my maternal grandmother, a remarkable woman. She had a life of sorrow and disappointment as the mother of six children and wife to a mentally ill WWI veteran, who spent the last 14 years of his life in a hospital. At 33, when my grandfather became an in-patient, she had six children from age 11 (my mom) to age one with little income and no employment. At 41, when I was born, she added me to the family.

She cared for and nurtured me, inspired me to love learning, and taught me to sing, which would nurture my soul all of my life. She also exercised corporal punishment—undeserved—with stripped tree branches, leather straps, and once, a lead pipe. She put me on stage in 1949 in Tony Grant's Stars of Tomorrow on the famous Steel Pier in Atlantic City, NJ, where I was born. I was shy and reluctant, but once I started singing, the endorphins took care of the rest. Gramma had a wacky sense of humor that is in my DNA. Most of the women in my family share the gift of gab and nutty way of seeing life. To this day, I enjoy telling a good story. Singing continued through my adolescence when I began to sing in choirs (there's safety in numbers). My grandmother put me into various talent contests, whether I liked it not. It didn't matter if the prize was six candy bars or nothing but recognition.

We discovered that I qualified for educational benefits from the British Ministry of Pensions, so I enrolled at the University of South Florida (Tampa) instead of becoming a hairstylist at the local technical school. I performed in various plays and concerts as part of my fine arts major and studied linguistics and foreign languages. I fell in love with a quiet, brilliant, handsome student from the Northwest. He returned home, and I followed with a few belongings and a heart full of hope. I left home, and all that was familiar and traumatic. My regret was leaving my grandmother alone, especially when she died nine months later when I was 20.

We applied for our marriage license on the day John F. Kennedy was assassinated. Jeff was my world, but he had a secret life and left me alone while he hitchhiked to Central and South America and throughout the United States. This was the only intimate relationship I had known. The separation and divorce were painful, and caused serious depression and panic attacks for the next few years. Luckily, with "a little help from my friends," I survived. Sadly, after two more wives and three daughters, Jeff died in 2015. I cried. Dimitri said, "Once you love someone, you always do."

A professor heard me singing a Mozart aria to myself before class and offered me a role in an original Commedia dell'Arte musical he had written with a local composer to introduce children to opera. It was my first professional Equity contract touring Washington state and performing in schools, co-sponsored by Washington State Cultural Enrichment and Seattle Opera in 1972.

Later that year, I met my beloved spouse of 47 years, a native-born Greek who came here as a foreign student. One month after we met, I was hired at Seattle Opera for the next 20 years as a member of the professional resident chorus. After leaving that beloved employment at age 49, I continued to sing in an a cappella quartet, the Angelou Vocal Ensemble, with many talented singer colleagues (a roster of 16). Eight years followed with the Seattle Symphony Chorale, and I am currently singing with The Medieval Women's Choir specializing in music from the middle ages. I am grateful to express my soul in song.

I have manifested myself as a warm-hearted, easy to cry, generous person who cares about those who hurt in the world. I speak to strangers easily, and quickly get into deep conversation. I learn so much from other human beings—their stories, their pain, their joy. I believe that we are all connected and that love, forgiveness, and sharing are the only ways to survive and thrive.

I don't entertain the "poor me" attitude from things that have deeply frightened me. My losses include the shock of my mother's brutal murder when I was 39, and she was 57. I remember the swirls of blood on the floor and reading her autopsy report. I returned from Galveston to warm, caring colleagues at the Seattle Opera and rehearsals for a comedy, "L'Elisir d'Amore." Singing saved me and helped heal my wounded heart. Later, when we performed "Lucia di Lammermoor," I had a flashback and panic attack on stage when Lucia came out with blood on her nightgown and a dagger in her hand. Despite the sweat and pounding heart, I knew I couldn't freak out and ruin the performance, so I quietly whispered to my tenor friend that I didn't feel well, and he held my hand until the scene was over and I could explain what had happened once we were off stage.

I share my life with a loving spouse. Each remaining day of my life, I will wake up with the intention of making a difference in the world. I will see beauty and goodness all around me and look for the humorous and a chance to laugh until my gut aches. Be kind and see the divine in others. You won't regret it.

# Manifesting Monster Sized Adventures
## By Crystal Frame

I'm a big believer in the law of attraction, which is the principle that you can attract success or failure based on your thoughts. Well, I'll never forget the time I decided to put the law of attraction to the test and manifest something crazy—me becoming a monster truck driver! It was comical—I had absolutely zero experience driving one of those big rigs. The odds were astronomically low that I would ever be featured on the television show, *Monster Jam*, sailing through the air in Grave Digger and crushing cars as I landed, so I decided to treat this wacky idea as an experiment. The first step was to spend a few minutes imagining what it might feel like to drive a monster truck. I genuinely put myself into the scene and asked what it would take to make my idea happen. After that, I let my daydream go and remained open to receiving signs from the universe. Then, some strange things started happening. A few months later my company had a sweepstakes where the winners got a trip to Monterey, California, to ride with Mario Andretti in an Indy car through the infamous "Andretti Hairpin" turn at Laguna Seca Raceway, then have professional drifter, Tanner Foust, teach how to drift in a race car, and, best of all—meet Dennis Anderson and drive his monster truck Grave Digger!

Now, I worked in an office on the east coast and *never* traveled. There was zero chance that I was going to that event, right? However, through a series of unusual circumstances, I somehow ended up in California working behind the scenes, when, lo and behold, I was given a chance to drive the legendary Grave Digger monster truck. The winners of the sweepstakes had moved on, but the instructors kept the Grave Digger event open for a few minutes longer, knowing others would want to drive. I almost missed my opportunity, because I had been working from the hotel most of the morning, but thanks to the law of attraction, I managed to suit up and climb into Grave Digger.

Seeing it up close was a humbling experience. The enormous size of the truck made me look like a little kid wearing an oversized helmet and trying to climb up monkey bars. When I was strapped in, I could barely reach the gas pedal. My instructor taught me a few basic rules for driving a monster truck. After several minutes of instruction ("flip these four switches here, push that button there, put it in drive and go for it"), I was almost ready. I had one final question: "How do I know if I'm following the course?" The instructor said, "Go to the first hill you see and hit the gas." I saw a huge mound of dirt straight ahead and slowly drove toward it. The hill matched the many images I'd seen on television of monster trucks sailing through the air over a row of parked cars waiting to be crushed. As I inched closer, I realized I was being pretty lame. I was driving the legendary Grave Digger after all, and I should go for it! I certainly didn't want to go back to the office and have to explain that I was too scared to finish the course. It was now or never! I floored it. The next thing I saw was sky, as Grave Digger shot straight up in the air perpendicular to the ground. There was a slight pause before we came crashing down. The left front tire hit first. Boom! Then the right one. Boom! The engine immediately cut off, and several extremely concerned men came running over. "Are you okay?" asked my instructor. By this point, I had an adrenaline rush that ten cans of Red Bull couldn't match. "Whoooo!" I yelled, raising one hand in the air. "Don't worry," he said. "We'll get you back on the course in a minute." The course? It turned out that the huge hill was essentially a mound of dirt they were going to use for Dennis Anderson's Grave Digger exhibition. The real course was much tamer, more like a kiddie version of Monster Jam. Oops. When I climbed out of Grave Digger, Jason Britton, a professional stunt driver, came over and said that he had wanted to do the same thing, but was afraid he would get in trouble. That was when I realized that

I had manifested a once-in-a-lifetime moment—and it all happened because of a mistake!

**Exercise**

As a fun experiment, pick one item that you want to attract into your life:

1. Identify what you want to manifest.

2. Close your eyes and imagine that this has already happened. Spend at least five minutes visualizing it. Get into the scene, and use your imagination. What would it feel like? Who is with you? What does the environment look like?

3. Ask, "What would it take for (your goal) to happen?" Be playful and flexible with the answer.

4. Ask the universe for obvious signs that this dream is about to occur—as obvious as seeing a marching band during a ticker-tape parade!

5. Make it a game and follow the signs! These can be found anywhere from song lyrics to conversations with friends, or even signs like giant billboards on the side of the road. Keep a journal of these signs, and soon you'll recognize a pattern.

6. Say yes to opportunities as they pop up! This is especially true if they don't match the exact idea of what you thought would happen. Please remember the universe is taking care of things behind the scenes and is moving people, places, and things around to bring this dream to life.

7. Don't be afraid to make mistakes. These mistakes can become part of an amazing once-in-a-lifetime story shared for many years to come. Go for it!

# What Is Manifestation And How Can You Do It?
## By Jami Fuller

What if I told you that you do it every day? Many people feel it's a practice attributed to "gifted" people, when it's actually done by everyone. Let me explain. Manifestation is the process of creating your reality. Every day we choose what we're going to encounter that day. Everything is a choice, and how you feel about those choices is important. The things, people, places, situations, and feelings that we encounter are all potential influences of our moods. This is important. Manifestation starts with feelings and ends with believing. Feelings all have different vibrations, which the universe—God, angels, creator, source, or whatever term you choose—then translates into your desire. It is going to give you what you're asking for, even if it isn't what you want. The law of attraction dictates that *like attracts like*. So the first step in conscious manifestation is to clean up your feelings.

We're not always happy, and there's nothing wrong with that. However, you do have a choice of how you choose to continue. You can actually decide how you feel. Remember the law of attraction? It has to matter to you that you feel good. You have to be the most important person in your existence. You matter too much for it to be any other way. Your mental, physical, emotional, and spiritual health needs to come first. It's about balance, but most people put their needs aside for their loved ones. Fill your cup first. How? Think about all the things that make you feel good. Are there activities you enjoy? Something that you used to do, perhaps? Jumping into these things is a great way to raise up your vibration. Remember, you attract what you put out. If you're doing something that makes your heart sing, you attract more things that make your heart sing. This is manifesting! Pay attention to your moods and the outcome. Shift your focus to shift the momentum. If I'm grouchy, then the only thing that helps me not to be is either meditation or a nap. If I'm at work, and things are not going as I'd like, then I know I need to check in with myself and shift my attention to something more fun. Be playful, laugh, dance, or if you're not in an environment where you can do that, think about a funny memory or take a walk. I like to make my work into a game, and when I meet goals, I reward myself. The reward is your choice. Make it something that feels satisfying and deserving of the work you're doing!

We've looked at your emotional health. Let's look at your mental health for a minute. You have to *know* how perfect you are, exactly as you are. You can never truly make a mistake. Oh, I know that it feels like we can, but a tiny shift in your perspective, and you'll see that all those "mistakes" are actually learning moments. Take a look back at one of those "mistakes." What came out of it? Maybe you only learned more about what you don't want, but maybe it pushed you towards something better that you weren't willing to take the steps needed to get to. The best analogy I've ever heard was from Abraham-Hicks. They speak of a baby learning to walk. When you're watching this baby, are you dumping on them for falling down? No! You're cheering on the first steps! Why, then, do we kick ourselves when we're down? Instead, I want you to practice congratulating yourself for all of the amazing things you do. First thing in the morning start cheering when you wake up, "Thank you, Creator! I'm awake!" Appreciate everything you have, and then take the time to reward yourself with a nice hot shower. Did you do the dishes? Woohoo! Time for a reward! Did you pay your bills? No? Bills are a huge stressor for many. Let's try another perspective shift—"I'm grateful for my phone bill because I get so many awesome benefits from it. And I get to support the people who work for the company, along with their families. I am happy to pay my bill because I get to help others by doing it!" Do you see where I'm going with this? What it comes down to is how you're looking at your reality. Focus on the desire and not the lack of it.

Let's talk about the physical part, and this is brief and specific. Honor your body the way that it deserves to be honored. If you're tired, rest. You aren't lazy. If you're hungry, eat. You need to fuel your body. If you're full, stop eating. You can always eat it later. Move! Your body was made to move. I'm not saying you need to go to the gym and lift hundreds of pounds of weight. Simply move every 30 minutes or so. Go for a walk. Connect with nature. Honor yourself.

Okay, here's the last part of manifestation and often the hardest—trust. Trust that you are loved and supported as you are. Trust that you will always have what you need when you release the need for it. Trust that you are exactly where you need to be and are doing exactly what you need to be doing. *You are enough.* Schedule yourself some free time, and do what you're called to do. All those urges to do something, see something, call someone, are God guiding you toward something more. Maybe you'll have a beautiful experience, or maybe you'll meet someone who will introduce you to someone else who will hire you for your dream job. A step to a step to a step. Our job is to desire. Our job is to grow. Our job is to love. Focus on what you want and not the lack of it. Allow yourself to believe that you are worthy of it all, and you cannot help but to receive it.

# Creating The Life You Desire
# With The Power Of Your Mind
# By Karen Gabler

"If a tree falls in a forest and no one is around to hear it, does it make a sound?" ~ George Berkeley

Philosophers and scientists have long debated the meaning of "reality." Quantum physics researchers have theorized that reality exists only as we perceive it. Thus, instead of asking whether a falling tree makes a sound if no one is there to hear it, the better question would be, "If no one is there to see or hear the tree, is there a tree at all?"

The law of attraction posits that we can draw what we want (or what we don't want) into our experience based upon the power of our thoughts and actions. Fortunately, you don't have to be a scientist to understand how to manipulate your view of reality to alter your day-to-day experience. We can literally change our lives merely by changing our perception of our lives. How do we do that?

Before we can manifest our desires, we have to know what we truly want to bring into our lives. Set a goal that is something you actually want for yourself, rather than something you have been told to want. We may block ourselves from achieving what we say we want if we never genuinely wanted it in the first place. Stating our greatest desires should make us feel excited, hopeful, and energized—not burdened, overwhelmed, or defeated.

Make sure your goal is believable to you. You can manifest anything you desire, but if what you want is so fantastical that you can't imagine it happening, you may subconsciously block it. If we set an overly lofty goal ("I'm going to win ten million dollars in the lottery!"), our ego-mind argues with us ("That will never happen! Who are you kidding?"). We may need to start with something that feels more achievable, such as: "I will bring in enough income to give me everything I need this year." Use incremental steps if you need some time to grow into your desires.

Avoid focusing on what you want to leave behind, instead of embracing what you want to bring forth. When we want financial abundance, we say, "I want to get out of debt. I want to stop feeling like I don't have enough." We think we are manifesting abundance, but the energy we emit is one of lack: "I'm in debt. I never have enough."

Instead, if you want financial abundance, announce: "I'm going to double my income in the next 12 months! I have more than enough money to buy anything I need!" To manifest our greatest desires, we must use words that bring energy, joy, and beauty into our lives. Sit with your desires, consider what you want to change in your life, and create a positive statement about what you truly want to manifest.

Once you have a believable and positive manifestation statement ready to go, begin integrating it into your daily life. Write it on a sticky note and attach it to your bathroom mirror. Put it on a meme and make it your cell phone home screen. Send emails to yourself. Write it on your hand. Start with gently and slowly repeating your statement for five minutes in the morning. Set a reminder to do it again at lunch, and again before you go to bed. By doing this each day, you will start to notice a shift in your thoughts.

Next, verbalize or journal your gratitude about your manifestation statement, as if it has already occurred. If you want to manifest financial abundance, you can say or write: "I'm so grateful that I have all that I need. I'm so grateful that I have plenty of money and can buy whatever I want. I'm so grateful that I am able to share my abundance with others around me."

Sometimes we become frustrated when negative events continue to occur. Don't give up! Continue to express your gratitude, and your reality will begin to catch up with your new energy output.

Sometimes, our ego minds argue with us: "What are you talking about? We don't have what we need! Have you lost your mind?" That's okay! Most of us have spent decades listening to our inner critic. It takes practice to shift those negative thoughts into thoughts of abundance, fulfillment, and joy. Take each negative thought and turn it into a positive thought, and keep returning to your gratitude statements.

Next, create a shift in your behavior, so your actions aren't contradicting your manifestation thoughts. To do this, you must live as if it has already happened. What would your life look like if this thing you want to manifest had already occurred? What would your day be like? What would you do if you were that person?

If your manifestation statement is "I live in a healthy body, and I move my body every day," consider how you would live your life if you had already manifested that reality. You wouldn't say to yourself, "As a healthy person who moves her body every day, I sit on the couch and eat a bag of Oreos." Instead, you would say to yourself, "As a healthy person who moves her body every day, I like to walk in the morning." You then live that reality: you get up in the morning and go for a walk because you are a healthy person who moves her body every day, and that's what you like to do with your mornings.

If you take these steps, your life will change rapidly and dramatically. You will notice a shift in your attitude, which will turn into a shift in your life. By determining what you honestly want for yourself, stating it with positive and abundant language, expressing your gratitude for having already received it, and living your life as if it had already occurred, you will experience the tremendous power you have to manifest the reality you want to create for yourself.

# If You Want To Build It, It Will Come
## By Karen Gabler

The air was crisp and cold. Thunderous waves crashed onto the coastline to the west; seagulls dove for fish in the gentle river flowing to the east. The mountains rose in the distance, their majestic pine trees ascending to the heavens.

It was New Year's Day in 2018; we were visiting our favorite Oregon coastal city. It was our fifth holiday break spent exploring the community, daydreaming about our future retirement and the life we would live there.

"Let's go visit The Reserve!" I exclaimed. Our desired neighborhood was still under development, and available lots were rapidly disappearing. I knew we wouldn't be ready to retire for at least five years, but we drove through the development each year, occasionally stepping out to walk an empty lot. I would stand under the trees, imagining what it would be like to have our living room on that spot.

As we drove past the remaining land for sale, I noticed a now-familiar sign advertising the real estate broker for the development. We called him and explained that we were visiting for the week, and hoped to gather some information about The Reserve. "Come on over!" Tim said.

A warm fire crackled in his cozy office as we told Tim about our annual drives through The Reserve. He said, "Let's look at what we have available over there," as he pulled out blueprints and information binders.

"I think this one is the best lot," he said, pointing to a 2.5-acre parcel. "Let's go take a look!" I told Tim that the lot had been one of our favorites, but hadn't appeared in my ongoing online research. Tim confirmed that the property was still for sale and expressed surprise that it hadn't been sold long ago. "It's like the lot has been hiding or something—maybe it has been waiting for you!"

At Lot 98, a short walk led to a wide clearing nestled in a forest. A berm of towering trees hid the property from the street. A mountain range decorated the north. As I closed my eyes, I felt as if I had been there before. The resonance of the nearby ocean waves chorused with the breeze rustling through the pine trees. I took a deep breath and could feel my heart swelling with joy as I thought, "We are home!"

I was suddenly hit with a wave of sadness, realizing that there was no way to preserve this awe-inspiring portal until we were ready to move. Tim explained that real estate was slow in the winter, and the developers were offering enticing financing options to build out the neighborhood. With no development deadline, we could buy a lot and build when we were ready. I held hands with my husband and daughter, and said, "Let's do it!"

We returned to Tim's office to write an offer, then left to have lunch while he presented it to the owner. He promised to call as soon as he had a response. I was buzzing with excitement as well as apprehension as we sat at a waterfront restaurant. With this remarkable opportunity seemingly falling into our laps, I was suddenly afraid it would slip through our fingers.

"Okay, family, here's the thing—we need to manifest this property! Let's make this happen! Do you remember that trip we took to Oregon in January of 2018 when we found the lot for our forever home? Do you remember how nervous we were when we were waiting to hear about our offer? Do you remember how our favorite lot was simply waiting for us? Do you remember how amazing it was when it was finally ours?"

My daughter jumped in: "Yes! I remember that trip. It was so incredible when we first heard that the property was ours. Do you remember how happy we were? We jumped up and down and screamed!"

My husband smiled and said, "I remember it too—we knew it was right. We found our home, made our offer, and within a day, it was ours. It all fell into place, as if it was meant to be!"

As we strolled through the local shops, we continued to remind each other about "that January 2018 trip when we bought our property." We marveled at how happy we had been when we found out it was ours, and how much fun it was to build our forever home on that awesome site. We laughed about how nervous we were and how we were overcome with joy when Tim confirmed that it was ours.

After several hours of reminiscing, telling each other stories of that "long ago" trip when we found our Oregon home, my phone rang. I held my breath, and my husband and daughter crossed their fingers as Tim announced, "They accepted your offer! The lot is yours!"

We returned home at the end of our trip, elated about our plans. I began organizing my Oregon photos, daydreaming about our future as I surveyed years of coastal memories. While scrolling through old photos from 2013, a familiar image caught my eye. I scanned the now-familiar open lot, nestled among its majestic forest. A mountain range rose in the distance; a berm of trees protected it from the street. It was nearly identical to my 2018 photos of our future home.

Stunned, I showed the photos to my husband, who said, "I know! Don't you remember? We walked that property years ago. You announced that we were going to live there someday when we retired. You've been manifesting that lot for five years now."

I placed the 2013 and 2018 photos next to each other and marveled at how our vision fell into place. Sending silent blessings to our land, I thanked the universe for preserving our dream. I turned to my husband and said, "Honey, remember the first time we opened the front door to our beautiful forever home? Wasn't that a great day?"

# Manifesting My Best Friend
# By Sarah Gabler

L et me tell you about how I manifested my best friend. I love him so much! He is beautiful. He has long, blond hair, and deep brown, soulful eyes. When he looks at me, it's as if he is looking into my soul. He is always there for me. He sits quietly with me when I need a friend. He goes on walks with me and listens to me when I need to talk. He holds my hand when I'm lonely. He is always willing to play with me and is never too busy for me. When I'm sad, he leans into me and licks my face.

If you haven't figured it out already, I am talking about my dog! I have a golden retriever. His name is Beau, and he is nine years old. He is the "little brother" to our toy apricot poodle, Brandy— although Beau is about 80 pounds and several feet bigger than Brandy! Beau has been my best friend for the past nine years.

It started when my first beloved golden retriever, Teddy, passed away unexpectedly when I was four years old. I missed him terribly, and I was lonely without him. Brandy was sad to be alone, too—she needed another brother! I love golden retrievers, and I begged my parents to let me have another one. My parents would say, "maybe" and "someday," but we weren't taking any steps to find a new friend for me.

I didn't truly know what manifestation meant when I was four years old, but I decided that I was going to bring a new golden retriever into my life. When I lay in bed at night, waiting to fall asleep, I talked to Teddy and told him I missed him. I asked him to send a new golden retriever friend to me, someone who needed a home and a little girl to love. I prayed that a new dog would come into my life. I visualized us playing together in my yard, throwing a ball, and letting him chase it and bring it back to me. I imagined us snuggling in my bed, feeling his soft fur and warm body next to me. I pretended that we were going on a walk together. I thought about how it would feel to hug a golden retriever again, seeing his eyes shining at me as he reached out to lick my chin.

One day, my daddy and I were taking Brandy to the pet groomer for a bath and haircut. As usual, I was asking my daddy if we could find a new golden retriever. As usual, he said, "Yes, someday!" We walked into the groomer's office, and there was a man standing there waiting for an appointment—with a golden retriever puppy! I was so excited to see the puppy. I began petting him and hugging him. He was excited to see me, too, and he immediately rolled over so I could scratch his belly.

My daddy started talking to the man, asking him where he found his golden retriever puppy. He said he had adopted him from an elderly lady who couldn't care for him. To our surprise, he then said that he and his wife had recently had a baby and couldn't care for the golden retriever puppy in their tiny home any longer. He said he was bringing him to the groomer to make him look his best because he was taking him to a dog shelter to give him up for adoption the next day.

I was jumping up and down and pulling on my daddy's arm, begging him to let us adopt the puppy. I knew that this was the friend I had been waiting for! My daddy exchanged phone numbers with the man and told him that we might want to take him. They agreed that the man would bring the puppy to our house the next day to see if he would be a good fit.

The next day, the man came over with the puppy to let him play with our poodle, Brandy. After a few minutes of sniffing each other, they were bounding around our yard like the best of friends. I asked the man for the puppy's name, and he said his name was "Beau." I called Beau over to me, and we started wrestling. After a few minutes, he fell asleep on our living room floor, and I curled up around him to hug him. I was ecstatic, and I immediately fell in love with him.

I looked up at my daddy and mommy, pleading with them to let us keep him. I could tell from the looks on their faces that they were already in love with Beau, as I was. The man was glad to see that Beau would have a happy home, with a child to love him and another dog to play with. We went to the store and bought new toys, dog food, and a soft bed. I told Beau that he was a part of our family now and that he would never have to go to a shelter. I told him that he would be safe and loved forever.

Later that night, my mommy was talking to my daddy about Beau. She said she couldn't believe that we had recently been talking about finding a golden retriever, and Beau fell into our laps that easily. I told my parents that I found Beau for us because I asked Teddy to send him to us. I told them that I dreamed about him and imagined what it would be like to have him. I told them that Beau was always supposed to be a member of our family, and I was happy that we waited for him to arrive.

That's how I manifested my best friend—and I am so happy to have him. Beau is the sweetest, most lovable dog alive—I am sure of it!

# Pocketful Of Pixie Dust
## By Jaime Lee Garcia

I was known to be a sunny and happy child with a smile on my face and a bucket full of love in my heart. I realized early on that I was too empathetic for my liking. Being around negativity would make me physically ill. Therefore, I vowed to live my life as positively as I could. I imagined carrying a pocketful of pixie dust to spread happiness around me magically.

Trudging through life's challenges with the same positivity I held as a child, I hadn't yet understood the power of thought and intention or their importance when experiencing huge life changes. I would soon learn the significance.

Married at nineteen to my brother's good friend, we had two daughters throughout our twenty-year marriage. As we "grew up," we grew apart. It was time to separate. Things spiraled from there. We lost our jobs and were forced to remain roommates, which was not ideal. The house we lived in prior to this was my favorite. I fondly called it the "Portside House" after the street it was on. Many of my favorite memories were created there. Weeks after moving in, our youngest was born. I had found an instant friend in my neighbor across the street, and the neighborhood kids surrounded my girls and me daily. They were "my kids." Their presence brought so much joy. We planned neighborhood parties for every occasion, building cherished memories. I would have stayed there forever, but it was time for us to buy a home. As the moving truck drove us away from my friends, neighborhood kids, and the Portside House, I sobbed.

Here I was unemployed, going through a divorce, foreclosing on the house, and filing bankruptcy. I was known for my positive outlook and tried to maintain that for my daughters. However, a dark and gloomy cloud was hovering over my life. I took refuge in the bookstore that became my sanctuary. It was there that I remembered a life-changing book my friends had mentioned. I searched for the title. Due to its popularity, there was only one copy remaining. It was fate that it was now in my hands. I found a cozy chair, cuddled up, and slowly ran my fingers over the front of the book. The magical cover evoked a spark of hope. As I began reading the words, I realized what I had been doing wrong. While I thought that I was thinking positively, in actuality, I was focused on the negatives and the dismal reality that I was reduced to living in a guest bedroom, in my parents' home, with a few remaining possessions. These thoughts were only bringing more unfortunate events into my life.

Reading the first few pages, I learned that to manifest greater things in my life, I had to change the frequency of my thoughts to that of positive intention, letting go of all doubts, fears, and negativity. I had an epiphany and realized what I needed to do. By page five, my phone rang with an offer to purchase my bedroom set, which I needed to sell by the weekend so I could pay a bill. I left the bookstore as fast as a speeding bullet, with this magical book in hand, and set out to change my life.

That night I curled into bed and finished the book. Everything turned around quickly. I closed my eyes and began to manifest everything my heart desired, using the principles I had read about. Believe me when I say it worked like magic! Before I knew it, my life began to change. The dark cloud looming over my life was whisked away and replaced with blue skies, sunny days, and rainbows reflecting beautiful colors.

Suddenly, an old job from six years prior landed in my lap, beginning a chain of wonderful things to come. A replacement car was lined up for me at a friend's local dealership after my previous one had been repossessed. This was a car I would typically not pick out for myself. The magical book came to mind, and I decided to use positive intention. I kept my focus on manifesting a better car. When I arrived, the management announced that they had a surprise for me. As we approached the car originally set aside for me, my heart sank a little. However, they kept walking, and we soon stood in front of a beautifully-used, fully-loaded Honda. I fell in love with it. The manager smiled and said, "The owner drove this car for a while and decided to return it today. You immediately came to mind, and we wanted you to have it instead of selling it on the lot." Intention was working!

What came next was truly astonishing. After getting a reliable car and my old job back, it was time to move out of my parents' house. Browsing hundreds of listings for home rentals, I mentioned to a friend that I wished I could have my Portside House back, as that was the home that filled my heart with joy. She replied, "I know you loved that house, but someone has been living there for nine years now, so that is extremely unlikely." However, I kept my focus and intention on the house. Days later, I decided to browse the rental listings again. I was suddenly drawn to a particular posting, and the monthly rental amount was in my budget. I scrolled down to see more details and almost fell out of my chair. The address read "824 Portside Circle." This was my beloved Portside House, magically available for rent again! I reached for the phone, and within a few days, the house was mine again! My dreams were manifesting before my eyes. The little girl in me was standing there with a pocketful of pixie dust, once again. It was time to help others manifest their greatest desires!

# Heart Flutter
## By Jaime Lee Garcia

On the other line of the phone, I heard, "Hey Jaime, it's Christopher Garcia." I almost dropped the phone. Hearing his voice evoked a lot of emotions. The familiar heart flutter I had at sixteen returned instantly, although it had been twenty-six years since we first met.

Always a romantic, at five-years-old I adored sappy love songs, and Cinderella was my favorite movie. I dreamed of finding my Prince Charming to marry and live happily ever after with. At sixteen, I was still that dreamy, romantic girl, and was entering my junior year of high school. I remember the first week of school and meeting Christopher while working as a teacher's aide. He entered the office one morning, having transferred from a different school. Known as a friendly, people-person, I approached him with an encouraging smile and introduced myself. I knew how intimidating it was to change schools. The first thing I noticed when he turned and told me his name was his adorable smile. He had perfect teeth, hazel eyes, and thick, wavy blonde hair. I was mesmerized by his smile and personality. We became instant friends, and I would check on him periodically. Hearing his name spoken by friends would always make my heart flutter, but dating wasn't in the cards for us then.

At 19, I was newly married. It was then that a friend brought Christopher over to say goodbye to me. He had joined the Army and was heading to Germany. I was happy to see his smiling face, and wished him well on his new life in the military. At this point, I thought I would never see him again.

After twenty years, I found myself divorced with two daughters. Always a hopeless romantic, I vowed to never give up on finding true love. However, divorce brought many financial challenges I felt I could never make it out of. It was then that I opened a life-changing book and learned about the law of attraction and how to use the principals to manifest great things into my life. I would later use these principles to manifest my soul mate.

In 2009, Facebook had become popular. While browsing the newsfeed one night, I heard a chime signaling a private message. I was shocked to see Christopher's name displayed. We hadn't talked since he joined the Army, and twenty years had passed. I opened the message, and a smile spread across my face as I read the words, "Hi, Jaime, I wanted to reach out and thank you. During our junior year, you were the first to approach and welcome me. I never forgot your kindness. Because of you, I taught my soldiers how to properly welcome people." I couldn't believe he remembered and was thanking me for this so many years later. Our communication was sporadic after this email—I was now dating someone, and Christopher was still married with two daughters.

A year later, we had a rare chance to meet in person. He was in town visiting family before deploying to Afghanistan. We were now forty years old and excited to reconnect as friends. However, while he waited patiently for me at Dave & Busters, I had a family emergency come up. We were disappointed to miss each other, but fate had intervened. It wasn't yet our time.

Two years later, I was single and despising the dating game. I desperately wanted to find "the one" without weeding through candidates. Several guys were taking me out, none of with whom I had chemistry. Suddenly, I remembered the power of intention and how it worked magically for me after my divorce. I decided to put the principals to work on my love life and focused on manifesting my soul mate.

On a lunch break, shortly after, a friend asked which guy I was going to choose, and I replied, "None of them." She frowned and said, "Why not? One guy is giving you gifts, one is taking you to shows, and another is a family friend." I explained that none of it mattered if there were no sparks. I wanted my true soul mate and would know him by how I felt when I met him. Saying this, I had a strong feeling this would be soon, as I had already put the law of attraction to work.

That same day, life-changing events were about to unfold. Three hours after my lunch date, my phone rang and displayed an out-of-state number. On the other line, I heard, "Hey Jaime, it's Christopher Garcia." I almost dropped the phone. Hearing his voice evoked a lot of emotions. The familiar heart flutter I had at sixteen returned instantly. This time we were both single. We talked for hours as if no time had passed. Something magical was happening, and it was more than friendship. Who knew we would meet at sixteen and fall in love twenty-six years later?

We were living across the country from one another, but knew our reconnection was meant to be. I happily shared the news with my friend and explained that my "soul mate" had called only hours after our lunch date. She was as astonished as I was at how fast this manifested.

Things progressed quickly after that first phone call. Four months later, Christopher dropped to his knee and proposed to me at the airport during a visit to see him. Months later, with the blessing of family and friends, we packed a moving truck and relocated me across the country to start a new life together. Our romantic wedding took place that following Christmastime. Surrounded by our children, family, and friends, we said our vows in a magical evening ceremony under the stars, with lights and candles flickering upon us.

Six years have passed, and Christopher still gives me that heart flutter. We love our blended family and have five grandchildren who bring us joy. I will always be thankful to the universe for manifesting this true love.

# My God
# By Roxy

"**B**ut my God doesn't need me to kneel down and pray. We talk to each other all the time!" This is one of my earliest memories of my spirituality, and ultimately, my ability to manifest. I was about five years old. Now, I consciously manifest parking spots or finding the perfect object when I enter a store, using the laws of attraction and gratitude. But I now realize I have also manifested my health and my life since a young age.

Sickness tried to end my life at five years old, and again at nine years old. I knew nothing of my illness, but never once believed I would die from it. My God would guide me to thinking about life—riding my bike, petting my cat, going into a higher grade at school the following fall. I wanted all these things forever, so I somehow made them happen. A few years later, I experienced a near-drowning while playing in the water with a friend and my parents supervising. At first, I was scared of this being the end, but then I decided that I had too much life left to live! I found some strength to yell, and help came running. Thank you, my God!

Fast forward about 40 years—two marriages, two beautiful daughters, two divorces, and a second dream job later. (The number two seems to be prevalent in my life!) I was involved in a near-fatal single-car accident with my youngest daughter. My only thought was of her safety. I would be fine. I use the word "fine" quite loosely here—at least I would be alive! A broken neck and many broken bones later, I manifested my health to conquer these roadblocks. I didn't waiver. A certitude of returning to my previous self was ever-present. I worked hard physically, emotionally, and psychologically for over two years, and I manifested myself back to life as we know it. But you know what? I'm not the person I was before. I believe that we manifest every occurrence in our lives. So, maybe you're wondering if I manifested my car accident. Well, yes, I think I did—to grow into my "new me." Had I not had the opportunity to see the preciousness of life up close and personal, I might not have opened my heart, spirit, and soul to all the possibilities of life.

I have advanced to level two of Reiki, have done a bit of public speaking on perseverance and the importance of sisterhood, I am writing this short story for this book, and I am working on preparing myself to share my gifts of healing with the world! Yes, I manifested all this. No, I did not surround myself with crystals under the full moon planning these manifestations, although I love crystals and precious stones and their properties, and stare at the full moon regularly. I created through talking with and listening to my God.

So, who is this regular-talking, precious being who has accompanied me through all the ups and downs, that I call my God? Call him or her God, Allah, spirit, Mother Nature, power, Universe, or whatever you prefer. But somewhere deep inside of me, I know and have always known, that manifesting starts with me. I *am* my God! We all have this super-power in us, and we can tap into it using all kinds of methods, such as crystals, rituals, chants, tapping, and praying. Do what it takes to connect with and believe in your God—in yourself. You and only you can manifest the life you want to live. Of course, it takes hard work as well, but you can do it! Whether it be consciously like after my accident, or subconsciously like when I was a child and knew I had more to give to the world. Believe, trust, and go for it!!

Sending you all love and the blessings of health and a life worth sharing!

# Map A Life You Love
## By Anonymous

Concentrate. Focus. Rehearse. Acting training emphasized the importance of these skills. It didn't occur to me to use these techniques to manifest the help I needed when life as I knew it suddenly ended.

It was one of those early spring days when the first green grass appears. I was driving to work and feeling blessed to live in a river city, when my cell phone broke the reverie of my commute.

Caller ID showed it was my husband. I quickly picked up, "Hi, I'm about to park, can I call you after?" His reply was equally brief. "We need to talk about sharing custody because I'm done being married."

Ours was a tumultuous relationship between two passionate personalities. We met while I was an actor and he was an engineer exploring acting. We were cast as husband and wife in a community play. Life soon imitated art. We married in less than 12 months and started our new life in a top floor corner apartment near the park. Together we acted, produced short films, completed the NYC Marathon, founded companies, and created a son. We adored each other.

Early in the courtship, he mentioned his father was an alcoholic. He was proud of his father for going cold turkey and remaining sober. Toward the end of my pregnancy, when his drinking escalated, I wondered if he somehow associated the behavior with fatherhood. I felt crushed when he wanted to join his friends at the pub a few hours after I delivered. Before our son turned two, the hours he spent at the pub almost equaled the hours he spent at the office. Still, at least once every week, the three of us enjoyed an idyllic family experience. I was a new mom, nursing on demand, disoriented in body, mind, and spirit.

As his time away from home increased, a co-producer invited him to an AA meeting and me to Alanon. One night, I was drafting a fearless inventory of my strengths and weaknesses. The exercise resulted in a letter I wrote to myself, explaining how I felt when he no-showed night after night. I suddenly got up, scooped up our sleeping child, and walked out of the apartment. Since he arrived home well after the bars closed most nights, I was completely surprised when the elevator opened on the ground floor. There he was, leaning against the lift, flashing his boyish grin. A few minutes sooner or later, and we would not have overlapped. He was proud of himself for coming home "early." Midnight was not my idea of date night. He kept cajoling. I kept walking.

My broken heart yearned for a tranquil home, love worthy of commitments kept, and emotional stability. I ached for a full night's sleep and a change of scenery to sort out what honoring our vows might look like going forward.

The separation lasted a few weeks. Later that year, we bought a house he was excited to renovate. After months of repairs, with many more needed, we moved in. He spent one night there before I got "the call."

The new neighborhood could be considered transitional at best. It was the kind of place where stolen bikes and used needles end up, not a place to raise a child alone. We had painted the wall of our bedroom red and hung a large round mirror there to promote marital harmony. So, how had my spouse lasted only one night? Reflecting on the sudden divorce, my attorney mused that the Feng Shui had worked. Without a marriage, there was no marital discord. No disorienting late night arrivals. No tense early morning departures.

I didn't contest the divorce. I didn't contest his request for joint custody. I naively believed he was well enough to care for our two-year-old son. I couldn't imagine the man I fell in love with could be capable of endangering a toddler. Neither of us paid or received alimony or child support. Our son was suddenly thrust into two extremely different households. My partner's separation from me was immediate and complete.

This lowest point of my life did not feel like a manifestation at the time. It looked and felt like a series of failures. Our companies closed. Shared custody proved challenging. Our young son logged hours in local pubs. Hindsight revealed how the divorce served as a catalyst. As excruciating as the unanticipated emancipation was, I began experiencing a stream of unexpected, encouraging events.

The seeds of my heart's desire were planted in the demise of my marriage. Decisions were filtered through two priorities: 1) does this keep my son safe, and, 2) will this choice create an environment where he can thrive? Those two criteria became the fertile soil in which my desires took root.

Life seemed to be conspiring to support me. In less than a month, a chance meeting during a car repair led to flex-time work, my college love re-entered my life after 12 years of no contact, and friends recommended tradesmen to improve the house at rates I could afford.

I met people able to teach me how to harness feelings. I learned that what I think about grows stronger. I began forcing my scared self to interrupt the anxious thoughts by focusing on how I would feel if I achieved my desires. I imagined what a safe and tranquil home felt like. Within a year, I was earning five figures a month and enjoying a fulfilling relationship that continues to this day.

The practice of focusing on desired outcomes activates unforeseen forces of synergy, creativity, and assistance.

Do you know what you *most* want to feel? Secure? Appreciated? Supported? Valued? You can find out by:

- noticing when and where you feel your best
- keeping a list

- using the list as your treasure map
- navigating each day by repeatedly choosing thoughts and actions that promote your desired feelings

Give it a try. You are worth it.

My path evolved from business school through a decade of professional acting to the study of touch and energy medicine therapies. My passion is to learn and teach ways to relieve suffering. My professional work involves partnering with physicians and patients in designing a care system that continuously improves health. As the poet Rumi suggests, "Out beyond ideas of wrongdoing and rightdoing there is a field. I'll meet you there."

# My Perfect Job
# By Jae Hart

It is an understatement to say the fall of 2018 was a challenging time in my life.

I had recently been laid off, my mother's dementia was rapidly taking over her brain, and my son, a junior in high school, needed his single mom around. I needed a job—but most importantly, one that would allow me the flexibility to be available to my mother and son.

Having always been a spiritual person, I was ready to take it on with the power of positive thinking, and put my manifesting tools into action. I decided to define what I wanted for my perfect job. I wrote out four possibilities, three that would work for me, and the fourth, God's plan. I thought this would clearly let the universe know what I was "willing to take."

After a slew of interviews, some seemingly going well and others not, nothing turned up. Months passed, with no success. I began to get frustrated that this manifesting thing was not working so well. I discussed my disappointment with my sister and friends. I finally figured out what I needed to do. I needed to focus on one ideal situation, rather than a multitude of choices the universe could try to grasp. I eagerly wrote a honed in, detailed account of exactly what my perfect job looked like, spending extra time distinguishing between what I wanted and what I would accept.

After finalizing the precise description of my perfect job, I posted it on my bathroom mirror. Several times a day, I would take time to set the intention. I would act out how I would feel once I got the job, and would roleplay, telling my friends all about the perfect job I had received.

A week later, out of the blue, I received a call from a previous coworker I had not spoken to in years. She asked if I knew anyone looking for a Human Relations (HR) job because her company was in need of filling this position. Coincidental, isn't it? Ha! I immediately sent over my resume, and they called me for an interview. The interview seemed to be going well, but at the end, I had to ask the important question. The most crucial element I needed for this to meet my perfect job criteria was the flexibility to be able to be available for my mother and son every afternoon. Typically, this is when things went south in previous interviews. Surprisingly, they were supportive and understood that I needed to put my family first. The CEO and the COO were kind, gracious, and thoughtful. In addition, they wanted an HR professional who would build relationships with their associates and find ways to show the team how much they are appreciated. This sounded too good to be true. It truly was my perfect job!

After the interview, I began pretending that they had offered me the job with all of the authentic emotions to match. Four days later, they called and offered me the position. I was beyond excited! The only detail that was disappointing was the pay. Although it was the same rate that I earned ten years earlier, I still accepted the job.

Looking back at my "perfect job" list, I could see that most of the items were checked off with this new position, including my willingness to take less pay for additional flexibility. Why did I say that? Why didn't I believe I could get paid a fair wage and have flexibility? I was stuck in believing that I had to sacrifice something to get what I wanted. I knew better, yet I still allowed myself to manifest this! After a few weeks in my new position, it began to press on me that my salary was less than I was worth. I decided to manifest further! I started repeating over and over again, "I'm worth more." I repeated this mantra all day long, and even in my sleep. I did not express anger or frustration; I simply stated it as a fact. I had decided that at my 90-day review, I would ask for a pay raise.

During my sixth week on the job, I received an email from a previous employer offering me a similar job, yet with a higher salary! However, rather than risk losing the flexibility and other benefits of my current job, I negotiated with the potential employer. They matched the flexible hours, bonus pay, and insurance of my current position, but with a higher salary. It was unbelievable!

Knowing that I liked my new job and I didn't want to leave, I decided to talk this over with my current employer. I told them the details of the other offer. My current employer didn't want to lose me, so they immediately matched the other offer. In the end, it came to a 65% yearly pay increase!

I am so thankful that my background thoughts were positive. I thought, "I'm worth more" rather than, "This is a bad deal," or, "They are taking advantage of me," or, "This is unfair." Had I possessed negative thoughts with emotions to match, I don't believe the pay raise would have happened. Now I love my new job and my raise!

I learned a few lessons through this experience. We don't have to sacrifice something to get what we want. Also, it is important to have clarity and be precise about what it is we are wanting. And finally, we need to be aware of our automatic chatter. Take a moment to listen to what's being said in the background—it can make or break the deal.

It is exhilarating to have my dreams become my reality. Yours can too!

# Dare To Create Your Dream
## By Debbie Helsel

Have you ever hoped for something or dreamed for years of doing something that has never left your heart? A burning desire down so deep that it is embedded in your core, and deep down, you know it's your life's path but are unsure of how to get there? Have you had it happen to you several times?

Everyone has hopes and dreams. Most give up before they see them come to fruition because they are not willing to invest the time or energy sometimes needed. They are like forethoughts of what could be—well, hopefully, the only good ones.

When you have these hopes and dreams that you want to see come to pass, it takes a lot of effort in the area of faith and a belief that anything is possible. But you have to work toward the goals you have set to see them happen. When it comes to manifesting things, they can be small things that will perhaps come sooner or large things that may take additional time, depending on the complexity.

I dared to dream, and I dared to be different. I dared to have a dream that I would make the basketball team in high school with no real experience. I made the team all three years of high school. I didn't play a lot, but I had greater determination when a friend told me I couldn't do it. It pushed me to prove him wrong.

I dared to dream of a job working with wildlife. It happened when I was 25 years old. It took all the effort on my part, but when a door was shown to me that led me to my deepest desire, l stepped through it and never looked back. In working with the wildlife, there was always a goal to move to a larger space and provide natural surroundings and better accomm-odations for the animals, as well as educating through the environment, while thriving in the process.

This one took a little longer, but with the right combination of factors and 25 years of hard work and dedication, we made it happen. Yes, I say, "we." This didn't happen because only I wanted it to. It happened because of the collaboration of many people who shared the same dreams and desires for our facility and for themselves as well. There was a common denominator that we all shared, and it was that we loved our wildlife refuge, and we wanted to see it reach its next chapter in its growth, and we wanted to be a part of it somehow. We all believed in the same dream and shared the dream with others who believed, too, which drastically raised the vibration and brought it into reality.

Now, my story doesn't end there, either, as I had and still have more daring dreams. As faith would play another role in between all of this, I learned several forms of energy healing and became a minister. I then studied for my doctorate in metaphysical studies and spirituality. I thought that becoming a minister would help me with the legalities of doing energy healing, which it has, but I never thought it would change how I felt about helping people too.

I have evolved into a much better person through my journey, and I have learned to see things from many different perspectives, not only mine. I realize I must have been self-centered in that I believed my thoughts were always the best and the only way sometimes, which is actually the farthest thing from the truth and likely held me back. I found that I had a desire to help people as much as I did animals, and most times, my series of paths intersected, as I am "multi-pathed" with my inspirations and my aspirations. Being on more than one path simultaneously gets complicated, but is fulfilling and pretty interesting most of the time.

My path has led me through a ministry of many different meanings and concepts, has led me to go places and see things I have never gone or seen before, and finally, has given me a desire to travel and see things I never realized I was missing out on. Those days have been happening frequently in recent years. I am seeing my life changing yet again as I get older, and after a few incidents through the years, I realize I cannot keep the pace I always had because my body won't do what it used to.

It takes effort, and yes, it takes time and dedication to your cause. I don't know anyone who dreams it up, and suddenly, it is a reality. The first step is to get out of your way and believe that anything is possible. Ask for help from whomever you believe your higher power to be, and listen from within for wisdom, insights, and subtle messages that will steer you in the direction you need to go. Yes, it may be uncomfortable, and it may create a bit more work and effort, but if you dare to believe and are willing to work for it, anything is possible.

Our wildlife refuge is 30 years old now, and for a non-profit, that is quite the accomplishment. We are at the threshold of another new start that will not only change our entire essence, but it will up our game to a level we have never before experienced. The challenge will be having the right people to move it forward and the funding to continue the work. But with the collaborative efforts of all involved and the desire to see this happen by so many people, we will accomplish this too, easily and seemingly effortlessly. After all, why manifest a dream this big and not the means to succeed?

# Manifest, Then Voila!
# By Dr. Vicki L. High

According to Merriam-Webster, a manifestation is a public demonstration of power and purpose. Would you believe me if I said you are constantly manifesting? Well, it's so true! Look at what you are manifesting. What results do you see? If you could track your desires, focused thoughts, words, expectations, and outcomes for twenty-four hours, what would you discover about your manifestations? Where do you target your energy, and what are you creating?

I am a creator. My hometown of Plano, Texas, has grown considerably during my lifetime, and the changes make some areas unrecognizable to me. I remember the small-town atmosphere, the feeling of knowing others and being known, a feeling of community, faith, and belonging.

Fast forward to 2019. I live in Frisco, which neighbors Plano to the north and is currently the fastest-growing city in the nation. It is estimated over a million people have moved into this area as a result of major corporations relocating in the last year. Although I work from home and am happily cocooned in my space, I occasionally venture out into a world with more cars, more people, more traffic.

I groused about the growing population, the perceived changes and diminishing "Texas hospitality," and the extended time needed to travel to and from destinations. My grousing was concentrated, emotionally laden, and repeated often. I was unconsciously manifesting. Within one month, the lessons showed up for me—these results of my manifestations. In the analogy of pebble, rock, brick, and brick wall, the pebble came in the form of road construction. I was directed to drive through what seemed like wet concrete on my black car resulting in a damage claim against the road construction company. Within two weeks, the rock appeared as

I received a speeding ticket complete with a lecture from the officer, lights, and sirens as if I were a potential flight risk, and then a thank you for my courtesy. Less than a week later, I received the brick in a warning from yet another policeman. It had been years since I had been stopped and ticketed.

Then I received my brick wall lesson in an actual full-circle moment. I was driving back from DFW Airport when the car in front of me sent a tire remnant in the shape of a complete circle hurling twenty feet through the air, colliding with my front left bumper causing over $5,000 in damage. I knew I had to stay in my lane, not swerving to hit a vehicle in the next lane or the concrete wall to my right. The defensive driving course that I had completed for the speeding ticket served me by keeping me calm and able to maneuver safely on the road.

Then the light bulb came on! I realized I had manifested every single incident. Every obstacle I encountered was a result of my deliberate focus, desires, expectations, and actions. I had unwittingly created conflict with my community, the roads, safety and my environment. Our power to manifest can be either conscious or unconscious. When we have that kind of power, shouldn't we be fully aware of what we bring into reality? Let's consciously use our power to create situations that bring us joy, peace, love, and abundance—that soothe our souls.

When I'm living my *conscious* truth, I am here to love the people who move here. These people are members of my global family, and they are here for a purpose. They bring their gifts and seek enlightenment. Throughout my career, I have traveled to each of the 50 states. In each state, I encountered friendly people, exciting experiences, beautiful scenery, and was welcomed. It's ironic that I have been guilty at times of not extending that same courtesy to others visiting or moving to my state.

I consciously manifest healing outcomes when providing Heart 2 Heart Healing with deliberate focus and intention for the highest good for the client. My thoughts, desires, and words are in alignment with that intention. God, source, or the Universe manifest healing and unconditional love in the client. I find this manifestation easy because it happens every time. I see the results. I know God delivers.

The manifestation formula is simple with conscious (or unconscious) manifestation. Decide what you wish to manifest. Then feed that burning desire with focused, deliberate thought. Monitor your thoughts and words to constantly and consistently align with your desire. See the results you desire with the expectation that it occurs now in the present. Focus on the manifestation result—what rather than how it will appear. If the results are not what you expect, check the factors in the formula, and adjust as needed.

Perhaps you have wondered if you have the power to manifest what you want. You do. You have the same creative power that is available to each of us. You hold the key and determine how and when you use your key to unlock riches designed especially for you. Choose to manifest consciously and then, voila!

# Manifesting Shangri La
# By Lisa Holm

I had to surrender. It was the only option. My bi-polar daughter had also become an alcoholic, and her moods and raging were off the charts. I had let her move in with me, thinking it would somehow work out. It did work out, but not in the way I had anticipated.

I knew that I created my reality, so why was this happening? We can only experience that which is a vibrational match to the frequency or energy that we hold. We are creating or manifesting our experiences constantly. The Universe responds to our most dominant vibration. I had to face the fact that I was out of alignment with the positive flow of life force. I had unconsciously manifested a situation that was full of opportunity for growth, but why had I, on some level, chosen such an extreme scenario to unfold?

We often find ourselves in dramatic circumstances because we have not been conscious of our deepest thoughts and feelings. Extreme circumstances offer quantum leaps in our spiritual growth but can be rather painful in the process. As we mature spiritually, we can create gentler ways to expand, and many of us are doing exactly that.

When I felt the shift within that took me to a place of total surrender, everything changed. It changed in me, at least. I asked for my higher self to fill me, and I gave up my old way of handling this situation—trying to figure it out in my mind, which was not working. As I gave up the struggle, I felt a warmth and light within me begin to glow and then expand. It was a profound experience. I could breathe deeply for the first time in months. Relief was blossoming within me.

Soon I was led to realize that the best option was to find a place to move to, as I saw that my daughter was not capable of moving out. I could not be in the same space with her and maintain balance and harmony. I began visualizing how my new home would look and feel. I was specific. When we wish to manifest something new, whether it is a place to live, a car, partner, job, or anything, it is important to be specific with the details only if we are coming from a place of harmony. I spent time imaging or imagining what this place would feel like. I wanted peace in me and my surroundings. The physical space would be exactly the right size for one person with the following criteria:

- A daylight basement apartment with French doors opening onto a yard
- All utilities included at an affordable price
- A wood stove or fireplace
- A great landlord who also had and loved animals and would welcome mine
- A quiet environment to connect with source and nature

I began looking on Craigslist. I always looked at the apartment rentals, but one day looked in room shares. Not looking for a room, I wasn't sure why I had been led there. Then I found it—a daylight basement in a house in the country with a propane woodstove, all utilities included with a sliding glass French door leading out onto a patio on 16 acres of pure bliss. The owners had animals and were fine with my dog and two cats. It was less per month than what I had been paying. The energy there was serene. The name of their acreage was "Shangri La."

The owners and I began exchanging emails, and I drove out to see it. It was beautiful. The energy there was so different than in town. My body and mind relaxed immediately. We discussed and agreed it was a good match for their family living upstairs and myself. Then one issue surfaced. My work required reliable internet. It turned out there was no more availability out there and only the one provider, so I could not get the internet. This was a deal-breaker. I had to let it go.

I handed it over to the Universe and kept seeing myself in the perfect home for me with all of what I wanted. I knew that the right place was already manifested vibrationally, and it would rendezvous with me in perfect timing. I kept looking on Craigslist and putting it out there. A few days later, I got a call from the owner of Shangri La. She said that they genuinely wanted me to be there, and her husband had agreed that I could share their internet. I was overjoyed.

I had three months left on the lease of my current duplex. Somehow, I was able to pay double rent for three months! When we are in alignment with the flow and know that anything is possible, amazing things can happen.

This all occurred several years ago, but is a clear example of manifesting a desire. If I had not given up my discordant thinking, my angst, the Universe could only reflect to me *that* vibration. The discord was not a vibrational match to my desire. We do have the power to shift our frequency, our thoughts and feelings, our expectations. When we are focused differently, we have a different experience. The simple phrase I love is: "Whatever we focus on gets bigger in our reality."

How do you want your life to look and feel? Manifesting is not only about getting things; it is about a change in our energy and expectations. We hold a vibration that matches that which we desire. We visualize and then release and let the Universe do the work of bringing the pieces together for the fulfillment of that desire. Deliberately creating or manifesting is a collaboration with God, source, Spirit, the Universe, or whatever your name for it is. We hold the vision, and the Universe does the heavy lifting.

# Blueprints
# By Caitlin Hurley-Jenkins

I believe that manifestations result from the ego and soul coming together with the blessing of spirit to create what has not been done before. I have been blocked, unable to write for a long time. I would start and stop, delete. Start and stop again, delete. I forgot that the muses are not something we control. On the contrary, we must listen for the right words like secrets on the wind. Sometimes they come in whispers; other times, they come through with gusto, demanding to be heard. Last week I was struggling with several decisions at once, and the noise had become deafening. I forced myself to get still in my body and accepted some radical healing.

What came up for me was an old wound on my heart, in the form of a dream about an old college boyfriend who had hurt me deeply. In this dream, our souls met in a deep embrace as friends, and I said, "You know I loved you, deeply and truly." We cried on each other, and all was forgiven. There was a turquoise blue misty light that surrounded our souls while we clung to one another, absolving each other of all past hurts.

This was the one guy I swore I would never forgive. "Good riddance," I said, and proceeded to pretend he no longer existed—poof! Like that, he was gone from my world. Yet, I was haunted by the pain of this heartbreak, so my perception of what happened became the dark misty shadow through which I saw the rest of my life. It was the lens through which I viewed every guy I subsequently dated—a strong, unrelenting undercurrent, which pulled me away from other intimate relationships I attempted to engage in.

This dream was a definitive nudge for me to reach out to the one person I'd been afraid to talk to for the last 15 years. In many ways, his shadow was the albatross I carried through my life. He was not on Facebook, but his wife was, so I knew at least he had married and started a family. I looked on Instagram, and there he was. I chewed on the idea of contacting him for a bit. This was scary—was I willing to open a door that had brought me pain for most of my adult life?

Then I reminded myself that I am not the same person I was back then—I am not the same person I was a year ago. I am stronger, wiser, and I know a hell of a lot more about self-care through the process of my journey.

I wrote to him, and he wrote back quickly. This wasn't the same man that I knew before; thank God. We were able to have an honest conversation about the trauma we went through, probably because we had both sought help, each in our individual time and way. I finally asked him, "Who was I to you? I have eight years sober, so it's been a long journey for me to figure out what happened. Alcohol nearly killed me. I came to Arizona when my parents took drastic measures to keep me alive. In part of the healing journey, you came up a lot. I may be asking too much, but if I don't ask, I won't know."

He responded, saying that he had no problem sharing what he remembered about his life. He said that, in his life, I am a reminder of better times before the death of his sister. He was 21 when she died and didn't realize how much of his life he had lived with depression. He told me he could honestly say he would have loved to have met me as an adult and not as a 20-year-old boy. He said he didn't how to love a woman the right way at that age, but was grateful he'd finally learned what it felt like to love the right way. Then he told me that he hoped I hadn't changed, because he remembered me as stubborn, borderline funny, beautiful, and intelligent, and he apologized for whatever pain he had caused me. He offered to take the time to talk with me more if that would help.

Like that, years of pain and unknowing anguish lifted from my heart, and the old grudge I'd been carrying for too long melted away from my heart. Lord have mercy, forgiveness is powerful. Those words set me free, and I am so grateful for his courage, as well as mine, to speak our truths. The following day, my step was lighter and my smile brighter. I asked him to thank his wife for understanding my need to speak so intimately with him; my intention was to mend an old wound, not to break anything new.

Almost miraculously, right after such a huge emotional shift, I received a call from my attorney saying that, after fighting for my children for almost seven years, now would be the time to get the ball rolling if I wanted to move physically. I was stunned! For so long, I have felt tied down, not only by my past, but also tied physically to the place where I met my ex-husband. I finally have choices over my life. I am no longer a prisoner of the untrue stories I repeated to myself for so long, and I am no longer bound to the land on which I stood my sacred ground. I have much to think about, and no matter what, I know I will go where my children and I are happiest and can live out our best lives, wherever that may be.

What started as a dream, became the beautiful, healing, turquoise blueprint for my new reality. This, my friends, is how we heal and move forward. By the grace of God, go we.

# Perfectly Capable
# By Rosemary Hurwitz

**M**y beautiful, spiritual, Pisces mother, Rose, had passed on and been gone for a month when I started to feel her presence. She had crossed over peacefully with all of her family around her bedside. My mom had been a strong spiritual influence in my life, and as she died, I truly felt her drop her body and felt her spirit soar. Soon after, even through my grief, I could actually feel her around me. I had a few instances where it was so clear she was with me, inspiring me as she occasionally did.

Often during these experiences, the words are not as large as the experience. In other words, I knew in my heart when she was with me, but explaining it to someone else or giving an account of the spiritual experience at times, it fell flat.

Nevertheless, she was there. I knew it. This was not merely a "knowing in my head" kind of knowing. It was a head-heart-gut- or mind-spirit-body-aligned kind of knowing where you can truly hear the whisper of the spirit.

My husband, Dale, and I were experiencing financial distress at the time due to the failing of the company where he had worked for several years. I worked, but only three days per week due to our kid's schedules and needs. We had four kids and a home and a summer cottage. We had our kids in private school and were trying to keep up with it all. Life moved along at a fast pace, and soon, a year had passed. Always, when I prayed, I felt my mom.

"We might have to sell our summer cottage," Dale said. I was a bit shocked. I knew it was a spiritual haven for us, and that, with the fast pace of raising a family in the Chicago area, we *all* needed the downtime of that peaceful lake in a small Michigan town. We had rented it out in the past, so I said, "Can't we rent it? I will be responsible for any and all rental work." We agreed, and a realtor we consulted along the way reinforced our hope of digging out from under the overwhelming finances. She told us that people whose cottages she had sold came back to her saying they wished they hadn't sold their place, but no one ever told her they were glad they did sell. She advised, "If you love it, do what you can to keep it." We made it work by renting it both through the summer and school year.

Our financial picture was not improving, and I began saying a simple affirmation, "We are perfectly capable of participating in God's abundance." I said it many times a day, thinking of my mom in the glory. I did not tell anyone I was saying it, but I believed in us—our family—with all of my heart. As children of God, I believed we are all perfectly capable of participating and co-creating God's abundance. There would be a way.

I was in corporate recruiting work, and my husband would tease me, "If you want me to find a better paying job, see if you can find one for me!" I replied, "Okay, sure," and mentioned that I didn't often hear of roles in his field.

One autumn day, as I was working on recruiting and placing executive assistants and middle-management candidates, the CEO of a medium-sized company called me. He said that he was referred to me, and he asked if I had a talented operations manager or two in my files that he could interview for a position that was open. As I gained details about the position, it occurred to me that my husband, prior to his present failing position, had ten years of experience doing a similar job as this potential client was describing.

I replied to him, "I do not have anyone in my files with the experience that matches your job description, but my husband had ten years' experience in that field, and has been in sales for another company for the last five years. If you can hold on, I can ask him if he'd like to meet and network with you." He had a cheerful response, "That sounds like a great start." I asked my husband if he was willing to meet this client and hear more about the operations manager role, and he said, "Sure."

Faith is frequently a process that requires us to practice patience! My husband came home from the first interview happy enough, but unsure if the role was for him, because it would be a huge undertaking to help turn the company's operations around.

Again, my faith in us unwavering, I prayed, "We are perfectly capable of participating in God's abundance," not knowing what the outcome would be, but knowing that all would be well somehow.

The second meeting with my husband and my new client went a little better, and after the third appointment, Dale had landed the new role as operations manager with a much brighter financial future!

Our lives turned around. We were able to not only keep our summer cottage, but buy the other small one next door, and eventually trade those two small cabins for our dream cottage on our favorite nearby lake. At home, we moved closer to our children's schools where they could walk, and I got out of much of the carpooling that I was doing. Things settled down for all of us.

Although we were saving for college for our kids, I was able to hear a deeper call to go back to school for a Masters of Art in Pastoral Studies, and secured a scholarship. A wonderful new, deeply satisfying career of spiritual teacher, coach, and author awaited me! Our dreams were being realized, and I knew deep within that my faith in the affirmation, "We are perfectly capable of participating in God's abundance," helped manifest these new dreams.

# The Power Within
# By Foxye Jackson

One will manifest experiences despite believing in the ability to do so. The power of manifestation is given to all souls and accompanies them in their human form. Therefore, because these souls are having a human experience, and all souls are connected, each one is gifted with an innate ability to manifest their reality. Truly, the power within is there and only needs to be awakened.

Some common difficulties in manifesting experiences involve controlling one's thoughts, filtering one's beliefs, improving one's awareness, and acknowledging one's true intentions. Each of these affects the reality experienced when manifestation occurs. Thoughts have a tendency to be random and uncontrolled. Beliefs held by the thinker influence which thoughts are deemed true or irrelevant. In fact, beliefs can shape thoughts and intentions, and the individual may be unaware. Awareness means the individual purposefully and consciously evaluates each thought and belief and their effects. An intention describes the purpose of manifesting an experience or action. With that, the intention of this writing is for the reader to understand the amazing power that lies within, how to awaken it, and how to use it.

**Thoughts**

Buddha said, "All that we are is a result of what we have thought." Many do not spend enough time with themselves to know how they think, what they think about, or even which thoughts belong to them. Spending time with oneself, in this case, means studying oneself. Obvious ways to study oneself include journaling, meditating, and reflecting. Each requires some level of solitude.

Journaling involves the magic of writing, which combines the essence of being in the moment with allowing energy to flow from the mind to the hand, thereby enabling the thinker to release thoughts, negative or positive, onto paper. The thinker is then able to become aware of how they process events and information by organizing these thoughts. This organization of thoughts further empowers the thinker to connect their thoughts and experiences through journaling.

Meditation creates mental solitude and, with practice, the ability to quiet the mind and allow it to rest. With the absence of training, the mind will continue with such a constant flow of thoughts that one cannot rest, sleep, or heal. A picture of this would be the reins that bridle thoughts are in the hands of the thoughts instead of the thinker. Meditation allows the thinker to assume control of those mental reins and direct the mind on when to think, what to think, and how to change perspectives of thought.

Each second in front of a mirror is a moment of reflection. Placing a mirror in front of the mind requires honesty and courage: courage to see what is there and honesty to acknowledge what it is. For example, it is easy to hear the mind produce a thought such as, "You are inadequate." With courage, one acknowledges the thought, labels it as untrue, and begins to evaluate its origin. With honesty, the thinker debates the thought with the understanding that it originated from someone else's manifested thoughts and the belief that that person was correct. The importance of evaluating one's beliefs is demonstrated in this.

**Beliefs**

Beliefs are ages old and taught from generation to generation. Courage helps filter these beliefs into categories of which to retain and which to replace. Og Mandino stated, "Your only limitations are those you set up in your mind, or permit others to set up for you." Children are taught an initial set of beliefs from their parents in an attempt to keep them safe. Having no other conscious foundation of beliefs, the children believe the parents. The parents teach from their learned knowledge and experiences, and their beliefs may not always serve the children positively as they matriculate into adulthood.

A common example and one that has proven most influential on the children's growth is, "I love you." This statement, typically accompanied by actions or more words, creates an imaginary box full of descriptors of love. Descriptors may include hugs, gifts, and encouraging words or abuse (sexual, physical, mental). Either way, the connection between the proclamation of love and the actions demonstrated, creates a belief box that states if these descriptors are absent, so is love. Hopefully, one can recognize the importance of filtering beliefs (i.e., through journaling, meditation, and reflection) to manifest the desired reality, understanding that walking in that reality may feel awkward. Self-discovery, such as this, raises one's awareness of manifestation power.

**Awareness**

Awareness is simply being present and in the current moment—not thinking of the past or present. With the established routine of journaling, meditating, and reflecting, one gains thought control, aligns beliefs with individual desires, and experiences an improved awareness of the power within. Through awareness, cycles, processes, and lessons are uncovered. Awareness also reveals patterns of particular beliefs and thoughts manifesting into one's current reality. The self-discovery process revealed here takes that awareness and motivates the individual to become intentional about what reality is desired.

**Intention**

Once aware of the roots of one's thoughts and beliefs, and how they impact reality, it becomes almost automatic to set an intention of change. Obviously, changes will occur in the above-mentioned processes. Other amazing results are positive changes in reality. For example, one may change jobs, sever a relationship, or modify living arrangements all because it allows more space for spending time with oneself. Ultimately, the truest of intentions for anyone is to discover the power within.

## Conclusion

Thoughts, beliefs, awareness, intentions, and manifestation all are powerful. These abilities are innately within the reader, meaning the reader is powerful beyond measure; they need only believe. "Every intention sets energy into motion, whether you are conscious of it or not," said Gary Zukav. If this is true, my stated intention is already set into motion: the reader is now aware of and understands how to use their newly awakened power of manifestation, for this is the power within.

# Angels Of My Manifestations
# By Foxye Jackson

My preparation to write is often the same and involves a hotel room, a "do not disturb" sign, a silent phone, and food prepared in my room. Writing for this book was the same, yet different. In fact, from the moment the invitation to write was presented, everything was different.

Daily, I am aware of my ability to manifest my reality, and I am quite purposeful about doing so. I write down new moon wishes, my "ten most wanted," and even full moon releases. I regularly journal, meditate, and reflect upon my life. However, it seemed that life became awry once I agreed to write about manifestation, and nothing I did manifested what I desired.

Normally, life is routine and constant. When I decided to write for this book, I was working three jobs (8–20 hour days), running a nonprofit organization, caring for two children, and still squeezing in time to be a wife and friend. This meant minimal time was available for me to accomplish anything past preparing for my next shift.

Some time ago, perhaps several months, I formed the belief that we were not going to have enough money to care for our family. That belief invaded and, in hindsight, consumed my thoughts. I took on three jobs, and a few side jobs, under the shadow of believing in lack. As the law of manifestation goes, my thoughts and beliefs quickly manifested into my reality.

Despite listing expenses against projected income and always calculating a surplus, the financial books never displayed this. I continued to meticulously review our expenses for ones to eliminate or reduce. Consequently, my manifested thoughts created a funds shortage at the month's end. Gas prices, car repairs (one vehicle caught on fire), common needs of the children, and household maintenance consumed any calculated income overages. In those moments, my depression began to spiral, and I was simultaneously asked to write for *Inspirations: 101 Uplifting Stories for Daily Happiness.*

My beliefs of lack helped create a perfect excuse for not being part of *Inspirations.* The push to do so came from my intuition. That little voice inside me would not stop reminding me I needed to be part of that book. In the midst of my perceived lack, I decided to contribute my story to *Inspirations* to quiet that little voice. Little did I know, I would need that book to inspire myself.

*Inspirations* launched, and I immediately dissociated from it. For me, it was so surreal that it couldn't possibly be true. Unfortunately, I never experienced true excitement for this accomplishment. I'm still trying to grasp the reality that, in a matter of weeks, I became a best-selling author. The hard truth is that this accomplishment was a manifestation of my desire, and it put me in a state of shock.

During my annual vision board party, I entreated the universe with my supplications. In 2018, I listed the hope of becoming a best-selling author. In 2019, I added new perspectives of thinking and feeling that I wanted to manifest within myself. The universe answered by forcing me to evaluate my inner self with love and honesty. That reflection uncovered the need for me to intentionally heal from what I was attempting to replace.

I had failed to recognize my need to heal from deep-seated feelings of lack, inadequacy, and absence of capabilities. This failure created self-fulfilling prophecies and prolifically manifested into my reality. My poor beliefs convinced me to work more hours, manifest additional expenses, and have little time with my family. Each of these increased my feelings of lack, inadequacy, and absence of capabilities. Additionally, I became so chronically tired that I had great difficulty creating a sense of normalcy and peace in my life, which resembled a hurricane throwing symbolic emotions everywhere. The turning point was being presented with the opportunity to write in this book about manifestations.

From what I was experiencing, my ability to manifest was failing in the areas I needed it most. Then life began to send me messages. My friends would randomly comment that I was doing a lot and needed to slow down. Initially, I became defensive because my beliefs said all this was necessary. Then the universe said to slow down, increasing the pains and fatigue within my body. It was imperative that I slow down if I wanted to change what I was manifesting.

I slowed down and went back to my beginnings. I journaled, meditated, and reflected on my state of life. I evaluated my decisions and how I allocated my time. I made hard choices that put me and my desires at the forefront. I scheduled times for solitude, and I clicked the button to write a second chapter in *Manifestations: True Stories Of Bringing The Imagined Into Reality*.

As previously stated, preparing for this book was different than other writings. I booked a hotel and, upon arrival, noticed it was a new building located near the first hotel my husband and I booked together in Dallas. That night, I went to a restaurant with friends and noticed it was situated near where our massage therapist's office was located when we first met him. I pondered those synchronicities and immediately experienced an erasure of my writer's block. I realized that I had to return to my beginnings to understand my current reality.

Currently, my thoughts and beliefs are being challenged. My efforts to eliminate those thoughts and beliefs that manifest opposite my desires include returning to the roots of manifestation: journaling, meditating, and reflecting. I have set an intention to regain control over my thoughts, filter my beliefs, remain aware of what I'm manifesting, and to continuously evaluate my intentions.

Angels are messengers and surround me constantly. If you find yourself having trouble manifesting, slow down, go back to the basics, and listen. Writing in *Manifestations* pushed me to do that, hence the title of this chapter: *Angels of My Manifestations*.

# A Wish Came True
# By JamieLynn

A t the age of seven, I began to understand I could create my world. I began to make wishes and daydream about them coming true. I would look at the men in my life and pick aspects of them I liked. Many of these were inspired by my dad and the men he hung out with.

The aspects I admired the most were: tall, gentle, brilliant blue eyes, a passion for cars and a love to invent and work with a variety of materials, hardworking, and kind. Over time, I started to write about this man of my dreams in my journal. I would imagine what life with him would be like in detail—how we would communicate, where we were going to live, the kids we would have, and that I would meet him at the age of sixteen.

It was May of my fifteenth year, and I had not met him yet; I would be sixteen at the end of June. My spirit guides were pushing it.

My family and I went on a camping trip with my dad's best friend from high school. Others were invited too. It was May 19, 2001, and here was my dad telling me to have this guy teach me how to ride an ATV with a clutch. I took it as a sign. Four hours later, not only did I figure this clutch out, but I was hoping this guy wanted my attention. As he took off his helmet, releasing his wavy black hair, and having a full view of his sky-blue eyes, I said to my spirit guides, "Yep, that's him, thank you!" This was the man I would marry.

I had it that my dad already approved, and life from here was going to be amazing! The only thing was to tell him what I was going through and let him choose if he still wanted me. Fear of rejection set in. You see, I had recently released myself from eight years of sexual abuse by five family members, and we were well on our way through court proceedings; in fact, our first court date would be in August.

He wanted me to come with him to go get ice and some warm clothes from his cabin, the second sign. I sat in his lowered Sonoma, sleek and silver. The light feature flickered like lightning as I had a sobering thought—do I tell him now? Will this break his heart? I had not thought about how my past might affect my future, and at this point, I need to tell him before I fall any deeper.

He popped back into the truck. "What's wrong?" He was already worried about me. "What?" I came out of my trance. "Oh, nothing, just tired," I lied. I wasn't ready. We started to drive back to camp.

"Do you like me?" I asked.

"Well, yeah, I think you're nice," he responded, nervously. Good enough answer.

"I need to tell you a few things. If you do like me, these are things you need to know."

"Okay." His body shifted and his arm went up on the steering wheel like he didn't want to be there and, frankly, neither did I. This felt like a big risk.

I took a deep breath. "I have a boyfriend; I would have to break up with him first."

"Is that it?" He asked.

"No, there is more, that was the easy part. Well, I am going to be in court soon, not as the offender, I am the victim." When I said I wasn't the offender, he seemed to relax a bit, but said nothing.

"I was molested by my cousins, and they are going to jail. I don't know what the impact will be. I am told I might not know for a while. I might get angry, I might need therapy and prescriptions, I might do stupid things. I want you to know before you fall in love that this is going on so you can make a choice knowing." He nodded and said thank you. The rest of the night went as though I hadn't said a thing. I wasn't sure what to think of that.

We kissed in the rain before he left to drive three hours home. Two years of a long-distance relationship and the impacts did make themselves known. Still, eight years from when we first met, we were married in the rain. It's been a total of nineteen years now, and we have been married for eleven of those. Our marriage has survived the impacts of the molestation and thrived with two kids! Each year we fall more in love.

Here is the secret formula that works for me even to this day:

1. Believe to the core of your being and give a time frame that you believe. I *believed* in the depth of my being that this man was going to be in my life when I was 15.
2. Visualize every aspect. I *visualized* each of the features I wanted.
3. Know it will happen. I *knew* it was going to happen.
4. Take action when you feel it. Finally, when the time came, and it felt so right it was easy, I *took action* on what I wanted the most.
5. Practice gratitude. Now I am *grateful,* and this ensures I get more of what I want in my life.

I have manifested other aspects of my life, some in a matter of minutes and others over the years. This story is my favorite. Know what it is that you want? Believe you are worthy of it to the core of your being, see it, talk to it, talk about it, and then take action—say yes! And lastly, practice gratitude so you can keep it.

Lots of love to you, Wonderful. Go manifest your life.

# Raw, Risky & Real
# By Carmen Jelly-Weiss

When I was eight years old, I imagined myself creatively writing forever. As I stood in front of my grade three English class, bellowing my creative story out loud, I felt joy and passion. At nineteen, I wanted to be a journalist and an author, but when I got to university, I discovered psychology and fell in love with human nature. Finally, at the age of fifty-three, I came to the realization that I can marry my passions and be both a psychotherapist and a writer. The magical realization of manifesting my desires began six months ago.

Natalie, Suzanne, and I stumbled into our creative manifestations when we gathered at a cozy restaurant, eager to discuss our lives and new adventures. The three of us passionately shared our recent experiences of creating individual private practices in psychotherapy. With curiosity and courage leading our conversations, we soon leaped into a discussion about our deepest desires and visions. On that evening, the stars aligned, and we intuitively knew we were meant to create magic together. Natalie, with her vibrant red hair, oozed with exalted emotions and brilliant ideas. Suzanne's soft eyes revealed an abiding calmness and faith. Her power, which can part waters, was deeply apparent the moment we discovered our common purpose.

Our "power of three" synergy emerged like a soft waltz, pushing us together with grace and harmony. We wove our three business names together, and the power of creation was set in motion. Pow! The process of bringing something into existence had begun. "Imagine New Perceptions on Being Human" became our joint name and concept for healing wounds to wellness. Although not planned, our first manifestation quickly appeared before our eyes. This conversation became the birthplace of transformation and the first step in our beautiful dance.

From that day forward, our energy felt like a symphony of music guiding our clumsy feet forward and sometimes sideways and backward. Nonetheless, we plunged into a sea of vulnerability with intentional minds, hearts aligned, and souls on fire. We discovered an energetic connection that continues to develop and grow with each intention. We began to sense and feel ourselves becoming more real and authentic. Exploring wounds and the pain that lies beneath is woven into our fabric and has driven our collective intent to understand and heal our clients.

As three psychotherapists, we set an intention to collaborate, create, and strengthen our craft by creating podcasts. A faster tap dance together produced a second manifestation. Pow! There is no guidebook for bringing our whole three selves into this process, merely a magical feeling as we dance in our sea of creation. With our collective experiences and teachings, we imagined a podcast series entitled *Stories From Within* by WER3. With a goal to humanize healing, we created podcasts that are now published on Podbean, iTunes, and Spotify. Our interactions and podcasts became a platform that led us to another transformational discovery.

As the podcast series flowed from our souls, we began to understand that our messages would test us personally. They began to inform the way we conducted our lives as we practiced being present, open, and connected. This discovery allowed us to dance closer and faster together, and to fine-tune our rhythm and beat into our third manifestation. Pow! Raw, risky, and real emerged like the vibrant and playful tango. These three words define our personal journeys and encourage the development of sensitivity, clarity, and trust. We need these words to capture and hold our energetic power of three.

These words bring music to our ears and help us dance together so we can deepen and enrich our steps with clients. They are our navigation guide to bring us from our minds to our hearts and intuition. As the music plays on, raw, risky, and real has evolved to become a deeply experiential therapeutic process. Harmonically, we emerged with an individual and group therapy framework to reveal that what lies beneath can surface, and be understood and transformed. Our group, entitled Wounds to Wellness, walks others through our raw, risky, and real approach. The purpose of raw emotions is to move from suffering to a willingly bold and risky life dance. Risky engagement is changing your music and learning new dance steps to discover and create the real authentic you. In reality, we are manifesting new stories for ourselves and others who are tired of sitting this dance out on the sidelines of life.

During times of transformation, we can often feel lost with two left feet. Raw, risky, and real is our safe container, which allows us to explore different choice points and genres in our dance of life. In this pursuit, we awaken to our bodies with a powerful invitation to reconnect with buried emotions in our energetic and emotional states. This is where we change our dance steps. Our framework is a call to heal through creative expression, which requires us to risk leaving old patterns and trying new strategies. If music is the food of life, play on as we dance. Natalie, Suzanne, and I stepped into a cycle of learning that welcomes the body, mind, and soul to move together, understand, validate, and course correct.

With raw, risky, and real, the three of us entered the power of creating and manifesting a new chapter in our lives. On that magical night in the restaurant, our harmony together evoked a beautiful new song. A meeting of minds, hearts, and souls birthed three manifestations: New Perceptions on Being Human; WeR3; and Raw Risky and Real. With dynamic and energetic steps, our visions became our reality. We now understand that whatever we focus on, we will bring to fruition. With cadence and courage, we are hip-hopping into many more magnificent manifestations. My child and adult selves are smiling ear to ear.

# Manifestation, Mastermind and Miracles
## By Debra Kahnen

I started studying manifestation in the early '80s. The first book I read, *The Dynamic Laws of Prosperity,* by Catherine Ponder, opened my eyes to the possibility of creating what you want with a scripture-based process. I learned to scientifically and intentionally pray to bring things I wanted into my life.

I remember renting my first office space—a little scary. I had planned to sign a lease on a space the next day. That night, I looked at the list of everything I wanted and prayed for in that office or something better. The next day I received a call on a different office that was perfect, and leased it for even less than the first space. "That or something better" became a big part of my prayers in the future.

The next book that helped me manifest was *Ask and It Is Given, Learning to Manifest Your Desires* by Esther and Jerry Hicks. This book was loaded with processes to help train your mind and emotions to work with this universal power of manifestation.

I played with the processes in the book. It is similar to the healing work I do where you have to build your faith. As I worked the processes, I started noticing all the synchronicities that allowed life to line up, leading to the manifestation of what I wanted. What I learned in this period is whatever you give your attention to, negative or positive, you are attracting into your life. The trick is to decrease your resistance to what you don't want and be clear on what you do want.

For example, I was unhappy in my job as a nursing supervisor. I had all of this accountability and no authority. For years I kept saying to my mastermind partners that I wanted to change that. I spent years doing classes and working with entrepreneurial coaches, and I was still at the hospital. I know part of me felt secure in that job as a single mother. I also have a personality that is uncomfortable with not knowing where the next dollar is going to come from. Belief systems have a lot to do with manifestation. Then one day, I reluctantly volunteered to do a project to help the hospital. With my new mentor, I was able to save lives and money for the hospital. I published and presented my results at a national conference. This empowered me.

Because of this, instead of feeling trapped in my job, I made a decision that I was going to use the resources in that health care system to help me accomplish my goals of making a difference. Instead of resisting what I did *not* want—I focused on what I *did* want. Because I aligned my goals with the organization's, I had access to a research scientist, Institutional Review Board, statistician, public relations expert, an entire studio, rooms, and other resources—things I could never have had access to as a solopreneur. However, my entrepreneurial training had given me all the skills to be successful. I was able to complete several studies using mindfulness to help nurses with stress and individuals with chronic pain. I was able to publish and present nationally and internationally. The lesson here was in "lining up the energy"—intentions, thoughts, emotions, and beliefs all going in the same direction.

Over the last five years, two other women and I have used the eight steps into the mastermind consciousness developed by Jack Boland to continually elevate each other and create what we wanted in our lives. It got to the point that we knew if we asked the mastermind, it would happen, and we had to be extremely clear on what we wanted. Remember that job I had? Well, I got a new boss. She did not understand how what I was doing was helping her unit, because she did not think about the big picture like my last boss did. She made my life miserable. I kept saying, "I want out of there, but not yet. I want to finish this study. Wait, I want to get my bonus for doing the study. Wait, I want to take my vacation." Then, in one mastermind meeting, I said, "Okay, God—I give my job to you." The next week

I was laid off because they eliminated my position. Believe me, getting laid off from your job after 21 years is not easy, but there is something so comforting when another part of you knows everything is going to be okay. I was able to manifest a better job with top pay for that position.

I have noticed that, because of the faith I developed in the mastermind process, when something looks like it might be negative or unwanted, I can hold the faith that it is for my highest and best good and it will ultimately lead to something I do want. And it always does.

The other important aspect of manifestation I learned along the way is the need to act. You don't have to know all of the steps when you take the first step. After you take the first step, the next step becomes clearer. Each time you can successfully create what you intend, it builds your faith and belief. This makes it easier to act. A perfect example is a professional certification test I made a mastermind request to pass. I did not ask to pass the test and then arrive unprepared. I studied for three months and passed up many social events. During the test, I felt the anxiety build and self-doubt visit. I kept remembering my request and knowing I was going to pass this test. I visualized the passing certificate I had placed on my vision board and felt my mastermind partners support. I remembered all of the other successful mastermind requests and forged on and passed that test. Each success adds more evidence that the process works.

# Bringing Forth My Wishes
## Susan Marie Kelley

"What you think, you become; what you feel, you attract; what you imagine, you create." ~ Gautama Buddha

After all four kids left home, Dave and I decided it was time to downsize, so we moved to a grand, three-story townhouse. Crown molding graced every room, even in the basement. Palladian windows framed the wooded back yard, decks had been built off most of the rooms, and the gourmet kitchen had shiny granite countertops. For about six months, we were happy living there, until one day we realized we were spending all our time in the townhouse or in the car, never outside, and Dave and I liked being outside. Deep within, I recognized my need for acres of land to roam with peaceful places to commune among nature and spirit.

Having learned about the universal laws, I knew that it was possible to create what I wanted by putting forth my intentions because thoughts have power. Secretly I wrote a list. The property had to be at least ten private acres with centuries-old trees, and a pond would be nice. I put my desires away in a cabinet and thought about it from time to time, but never mentioned it to Dave, as I figured he wouldn't want to move to a place where he'd have to do yard work again. I had no idea where the money would come from, but I believed that it would become available, and I focused on getting what I wanted.

Not long after I made my wish list, the Homeowners Association got nasty and accused Dave, who was treasurer, of stealing money from their checking account. This was ludicrous because there was never any money in it. Furious, Dave announced one day, "I want to move."

"Okay, then, I know the kind of place I want," I answered.

And off we went in search of a farm. This took time, of course, but we did find our fifteen acres. Hundred-year-old oaks lined the driveway around to a six hundred square foot pole barn. Dave was sold immediately. The house was adequate and stood in front of a picturesque pond with plenty of frogs and dragonflies. Dave's mother died not long after, leaving us a sizable inheritance. We had manifested our desires.

Soon I began to wonder what else I could do, with my powerful thoughts. I decided to try it out. My twenty-something daughter, Annie, was visiting one evening in late September. The lights were low as we sat at the kitchen table, with a thick green candle burning steadily between us.

"I know we have powers we can use but have forgotten," I said to her.

"What do you mean?" she asked.

Staring at the candle, I decided to do an experiment. "I think we were able to manipulate fire in other lifetimes."

I put my hand next to the flame and raised it up. With this motion, the flame went steadily up one foot in the air. Shocked, I got scared, and immediately the flame died down. I realized that, indeed, we have the power to make fire move by our thoughts and intentions.

That summer, Dave and I, along with Annie and her boyfriend Jeff, went to the beach one afternoon. Jeff loved to surf, but the waves were being uncooperative. Knowing I could make flames move (after hearing the story), Jeff asked me, "Mrs. K, would you work some of your magic on the waves and make them bigger?"

Flames are one thing, but waves are huge. Not wanting to disappoint Jeff, I stood on the beach, cleared my mind, and imagined higher waves. At first, nothing happened, and then they started swelling and rising. Jeff, with his surfboard under his arm, looked at me and said, "Thanks Mrs. K," and ran into the water. He didn't care how it had happened; he only wanted to surf. Both our intentions were at work, and it created what we wanted.

I have learned that if I need a parking spot, all I have to do is visualize an empty space, and it appears. This works at the grocery store as well. Let's say you are in a hurry to get home, but decide to stop for some ingredients for that spaghetti dinner you are craving. You grab lettuce, pasta, and a loaf of bread, and then step into the shortest check-out line. However, the clerk insists on chatting with everyone, the woman in front of you has lost her credit card, and worst of all, the manager has to be called because no one seems to know the price of pickles. You fidget and roll your eyes as you feel the exasperation growing. And as it grows—everyone gets slower and slower.

One good way out of this situation is when you feel that exasperation building, STOP, take a deep breath, calm down, let it go, and say to yourself, "This line will quickly move." This actually works, and more times than not, another line will open up. Now, before I even get into the store, I say affirmations that everything will go quickly and smoothly. I am using my thoughts to control the situation.

Our bodies are here today, gone tomorrow. The only thing that remains forever is our spirit and our thoughts. We were created with the ability and power to create anything we want. By using imagination to create mental images, we can manifest all we desire. Jeshua has said, "Imagination is a most wonderful tool because it allows you to go beyond the boundary of what has been set as reality."

# Whipping Up A Little Wind
# By Susan Marie Kelley

There was a time when I was getting tripped up on the principle of the "All" or source or God. And then I had a dream. I was being pulled into an elevator by an incredible downdraft, but held onto a pillar to keep from getting sucked in. Standing inside was a balding, middle-aged man with a smile on his face. And then I heard the "big man upstairs" talking to people.

Somehow, I got up there with the bald man guiding me to make sure I got to the right place. We came to a waiting room where I was directed to sit and wait for my turn. And then the "big man" appeared right in front of me. It was a whirlwind, roughly in the shape of a person. This entity was a composite of all of humanity. From all the many people, I caught a glimpse of my eyes looking out at me and knew I was part of it as well, but I couldn't stay any longer. That must be the All, I thought.

Through my intuition, I realized what this dream was saying—that if we are part of the All, then we are in essence, God, so we have the power and ability to create what we want like God does. I had to imagine what I wanted—that was the mental part.

My guides explained, "The reason the imagination is so powerful is that everything in the universe is first created with thought."

The light was beginning to brighten. "So, does that mean there is nothing other than thoughts?"

"Bingo," they responded.

"With that in mind, can I conjure up anything and have it manifest?" I asked.

"You are where you are because you put yourself there," they reminded me. "Every nuance of your life, your relationships, jobs, even physical things like your house, car, and financial status has come to you by your thoughts."

"Then it stands to reason that if I brought everything to myself merely by thinking, I could change it to something else if I want."

"That's it. The stronger the intention, the faster and more direct the result will be."

I wanted to try out this little nugget of wisdom when Dave and I were RVing in the mountains of New York. It was a lovely day in May, so we decided to take the dogs on a hike. We hiked regularly and were in good shape—not great shape—and could do a couple of miles without exhaustion. Since Dave is in love with welcome centers, he spent a pleasant half-hour discussing the various trails with a nice lady, and came to the car with maps hanging out of his pockets.

"I think I know the right trail to take," he said confidently. I got our two Shelties out of the car, and we started our walk into the woods. The baby leaves were making their way into the world; sunlight cascaded down the branches, and birds sang praises to the heavens.

An hour into our walk, I asked sweetly, "How long is this trail?"

"The woman said about a mile," he responded.

"Gee," I replied, "It seems we've been walking a long time." I knew we could do a mile in about twenty minutes.

"We should be getting to the end pretty soon," Dave said.

"Let's stop up here and look at the map," I suggested.

After Dave and I took a long drink from our water bottle, we opened the map.

"I think we took a wrong turn," Dave said quietly.

I knew we were in trouble because it is a known fact that men don't get lost, and if they do, not even under threat of vicious torture will they admit anything.

I started getting a little warm. When I hit my fifties, nature had taken its course, and hot flashes would get so hot I could boil my morning coffee on top of my head. At that moment, I felt a wave of heat start rolling in the pit of my stomach and begin its ascent up through my solar plexus, gathering speed as it plowed through my heart chakra with the ferocity of a tornado. It ended in my forehead, with great drops of perspiration rolling off my face.

Many trees surrounded us, but not one of them had any direction markers. Feeling faint, I took off my jacket. I knew we had to move on, so I decided to whip up a little breeze to cool me down. Breathing deeply and closing my eyes, I imagined a mighty wind blowing through the trees. When nothing manifested, I gathered up my backpack and started walking, wiping the waterfall streaming down my face. Where was the puff of air I so desperately needed? Then I heard the trees above rustle slightly. With newfound hope, I waited expectantly. The wind moved down through the trees, then gathered speed and rushed past us, lowering my temperature. Relief washed over me, and I was able to pick up a brisk pace. After re-examining the map, we eventually discovered a trail and found our way back to the car.

As I gained more confidence using this new concept, I began manifesting everything in all areas of my life. I felt more in control, and with control comes power and then peace.

# Wordless Wisdom
# By Donna Kiel

I came home and discovered my dad wandering around the family room in his underwear. Only that morning, as I rushed off to my job as a school principal, he had wished me a good day and did his usual salutation of, "God bless you." I never knew why he wanted God to bless me, but it was important to him. As I left, he was doing some accounting work for a client.

My father had moved in with me after my mother died. At 84, my father was an intelligent, articulate, and engaging man. His ability to weave words into poetic phrases gained him notoriety. As an accountant, he had tremendous knowledge and expertise. Even at 84, he continued to do the accounting for local bars within walking distance, which was a clever way he could trade his accounting skills for free beer. My dad's intellect and expertise in all matters of mathematics were matched equally by his ability to weave words that could melt the heart of any man, woman, or child.

Finding my dad wandering around was petrifying. As I realized something was seriously wrong, I immediately jumped into problem-solving, and decided to take him to the hospital. First, I had to get him dressed. My father had a colostomy bag as the result of colon cancer surgery he had had 25 years earlier. His adventure of disoriented walking had him covered in feces. I had to shower my father, the man who had been my intellectual nemesis and my hero—the man I never saw naked.

Nothing in life prepares you for the odd emotions that accompany showering your father. Luckily my dad was compliant. I completely detached emotionally. I was scared.

My dad was diagnosed with sudden onset dementia. I placed him in a nursing home. I never weighed the pros and cons of that decision or even considered caretaking him in my home. Somewhere inside,

I knew I was too inept to give him the care he deserved and needed. The gift of language and articulate expression that had been my dad's hallmark were gone. He would answer questions and be compliant, but his intellect and power of words were gone.

The relationship I had with my dad was complicated. My dad loved alcohol, his faith, his country, cooking, and his family—in that order. As I grew, my dad was both my hero and my tormentor. He would write beautiful poems to me, and then when drinking, his words would cut and criticize. I could go from the most beautiful daughter to a stupid idiot in one day of drinking.

My father often chose alcohol over time with me. He chose work instead of noticing his daughter was slipping away. When my daughter was born, he became a loving, congruent, and reliable grandfather. I desperately wanted the love and care I saw him bestow on his grandchildren.

I would visit my dad in the nursing home. After a few months, he went on hospice. Hospice workers told me that I needed to give him permission to let go. My dad had few words, and I did all the talking, wondering if he understood. Our visits continued for two years, and each time, I would say it was okay for him to leave and that we would be fine. Somehow, he knew that wasn't yet true.

Sundays with my dad were a long goodbye consisting of my confessions of misdeeds, begging forgiveness, and sharing my wanting his love. I did all the talking and purging. My dad's health grew strained, and doctors determined the end was imminent and asked me to make a decision. I needed to decide if my dad should go to a hospital and gain the care that may extend his life a bit or leave him in the nursing home with comfort care to die. Fear filled my entire body, and the thought of losing him was more than I could bear. In the flash of an instant, I knew I had to try and give him the chance. I decided to have him hospitalized.

The nurses asked my dad, "Harry, do you want to go to the hospital?" They needed to follow the routine of asking his permission. Though he had not spoken, at that moment, he looked at me and said, "Whatever the boss says, she's in charge."

Over the next few days, my dad faded and was again nonverbal. His crystal blue eyes would open and flutter occasionally. On a bright sunny day, as I sat next to his bed, he opened his eyes and looked out the window. I leaned in and said, "Dad, I need to go to work; I love you." As I spoke the words, I finally felt the meaning. Yes, I truly loved him. No matter what had happened and what choices he or I made—he was my dad, and I was his daughter.

He looked at me and said, "I love you; I admire you; I adore you." I wondered if I was dreaming. Did this happen? Did he speak to me? In the moment of love, had I manifested the dream I had of a loving father?

The moment I released the need to control and write the script of what the love between my father and me would be like, was the moment I manifested the love I needed and that love which was his wordless essence. My father's final wordless wisdom created the space I needed to forgive him and me. Words often get in the way. Yet, when we can love ourselves and love those who we are given to love us, we can let go of the wanting and manifest love that is held within wordless truth.

# Permission To Live True
# By Donna Kiel

S he looked terrified. Most students who came to my office look petrified. After all, the principal's office is a scary place—even for the principal! Her school counselor accompanied her. I greeted them both with my usual gracious smile. I had become adept at exuding kindness and keeping any anxiety buried so deeply that no one could see.

Being a school principal, for me, was a complicated and unpredictable wild ride. My desire to rescue all my students and the burden that their care was on my shoulders was often too much, so I would pretend I had all the answers. The principal is supposed to have the answers, and I became great at the pretense. The counselor spoke first and unraveled a story that immediately erased my pretending to be calm. I could feel my body tense, and my heart pound faster. How could this happen under my watch?

I immediately moved closer to her. I reached for her shoulder, wanting to hold her and keep her safe. I desperately needed her to hear me. My entire being wanted to cry for her and with her. The desire to comfort her, to tell her she was alright, to let her know that I would never let anything happen to her became my single thought. I had to let her know I believed her. I had to let her know she was safe. This was personal.

Schools are supposed to be safe havens. They are supposed to be places free from harm for students and adults. Schools are far from safe havens, and even for me, the school became a place of secret violation.

Eight years earlier, as a new faculty member, and one of the only women on staff, I was anxious to fit in. When a popular male faculty member welcomed me with kindness, I eagerly accepted his friendship. We would joke around, sharing stories. We were

144

buddies. He'd often compliment me, and I liked his affirmation. He often stopped by my office to chat.

On one particular day, he stopped by my office, and things felt odd. He said how great I looked, then he moved toward my desk, saying, "Wanna see what you do to me?" I froze. He pulled down his pants. I said nothing. I felt the familiar detachment and emotional distancing I had gained as a skill the first time this happened to me at age four. He left. I never told anyone. I was so filled with shame and fear I pretended it had not happened.

Now, eight years later, I'm no longer his buddy, I am his boss listening to a petrified 15-year-old describe an all too familiar scene where, again, he is the perpetrator. She cried, "I don't want anything to happen to him, he's my friend." I reassured her, "You did nothing wrong." She began to relay the details. "He was talking to me after school. He's been helping me with boyfriend troubles." I could feel my heart pounding so hard I feared she could hear it. "He said I was beautiful and wanted me to see what I did to him. He pulled down his pants."

How had I let this happen? Had my silent shame, contributed to the heinous act? My deep fear that began so many years before had allowed this young woman to be victimized. My image as a powerful, strong woman of integrity who was a decisive and effective principal was all a façade. I hated myself. I had to find justice for this young woman and also find compassion and forgiveness for me. The task felt impossible.

My supervisor asked me if her story true. How could this beloved teacher do this? I knew the truth. The decision was clear. I fired him immediately. Faculty were enraged. Students were upset. I had stepped into my integrity and felt the shaming of a culture that denies things we cannot handle.

I was ordered by the school attorney never to share the details of the perpetrator's acts to protect him and the school's reputation. I complied. I went on with my work and kept moving. It is amazing how time moves forward, and we forget terrible things. School moved on, and so did I.

At the end of that school year, my evaluation from the super-intendent was exceptional. I had consumed myself with work as I usually did to hide from shame and pain. A month later, I was asked to meet with him. I never imagined he would ask me to resign. I had a stellar record, school planning was in full swing, and I had a signed contract for the next school year. He said the board didn't think I was a good fit any longer, and there were questions of my integrity. Shame flooded every cell in my body. I didn't disagree. I quietly, with overwhelming pain, submitted my resignation.

The moment I walked away from the school, it was as if I had been freed from prison. I had constructed a prison of silence, shame, and denial. The young woman who bravely shared her story of violation with me has been my greatest teacher of manifesting my truth and my purpose. She came into my office, petrified to speak, and left as a woman of courage and integrity. She risked all she knew to speak her truth. Manifesting the life of your dreams requires only two things—integrity and love. The moment I dropped into loving that young woman, I knew what was true. Deep within me was a calling to become a woman of truth who could help others own their truth. When we let go of shame, the freedom of integrity is born, and with it, we manifest the glorious peace of manifesting our highest and truest potential. To manifest the life of your dreams, begin by loving the beauty that is uniquely you, and embrace the truth guiding you.

# No More Fear Public Speaking Map
# By Donna Kiel

I'm not sure when the fear of speaking that consumed me for so long began to fade, but I do remember the moment it began. As an introverted, shy, awkward 12-year-old, the new seventh-grade teacher, Ms. Porter, was like the warmth of a blanket and a shower of joy. Her radiant smile and laughter were an elixir to my suffering middle school self.

Ms. Porter shifted my world. She was young, beautiful, passionate about our world, and unlike any teacher I had ever experienced. She talked *to* us and not *at* us. She would talk about the nightly news stories of soldiers dying in Vietnam and the importance of feminist marches. She awakened in me something I had no idea existed—a calling to make a difference and a belief that I mattered.

In Ms. Porter's class, I sat in the last desk in the third row. Teachers always seated me in the back because I was the good, quiet kid no one had to worry about. Next to me, on the right, was an empty desk. The day we had to give our first individual speeches, Ms. Porter came and sat next to me so she could listen. I was in heaven. She was sitting next to me, and I could absorb her courage, her dynamic personality, her kindness, and laughter.

When it was my turn, I walked up to the podium, and this odd rush of weakness filled my body. I wasn't sure my legs would hold me. I had been scared other times in my life, but this feeling was different. My hands were dripping with sweat. I held my hand-written notes and attempted to read as the paper shook. I felt faint. My voice shook as much as the paper. The rest of the speech is a blur. I don't even recall if I spoke the entire thing.

I quickly went back to my desk, forgetting Ms. Porter was sitting right there. I was humiliated. I wanted to be anywhere but in that classroom. I pretended to hold it together. That moment was the birth of deep fear and secret. I had to keep hidden my fear of speaking and my wanting to belong. With strong determination, I vowed I would never speak in public again and never tell anyone what happened.

That moment of humiliation in my first public speaking experience crushed my dream. I had desperately wanted the cool Ms. Porter to know me. I wanted her to be proud of me. I wanted her to know that I had been molested by my uncle, but bravely carried on. I wanted her to know my life was lonely and confusing. I wanted her to know I was a person who wanted desperately to make a difference and that I was brilliant and creative. That dream of being known was now dead. The power of shame was going to rule my life, and I would never allow that kind of suffering and humiliation into my world.

Living on this planet and going to school make it challenging to avoid public speaking, but I became a master of avoidance and lying. I was great at having spontaneous laryngitis and having several dying uncles whose funerals I needed to attend and would miss the presentation scheduled. Even in the midst of hiding myself, I found that your life's purpose has a unique way of haunting you.

"And the day came when the risk to remain tight in a bud was more painful than the risk it took to blossom." ~ Anais Nin

As I artfully avoided public speaking, I also accidentally discovered a powerful tool of manifestation. Avoiding speaking is a lonely experience. To ease the pain, I began a nightly ritual of story-making. I loved the music of Carole King, Janis Ian, and Barbra Streisand. I was convinced the words of each song were words my heart longed to speak. As a teenager (and even today), I would go to sleep soothing my loneliness listening to the music play. As I sang along to the songs, I would make up a story that I was singing in front of millions of lonely people and inspiring them to find meaning and joy.

I created fantastic stories with me as a rock star. Granted, this is an absolute fairytale as my musical talent is limited to playing a mean clarinet in high school. In the secret of my mind, late at night, I was rewriting my life story with me as the hero I wanted Ms. Porter to see. In reality, I was already the woman Ms. Porter had seen. There is this powerful truth in creating a fantasy story that defies what you believe culture is saying. By creating a story of the truth your heart is speaking, manifesting your true destiny takes hold.

My stories were actually a powerful part of me that knew the truth. I was the woman that I wanted Ms. Porter to see. I was everything I saw in Ms. Porter. Her vibrant personality and her commitment to social justice resonated because each of those qualities was buried within me.

If you feel trapped by shame, fear, or self-doubt, create a story that has you as the hero. Play with the story and play with the character that is you. Create the you that you want to be. I didn't know when my story had me as the rock star in front of millions that I would become a school counselor, then principal, then professor and someone whose daily activity is public speaking and inspiring others to live their highest potential. I simply wanted to be less lonely. Somehow, creating those soothing stories resulted in my truth being lived. I became that rock star though not playing music. Find your story, create your dream. You are a rock star, and the world is waiting for you to create the story that is your truth.

# With A Vision And A Yes, Anything Is Possible
# By Amy King

As I sit here, plugging away at what will become my first solo published book, I'm feeling overwhelmed with gratitude for the gifts of the past year. I'm fresh from a retreat in Sedona, and am readying myself for Thanksgiving week in Palm Springs with friends who are more like family. Autumn leaves are a reminder that almost a year has passed since the doctor gave me a breast cancer diagnosis. If you had told me then that this was where my life would be, I might've laughed at you. Now, I can't imagine my life if what follows hadn't happened. I haven't had a year this magical since the year my nephew was born.

In the spring of 2018, I had put together what must have been my tenth vision board. I had done this one with a laser focus, as I carefully placed each item on the board. As I attached each piece, I felt the feelings associated with achieving them. I believe that if you can see it and feel it, then it's on its way to you.

Three items on the vision board were of utmost importance. The first was that I wanted to find a fantastic life coach. As a life coach myself, I knew it was vital for me to have the support of a life coach. I felt the feelings that I associated with having a fantastic life coach, and onto my vision board it went. The second important piece was that I wanted an excellent publisher. I felt the relationship with my publisher as I placed it on the board. People have been telling me that I should write a book. I knew it too. I just needed the how.

Although I have many wonderful supportive friends, some of whom I've known for decades, I had the desire to expand my tribe of soul sisters. I found pictures of women laughing together and supporting one another. After all, isn't that why we are here? I felt the feelings associated with healthy, supportive friendships, as I attached it to the board.

In November 2018, I received a breast cancer diagnosis, had a lumpectomy in December, and began naturopathic medicine in January of 2019. As I was healing, I was seeing a barrage of signs pointing me to attend the International Women's Summit, taking place in Phoenix, March 7-11, 2019, approximately one year after I had created the vision board.

I understood that it was vital for me to make plans. I had attended concerts and comedy shows in the past couple of months, and this Summit was no different. Making plans and having things to look forward to was about living and moving forward. I registered for the Summit, booked airline and hotel reservations, and became a member of the Women's Summit Facebook page. I started to meet a plethora of friends. The bonding began weeks before takeoff. I even had dinner reservations, upon arrival, with several women. I was over the moon excited about meeting so many amazing women. I was open to the possibilities that lie ahead.

Off to the Summit I went. After landing in Phoenix, I waited for the shuttle to the hotel. Riding in the same van was a woman with a cherubic face and beautiful sparkly eyes, named Cindy. She was the first person from the Summit that I met. She is a true inspiration and one of the brightest lights. I feel fortunate and gifted with her friendship. After checking in and settling into my room, I had dinner with a lovely group of women. That night, I met so many loving women and enjoyed the opening keynote. The weekend was off to an incredible start.

Then came the day a famous life coach was scheduled to speak. Her message was inspiring and her energy magnetic. At one point, she instructed the approximately 1,000 women in the room to find a partner. It took a while for my partner to appear. Once partnered, we were to make scripted statements of encouragement to them while maintaining eye contact and holding their hands. While doing this exercise, I realized that my partner looked like the perfect cross between my mother and my grandmother. I was brought to tears having lost both, and I realized that I had some residual grief to work through. At lunch that day, the famous life coach was part of the panel discussion in the VIP room. The panel discussion ended, I was then able to express, through tears, my gratitude to her for what transpired with my partner. She hugged me with such warmth and love. Then she offered to take a picture together. Ultimately, she offered me the opportunity to be her client. She's been coaching me for the past seven months! Pinch me!

Eventually, the Summit came to a close. I spent an extra night so that I wouldn't have to rush to get to the airport. In the morning, I was sitting outside in my wheelchair, waiting for the shuttle to the airport. I saw Kyra, who it turns out is a publisher and who was also an integral part of making the weekend an unbelievable success, organizing her car. I thanked her, we hugged, and she said, "I needed that hug so bad!" I felt I needed it, too, and I was glad to have been there to give and receive. We said goodbye and headed to our respective homes.

One of the greatest lessons of this year has been to say "Yes" to opportunities. I have a great circle of supportive people in my life who I consider family. I'm being coached by one of the best in the world, and I'm currently working on my third publication, which will be my first solo book, for As You Wish Publishing. I couldn't imagine my life if I hadn't said "Yes."

## Even The Ketchup Tastes Better
## By Becki Koon

"Even the ketchup tastes better here, Mom!"

"Well, that does it! We are moving to Montana," I replied as I looked into my daughter's bright eight-year-old eyes.

She had wisdom that belied her young age, and, if the ketchup tasted better in Montana, how could we refute such innocent guidance?

Sitting in that old "Ma & Pa" diner made us feel hopeful for a fresh new start. There were several reasons relocation was in order, but most importantly, my son needed a fresh start in a school that did not carry his tumultuous history.

My son is a brilliant soul, and his early childhood years were full of life, sparkle, and energy. Then school started! He challenged his preschool teacher most of the time with his hyper antics, constant demands, and social awkwardness, yet had high intelligence, quick wit, and insight. First grade was more of a disaster, and he was thrown into a world of doctors, medications, counselors, and school modification programs.

Life became surreal—I was one of those mothers on a never-ending journey of seeking solutions to help my amazing child who didn't fit into this world, and who often wished he had not been born. One medication started then failed; another worked for a while, but caused side effects; another we tried until it stopped working. Take a deep breath, try another. Ten attempts to find medications that would help him function—none of them useful in improving his ability to be comfortable in his skin. He developed neurological tics, and his doctor was deeply concerned. We were exhausted!

Nearly one month after being hospitalized, we celebrated his homecoming. We thought it was a new beginning, but no, another dead end. At ten years old, my son was suicidal, and I was done! I found the strength to change course. We weaned him off medications, found nutritional supplements, holistic health practitioners, alternative healing modalities, and spiritual-energetic support. He began to heal, to smile, and his eyes sparkled with life. My son was back. But, it was hard for the school to shift and see him differently. We needed to manifest a compatible reality!

The decision was clear. Montana, it was. The events that took place in our new location were a divine manifestation we could not ignore.

A quaint little home was available through perfect timing in the small town of Darby. We made our move. Relocation went smoothly, and the local school seemed like an excellent fit for both of the children. Exactly how excellent, I would soon find out.

When my son's body cleared of the medication toxicity, he awakened to a healthier state of being, not only physically, but emotionally and spiritually. He exhibited signs of psychic awareness and intuitive gifts that were amazing. It was magical, and I never doubted his insights.

I enrolled my children in school. My daughter was excited, her teacher, lovely. I met with my son's new teacher, and the first thing she said was, "I'm not going to read the one-inch file from his previous school. I want to know him on my terms, not influenced by what others documented." *Hallelujah*!

I met with the new principal to discuss my son, stating his emotional well-being was of utmost importance. I also wanted her to know of the unique gifts that were beyond explanation, his psychic abilities. She then read his writings, poems he called songs.

When she finished, she sat in silence for a moment and then looked at me. While she did not understand what my son experienced, she was sympathetic to his gifts. She was raised by a mother who had psychic abilities and was familiar with the challenges that could follow such a gift. *Hallelujah hallelujah!*

A short while later, I traveled to a nearby town for a spring fair. I was cruising the health section, when I walked around the corner and, much to my surprise, amazement, and joy, there was a blue-green algae booth with several people waiting to share information. Algae had helped my son's healing. *Hallelujah, hallelujah, hallelujah!*

One of the people at the booth was a motivational author, speaker, and contractor with the algae company. Once he heard me enthusiastically share the story about my son, the word of hope quickly spread. Soon, hundreds of people knew our success story. I found myself on stage at the annual blue-green algae celebration sharing my experience with thousands. *Hallelujah, hallelujah, hallelujah, hallelujah!*

Once back in Montana, the phone calls started to flood in from people who wanted to hear more about my son's journey. It seems there were thousands of parents out there seeking alternatives to help their unique and gifted children. I freely gave of my time feeling blessed and divinely on purpose, and yet, there was more.

I became so busy that when the phone rang, my family would roll their eyes, grumble, and get frustrated. To alleviate family stress, I took matters into my own hands and wrote a book titled *Complicated Child—Simple Options*. I self-published the first two printings.

During that year, I sold thousands of books and was approached by a publishing company in California, wanting to add my book to their offerings. I gladly accepted, and we published in the thousands, with people from all over the North American continent ordering. Parents were grateful for the personal stories of encouragement and new ways to help their child. Thousands of children gained support through nutrition, and my experience was helping. *Hallelujah, and pass the ketchup*!

My son is happily finding his way in life. He is every bit the unique and gifted soul he came here to be. My wise daughter is married, the mother of two girls, and is still enjoying the ketchup that tastes better in Montana!

Life is a beautifully woven tapestry of divine manifestation through synchronicities that creates the fabric of our lives. Who knows, maybe the mustard will taste even better next time?

# Laugh Out Loud
# By Barbara Larrabee

We are powerful manifestors—creating all the time, good or bad. One of my biggest goals in this lifetime is to be more deliberate in manifesting what I want, and in harnessing the magnificent powers we have of mind, heart, and emotions. It's challenging for me to think big, visualize in vibrant color, let go of the "how," and have faith. And, hey, those are key to manifesting. So, I find myself joyously laughing out loud when my special something pops up! I'd like to share three of these experiences with you.

When I set out to buy a car in 2011, there was a lot of deliberation behind it. My husband had passed away a couple of years earlier from a long illness that kept us perpetually broke. I was employed, but barely getting by, and I was driving a car that had 250,000 miles on it. It desperately needed new air conditioning—a critical must in Texas! I was also working on manifesting a new career to get out of an emotionally tough job, but needed to qualify for a car loan before I made any change.

After narrowing the field down to the Hyundai Elantra, it was then a question of buying new or used. That caused some angst! I kept second-guessing myself and calculated the numbers with a savvy business friend. Because I was in my 60s, I was leaning towards a new car with a full warranty and fewer maintenance issues, but the idea of a five-year loan commitment was frighteningly daunting.

Isn't manifesting supposed to be easier? I can tell you that this car did not merely show up in my driveway with a huge bow around it like in the television commercials!

I needed to get off my duff and make a decision because Elantras were in demand. Prices for used cars were rapidly going up. The day I went to test drive a new car, there were only two models available on the lot. One was red and had an expensive upgraded package I didn't need. The other looked white across the lot, but as I got closer, I saw it was actually a misty blue.

I almost didn't buy Misty, as she has light tan seat covers. Really? Do these manufacturers not know that seat covers will get dirty? But other than that, I felt the excitement and joy in test driving her, and she was everything I wanted.

You can see that, although I had way too much self-doubt, I had a clear purpose, a burning desire, and was taking a lot of action steps towards having a safe and wonderful new car. It wasn't until a couple of months later that I had my "laugh out loud" moment. Misty was clearly a manifestation! Two things happened that gave me that new perspective. First of all, after a meeting one night, a friend and I walked out to our cars, which were in the lot across the street. He was a car guy, so I proudly pointed Misty out to him. She was showcased in a shimmering beam of light from the streetlight and magically glowed. He intuitively said, "That exact car was meant for you. It's from the Universe. It was supposed to be yours all along." Wow! What fun!

Second, days later, I happened to glance at my vision board on the wall, and there was Misty right in the middle! I laughed out loud!

I get great joy in creating vision boards, and yet, once on the wall, I often don't "see" them. So, I hadn't paid attention to the car picture on it in a while.

When I created the vision board two years earlier, the 2011 Elantra wasn't even manufactured. The car on the vision board was a different make. But it clearly had the same sleek design that Misty has, as well as the same swirl on the side panels. Misty's elegant essence was right there in front of me!

We don't always get the exact thing we are picturing, but it can excitingly be, "This, or something *better*." Thank you, Universe!

Even today Misty, is like a best friend. I talk to her, love on her, and find joy in every ride. She represents a big step in coming out of the nearly overwhelming jungle of grief and survival. She's a daily reminder that there is always hope. Knowing that the Universe and I partnered in bringing her into my life is joyous and uplifting.

While manifesting big stuff like cars is terrific, it's also joyful to watch little things pop up and amaze.

It was time to replace my bottle of organic vanilla. I was shocked at how prices had gone up. I looked in my favorite health food store first, then online. For a couple of weeks, I checked pricing, and finally resigned myself to paying more. When I went back to the store and reached for the shopping cart, there it was. A bottle of vanilla was lying in the otherwise empty cart! What are the odds?

Not only did I laugh out loud, but when I stopped by the vanilla section, that bottle was the best price. It was $7.77, and other bottles the same size on the shelf were over $9.00. Thank you, Universe!

Lastly, only this week, I manifested a koozie in four days. I haven't used koozies in years, but started thinking about one because my glass of iced coffee sweats so much. Not good for a lovely wood desk. Then—the worst—my hand slipped on the glass one day, and coffee dumped all over the desk and stacks of papers. Time to shop for a koozie. But before I even got out the door, I coincidentally cleaned out a bag of goodies from a trade show six months prior. Ha! Here was a koozie right here in my office. What are the odds? I laughed out loud!

# From Chaos To Calm: A Modern Day "You've Got Mail" By Christina Lawler

I t was New Year's Eve in December of 2016. I thought I wanted to get back together with an ex-partner because of the amount of time we had shared together, and the daunting task it would be to begin with someone new. The hourglass had made blurry the real reasons we split, and I was romanticizing our past. I had hoped to find lasting love in my authentic sexuality when my kids were much younger, rather than embarking on dating during their teen years, but sometimes life has other plans. The first divorce was never in the blueprints either.

On Facebook, I noticed a woman I had felt particularly drawn to, but we were always in different spaces with our lives. She had posted her Bitmoji, a cartoon caricature of herself, smashing the year 2016 with a mallet. It was odd (or was it) for me to even notice, as my mind was so consumed with other things, but for some reason, I did. Sure enough, the signs pointed to a break-up. I had admired her relationship, at least the public Facebook version of it. It was something in her eyes. She seemed so genuine. I felt that what you saw was what you got with her, and that prospect was alluring to me.

Occasionally, my natural impulsivity isn't all bad. I sent her a quick message that said, "This may seem odd, but it appears you are going through a difficult time, and I'm also going through a difficult time, so perhaps we could buddy up on some self-care activities?" And she responded, "If I'm being honest, yes, it is a bit strange. However, I have been saying I do need to make some new friends."

Of course, I knew there was some attraction; there had always been a spark. However, I was not wanting to become a rebound or put myself and my children through any more experimental relationships where the person was intrigued and taken with me, but had not truly thought through what it takes to love someone else's children. Let alone the patience that teenagers and a fully pre-made family require.

She's a 911 dispatcher and would often work crazy hours and overtime to make up for the bills that were left to her in the wake of her break up. So we began to write one another. We shared over 300 e-mails, finding that we could talk about anything—both hungry to be accepted exactly as is and to open up this realm of vulnerability through written processing. We wrote for about a month before we ever met in person. We both decided to go "floating" as our first self-care activity. This was a way to have a quick preview of the other in person, but also each go off to our respective locations afterward to process what that meant.

Soon we began taking walks, trying new things, and having adventures together. She was insightful, gentle, kind, and also angry and hurt at the way her relationship ended. Primarily, she was being hard on herself because she didn't end it sooner, rather than it ending in her partner's infidelity and only causing more shame. I was excited, nervous, and trying to break all of my patterns of diving straight into another person to avoid myself. We set intentions. We kept boundaries. We moved at what I refer to as a "quick-slow" pace. We became friends first.

Fairly soon after, she met my children casually, as we did not yet know what would become of this. She shared with me then that she was scared that I had children. My heart sank. I thought this is it. It's going to happen again. But thankfully, it didn't. Her being allowed to share her feelings without being judged, and the fact that I was able to hold space for them, is all that she needed. She turned out to be the perfect step-parent because she wasn't overbearing or unkind. She was careful and gentle with our hearts. And that is exactly what we needed—someone conscientious of the dynamic, which was greatly enhanced by the understanding we each were able to gain from our letters to one another.

We got into our relationship, each knowing the unmet needs of the other's heart and soul. We promised to hold those things gently in each of our arms, not only the other person. Responsible love. We knew we had to be responsible to ourselves first for this to work. I had only known chaotic love prior to this. A secure relationship gave way to a much more secure self. And a healing journey began that I never imagined. One without being terrified all the time and caught in a cycle of unhealthy attachment. I didn't know the person I could be before I knew what it was like to be in a relationship with her. That I could be gentle, that I could soothe myself, that I was funny, that I could play. Seeing myself through her eyes is a true gift that helps me love myself daily. It grows a secure, safe space inside my soul.

The biggest gift I ever received (or manifested), was a partner who sees me through generous eyes and celebrates me, something I never received in childhood. I couldn't have bargained for the healing that has occurred since then. As a result, my relationships with my children have changed as well. There is a lot more laughter and play in our lives now. The soft and attentive love that I was always seeking has settled over us like a warm and cozy blanket.

Soon we will celebrate our third wedding anniversary, and hopefully, a month or two after that, we will have the bundle of joy that we have tried so hard for. Relating is an art form. Our ingredients: honest communication, gratitude, vulnerability, laughter, holding space, kindness, patience, understanding, and sometimes, a few seconds of insane courage.

# Something From Nothing
## By Kenneth I Laws II

**M**any think of manifestation as something from nothing. By one definition, it is an event, action, or object that clearly shows or embodies something, especially a theory or an abstract idea. I can tell you from my limited experience, that which you put intention and thought into can become your reality. This I know on a deeply personal level.

In mid-2013, I had become quite a lost soul, and it took a single moment of clarity for me to do something to change the circumstances that I had created. My circumstances had led me to start my life over at age 43. I started from the ground up with what many might consider nothing. Despite this fact, I had become, in many people's eyes, one of the most grateful and happiest people they had ever encountered. They could not believe that it was possible for someone to have so little, yet be so happy.

I had discovered that true joy comes not from worldly possessions, but from the inside. This became important because I had stumbled upon something—when we free up enough space inside our heart and our minds, free it from all the clutter, we can bring into our lives that which we give our focused attention and thought to. I wanted peace, I wanted to love, I wanted to be free. I had come to understand that I must put something into it, put thought into it, put intention into it, and having cleared out all the clutter, both literally and figuratively, it all came.

I eventually became engaged to a woman I had known for a long time. I was now what I would consider a student. As the old saying goes, when the student is ready, the teacher will appear. I was being taught how to love again, how to live again. I was being taught the importance of all the little things in life and how they can become so much bigger when we allow them to. Tara, the teacher, passed away suddenly a mere nine months after we had reunited, and I was left with nothing more than tools. Although broken at the time, I had been given all the tools in which to bring unto you that which you think. To bring into your life that which you allow. I think most important would be how to love and accept another human despite faults and flaws, and the acceptance that we all have faults and flaws.

I began to focus on love and gratitude. As I focused on love, it came to me. As I became grateful for all the little things in life, the bigger things came to me. Little by little, it all started coming back, not only from a materialistic standpoint, but from an internal and spiritual standpoint as well. I do believe that being humble in the process of manifesting anything is of greatest importance, as well as not being greedy. I know the opposite of greed would be generosity. To put it into perspective, when we make a conscious choice to help another person as it relates to abundance, or anything for that matter, it must and will return to us. I can also say from my limited experience, that which you give away, will always return unto you, if not ten-fold, then a hundred-fold. I do find that generosity is of utmost importance as it relates to anything we wish to bring into our lives.

As I see it, manifestation is not a forced action, but one in which we allow circumstances in our lives to take place and unfold before us that which we think into it. One of the hardest things to do is to be patient with the process. I had to come to understand that the universe does not always work on our timetable. I cannot understate the importance of allowing. When we genuinely allow circumstances in our lives to unfold, without any resistance, this is when manifesting becomes a reality. We have to trust the process, as long as we have had the right thought and right action and allow for it to happen.

I had always said I wanted to live in a house in the country on five acres, and now I do. I definitely wanted to find love again, which eventually came. It did not fully come until I allowed it to, created space for it to occur, and most importantly, accepted it. As a result, I am now happily married to my amazing and beautiful wife, Suzann. Most of us think we have to force things into our lives, which leads to frustration and discontent. But when we put the right thought and right action into it, and then allow it to occur, life becomes amazingly beautiful and will unfold before our eyes.

We as humans fail to realize that when we focus on something, it becomes our reality. This goes both ways—when we focus on lack, we will always be lacking. When we focus on abundance, we will always have an abundant supply of that which we need. I consider this to be a form of manifestation. The most important thing, in my limited experience, is that one must accept that which comes our way, especially when our thoughts have been specific, one way or the other.

I am of the belief that anything that the mind can believe, we can achieve. When we put enough thought and are able to allow circumstances to be as they are, we can bring anything into our lives. Although we cannot always control the outcome of all our circumstances, we can control the journey. Focus on the good, and it will come. Be generous and serve others, and it will return to you. I know this to be true, again, on a deeply personal level.

# WeR3
# By Natalie Lebel

I have long held the belief that everything happens for a reason. Although my path has not been an easy one, every decision and choice I have made has led me to where I am today.

Over the years of providing therapy, I have witnessed clients learn to balance acceptance with change. I have watched as they reconnected with the essence of who they are and make choices to honor themselves. Clients have often told me that I should share my knowledge outside of the office. A part of me daydreamed of hosting a podcast or giving a Ted Talk—reaching people who might not otherwise be able to get to therapy. I wanted to share what I learned through my life experiences, my studies, and my work with countless individuals. I was excited to share that it is possible to change patterns and behaviors that are no longer serving us. Being human, we are wired for struggle. We seek certainty within an uncertain life. We seek to control that which is uncontrollable, which only intensifies our struggles and increase difficulties we will experience. I yearned to share this knowledge with a bigger audience, but kept telling myself I was dreaming too big.

I put this on the back burner as I found myself at a crossroads. I had to ponder which path I would take, the safe one, or the risky one. I decided to take a leap of faith and follow my intuition, which was telling me to take the risk, as scary as that leap was. This decision has forever changed my life. While I was facing this crossroads, two other women were also pondering life changes and facing their respective crossroads. I truly believe that we arrived at a three-way stop where we found each other, and our paths forever crossed. We decided to meet for dinner to check in and see how we were all doing. Suzanne shared with excitement and trepidation that she was preparing to start a part-time psychotherapy practice. Carmen and I were excited to share our experiences with Suzanne. Three years earlier, Carmen had started a practice and then encouraged me to get out of my comfort zone and also start a part-time practice. Three years later, we had independently made the decision to dive into our growing practices on a full-time basis, leaving our safe and secure jobs behind.

As we sat together, we were struck by how our energies, knowledge, and beliefs were aligned. As we talked, we saw how well we complemented each other—three women, strong and brave, facing new frontiers. This indeed is how we felt. We decided to get together in a month's time to regroup and brainstorm. We instantly knew that we wanted to do something together, a collaboration of some sort.

That fateful day came, and as we sat and connected on a deeper level, sharing our personal stories, we vibrated on how powerful our collective stories were. We talked about the themes we see in our offices and how we approach them. We had the idea of recording ourselves. We giggled as we got a microphone set up that Carmen happened to have in the house (her husband is a talented musician, and thus, has recording equipment—how perfect!!) and we hit record. There were blunders, including mispronunciation of names, forgetting words, and freezing up; however, there was a raw quality to it. We decided, "What the heck, let's post it as a podcast!"

This first podcast set us on a journey that none of us quite expected. Over the last six months, we have grown closer, collectively and individually. We had no idea how much these podcasts would inspire us professionally and personally.

Our initial collaboration name was *Imagine New Perceptions on Being Human*, which is a combination of our practice names. Week after week, we were energized by the creativity within our collaboration. Three women working together, encouraging one another's successes and soothing one another's failures. This was like no other collaboration I had ever been part of. Women often feel compelled to compete with other women—feeling the heavy weight of the glass ceiling and being taught to believe there is only so much tolerance for successful women. However, there we were, experiencing more and more feelings of success, creativity, excitement, and endless possibilities. We started to play with the number three: mind, body, and spirit. The three of us wholeheartedly believe if one of those three is out of sync, it will seep into the other two areas.

According to numerology, the number three represents the principle of increase, expansion, growth, and abundance on the physical, emotional, mental, financial, and spiritual levels. The number three resonates with the energies of optimism and joy, inspiration, and creativity. Most of all, the number three is related to synthesis, triad, heaven-human-earth, past-present-future, thought-word-action, demonstrating love through creative imagination, and manifestation.

As we reflected on the implications of the significance of the number three, our true collaboration name came to us: *WeR3*. As much as it represents the three of us, the three R's also represent *raw, risky, and real*. These were words we heard ourselves use a lot over the course of those first episodes. Raw, risky, and real has since become our therapeutic framework for groups and retreats. However, that is another story. This is the story of three: three women, three visions, a mutual path, and an infinite amount of creativity, joy, and growth.

# Laugh Your Way Into Your
# Wildest Dream Come True
# By Rhonda Lee

W e have this enormous power within us to manifest anything. Anything! Unfortunately, we spend a lot of time manifesting our fears instead of our dreams because energy flows where attention goes. We can change this trend instantly when we shift our focus and become aware of our actions. Awareness is the first step for growth of any nature. Awareness is powerful. Laughter is also powerful. Conscious laughter is a potent energy shifter.

As a professional Laughter Yoga Leader, I've had some amazing experiences when it comes to using laughter as a manifestation tool. Over the years, I have come to understand how laughter forces us to get out of our way and focus our attention elsewhere. It has the potential to stop our thoughts from running aimlessly and immerse us fully in the present moment. It's there in that moment when we surrender to laughter, that thoughts and ideas begin to settle and fall into place. It's the shift in energies that lets us look at things from a new perspective later. It's the shift in energies that allows us to become manifestation magnets.

Laughter is a higher-frequency energy that impacts all populations. It's an expression of energy that can move us out of stress, grief, confusion, and more. When used regularly and consciously, it can completely change the energy and tone of our daily lives. Science has proven that the health benefits of laughter could cost tens of thousands of dollars to achieve if you went the medical route. I have witnessed many of these health benefits in both my life and the lives of others. I have also experienced laughter as being the highest form of meditation within myself and others, as well. It is not only medicine for our bodies and souls; it is a creation point for our manifestations.

Laughter draws people and highly charged energy to you like a magnet. It clings to your personal energy field long after you are no longer laughing. Others can sense it, although they may not know what it is. This is your opportunity to manifest magic into your life. I also humorously refer to this as the "art of getting free stuff." Through years of expending my energies on using laughter as a creation point for health benefits, I discovered, quite by accident, that people would respond to that frequency long after I had stopped laughing. I found that I could spend 15-20 minutes getting in a good laughter session, and then as I later went about my day, all manner of things would manifest for me without me even trying. In the early stages of this (when I didn't realize what was happening), I began manifesting free coffee/tea, a meal, the extreme politeness of strangers, and unexpected money!

As time went on, I started to realize what was happening. I found that laughter not only had a multitude of health benefits but was truly a creation point of realizing manifestations that I consciously wanted. My manifestations evolved as I honed these skills. I never set out to try to get anything free from anyone, and I had to learn to release myself from the belief that I was taking something from someone. I had to open myself up to receive whatever was to be made manifest specifically for me. By "setting my stage for success," enjoying laughter and releasing the outcome, I found that I was able to manifest partnerships that didn't previously exist, money, trips, a new car, more adventurous opportunities than I can count and even new business ideas, to list a few. My experience continues to be vast as I evolve through this process.

Here are some steps that I have found to be beneficial when it comes to using conscious laughter as a manifestation tool:

1. Laugh! I know that may sound difficult at first, but by leveraging a few tricks, you can make it a natural practice. I highly recommended starting the easiest way possible. Watch a funny video. Listen to a funny podcast. Appreciate silly memes.

Whatever causes you to giggle, make a note of it, and simply do it. As you become better at your laughter skills, you can start to explore other ways to deepen your laughter. Learn to laugh for no reason at all. You can even fake laugh. It doesn't matter whether it is real or fake laughter since your body doesn't know the difference. You will still get the health benefits plus a magnetic change in your energy that draws all manner of manifestations your way. Take the time to cultivate a conscious laughter practice. Start with a few minutes a day and work your way up. The sky is the limit!

2. Release any attachment to an outcome from your practice. When you are attached to a specific outcome, your energy becomes stagnant, and you stand in your way. I recommend that you become the magnet for manifestations through laughter and allow whatever is meant to be made manifest to find its way to you with ease. Also, please note that when you hold precise expectations, you may be closing the door on something even better coming through. Be open to possibility.

3. Watch your attention. Energy goes where attention flows. To manifest anything from a dime to your heart's desire, you must learn to harness where you put your attention. Stay focused on your laughter practice. Make every effort to direct your energies. This is not to say that you can't ever feel bad or be sad. Life happens, and we were designed to feel a myriad of emotions. It's when those feelings start to occupy too much of our attention that we start to become stagnant in manifesting the things we want in life. Feel your feelings and then release them and put your attention back on conscious laughter.

Practice following these simple steps and start manifesting your wildest dreams in a creative and healthy way!

# Waiting For The Other Shoe
# To Drop -- A Cinderella Story
# By Stephanie Levy

If the shoe I'd ordered from Nordstrom's Single Shoe Program didn't arrive soon, I wouldn't need it. Days after I broke the fifth metatarsal on my right foot, I called Nordstrom and arranged for the delivery of a size 39 black and grey Dansko clog. The shoe arrived promptly, but they'd mistakenly sent a 38, and no amount of jamming my foot into the opening proved successful, so back it went.

The return required communication from many parties which complicated a simple process and caused endless delay. Finally, I picked up the phone and asked for help. The woman who answered my call was delighted to fill out the return form for me over the phone.

"The Single Shoe Return Form is the only form I've never filled out," she practically squealed. She composed herself, no doubt out of respect for the occasion, and said more calmly, "You don't get to do that every day. This has been my goal, and now I can say I've filled out every form at Nordstrom. You made my day!"

I wish I could have been as enthusiastic as she was. I'd had setbacks with recovery, but as the weeks dragged on, I finally began to wean myself off crutches. Having a left shoe that was the same height as the wretched boot strapped to my leg became critical for balance. Buff colored suede boots were the only shoes I possessed with any elevation. Not only was I tired of wearing that one shoe with everything, the suede was looking dingy, and I could feel the points of nails poking my heel through the thin sole.

Hobbling through a long day of errands with my friend Deb, I recounted my endless wait for the Nordstrom shoe. Deb was a former neighbor from Knoxville visiting Santa Fe and had been a willing and cheerful chauffeur. We were exhausted from shopping and had one more stop at the grocery when we veered off-course into Nina's Closet, a boutique consignment store packed with treasures. Ana, the owner, asked if we were looking for anything special. I detailed my search for a pair of shoes the same height as my boot. She guided me to a tufted stool in the shoe section, tucked my crutches into a nearby corner, and began bringing shoes to try on.

Deb meandered through the racks of colorful skirts and jackets, and I mentioned to Ana I'd been looking for a pair of cowboy boots. She brought over a pair with white lilies stitched onto black leather, perfect boots for my upcoming role as a soon-to-be first-time grandmother of a girl, due in December. Our son and his wife had recently settled on the name—Lily.

I walked back and forth, testing the comfort and the fit of the left lily boot. It felt a tad too high to wear comfortably with the orthotic.

"A Dansko would be the perfect height," I told Ana. She pulled out a pair of Dansko wedges that were also too tall. I related the story of the long-awaited single shoe from Nordstrom when I saw something click in her expression.

"Wait a minute!" With an air of surprise and determination, she lifted her forefinger and followed it like an arrow as it led her into the closet. I heard sounds of boxes shuffling and paper rustling as she rummaged around in search of something.

"I think it's in here," she called out to me. "I'm sure I saw it the other day. Hmmm. Where is it?"

I heard more shuffling, then, "Yes! Unbelievable!"

She emerged from the closet, smiling broadly, holding a single shoe in her hand—a black and white faux zebra fur Dansko clog.

"What size?" she asked, checking to confirm as she held the shoe to the light and peered inside.

"39," I said.

"Yep. What foot?"

"Left," I said.

"Here it is—a left shoe, size 39, Dansko clog!"

I beheld the miraculous shoe. Seemingly materialized from Nina's magic closet, the shoe appeared tailor-made for me—the right size, style, and height. I slipped it on, and exactly like Cinderella, the shoe fit perfectly.

"A woman amputee came in last summer and bought this pair of clogs. She only needed the right shoe and asked me to toss the left shoe or give it away," Ana said, shaking her head in amazement. "I don't know why I kept it. I've had it nearly a year, waiting—" she trailed off.

"Waiting for me," I said.

"I've already been paid for the shoes." Ana handed me the clog. "This is a gift."

I bought the lily boots, and Deb bought a silver necklace and a vintage beaded bag. I thanked Ana for her gift and left with the cherished zebra clog.

"That shoe was waiting here for you!" Deb said once we got into the car. "Things like this happened to you in Knoxville, and now they're happening for you in Santa Fe, too. You're making connections."

I marveled in silence over what had transpired and stared out the car window at the sunset and mountain peaks, the landscape of my new home. Walking up the path to the front door, I saw a Nordstrom box waiting for me on the doorstep.

# True Love
# By Stephanie Levy

"Where did you get this book?"

The guest at our bed and breakfast waved the hardback above her head with the urgency of a New Yorker hailing a cab. She'd recently returned from dinner with her daughter and granddaughter, making a special trip downstairs to inquire about the book. I'd been thinking about my grandmother as I set the table for breakfast, concentrating on pleating a napkin into an accordion. I slipped it through one of Grandma's silver napkin rings and spread it into a fan. The woman's question startled me from my reverie.

Small, almost frail, she looked young for a grandmother of a college-age student. Her deep-set brown eyes entrapped me, waiting for an answer. Was her tone accusatory? Curious? She seemed tentative as if holding something back.

I looked at the book she held: *True Love* by Robert Fulghum.

"My friend Jeanie sent that book," I said. "Jeanie's always going to yard sales. She sent a box of books to inspire me to keep writing my stories."

Too busy to read, I'd shelved *True Love* in a bookcase for the use of the guests.

I thought I remembered an inscription, an address label inside the cover. Maybe she thought I'd stolen the book.

"Where does Jeanie live?"

"Sacramento. But she also has a camp in Vermont. She could have gotten the book anywhere."

"It has an inscription on the first page." She pointed to the words. "To Mom, Happy Thanksgiving / Christmas 1997 Love, Roger."

I hadn't noticed the inscription, but now I wondered about Roger. Was he so cheap he wanted this one book to count for two occasions? Then I envisioned this being a long-standing joke between him and his mother. Suddenly I liked Roger, picturing him repeating this private joke every year with his mom.

"There's a return label inside the cover," she pointed out.

L.R. Milberger
Pleasant Grove, Ca.

My blank look must have reflected my confusion. She studied the inscription again before enlightening me.

"Roger was my husband. This is his handwriting."

At first, I didn't understand what she said. Then, I wasn't sure I believed her. Maybe she was senile. I hadn't spent enough time with this woman to evaluate her sanity.

She quivered with intensity. I worried she might collapse.

"Let's sit down," I suggested.

I guided her to the loveseat and pulled the rocker close enough to hear her story, our knees almost touching.

"He must have given this book to his mother. They both liked to read short stories. Roger died two years ago this December." Her voice wavered—the wound still fresh.

"His mother died before he did. She lived in Briar Creek, New York, along the St. Lawrence. Someone else handled the estate. Her books could have gone anywhere."

She was drifting, taking a path through time, her thoughts traveling like the book in mysterious ways, taking this unlikely turn, detouring there, landing far afield somewhere in the distance.

"Roger was the most loving man I've ever known. He was my second husband. Before we were a couple, we were family in a sense. He and I were married to a sister and brother. We spent holidays together, went to the same weddings, birthdays, and funerals. But our first marriages were bad. Our spouses cheated on us. Must have been a family trait." Her snicker sounded bitter.

"Eventually, both of us divorced. I became a single mother with two teenage daughters and little income. I had to find work without skills or experience. My daughter was wild." She nodded towards the bedroom upstairs. "She got pregnant and dropped out of college. Roger would call and commiserate. He'd drive six hours to visit and helped with my home projects. Sometimes he'd send money even though I never asked.

"Then, a few years later, after fixing my plumbing, he looked at me and said, 'You know, I think we should get married.'"

"And I said, 'To who?'" She burst out laughing.

"I didn't get it. I wasn't used to thinking about him like that, so I told him I'd consider it."

We laughed as she became animated by her tale. She wasn't senile. She was perfectly sane.

She continued, saying, "Time passed. Roger called every week and visited monthly. After a year, I figured I'd thought about his proposal long enough. I asked him if the offer was still on the table.

"Absolutely," he said. "When would you like to get married?"

"Soon," I said. "Very soon."

Her eyes changed focus. She smiled, and it seemed like she was pulling her thoughts from past to present.

"We married the next week. I'm so glad we didn't wait. We only had seven years. I loved every minute of our life together. He was a good man. For the last year or so, though, I've felt like he's left me without keeping in touch. But this strange coincidence, having this book with his handwriting in my room—he's sent me a message. I know he has. His true love endures even though he's gone. That's what he's saying. His love is with me still."

She looked spent, jolted into this incredible discovery, reliving the emotion of all those years and memories.

My friend had given me this book with all her love, as inspiration for my writing, repeating the gift of love from Roger to his mother, and the book had traveled a circuitous route appearing on a bookshelf in my guest room, finding its rightful place in the hands of Roger's wife to manifest and deliver the message of his unending love.

"This book belongs to you. Please take it."

"Are you sure?" she asked.

"Of course, I am." I placed one hand on top of hers as I gave her the book.

"Thank you," she said. Her eyes, glistening with deep emotion, connected with mine.

No, thank *you*," I said. "The gift is mine—the story of you and Roger, and your true love."

# Home Sweet Home
# By Donna Lipman

I was 45 before owning my first home. My husband and I purchased it in an area of the country I would never have considered visiting, much less living in. My English-born husband, Terry, and I had met through the late singer/songwriter, John Denver, and happily, we moved to Aspen, Colorado. We were in love, and Terry provided me the opportunity to live my dream— where the mountains created a stunning backdrop to our small apartment in the middle of town. I didn't care that the apartment was cramped and tiny. We had many friends from all walks of life, enjoying deep conversations and outdoor activities. Depending upon the time of year, we hiked or skied. It was the first time in my life since I was 14 that I didn't have a regular job or two. I felt happy and in love with life and my husband!

Three years into our marriage, hard times fell upon us financially. It was something we hadn't anticipated. Although we were happy in Aspen, it was an expensive place to live, and we couldn't see a way of supporting this lifestyle for much longer as neither of us was working. A friend of ours, money guru, Robert Kiyosaki, observed we had money going out the door, but nothing coming in. The reality was shocking and moved us into action.

Somehow, we found ourselves in a conservative, small town an hour outside of Austin, Texas, in 1994. That I was not a happy camper to be living in this comparatively desolate place is probably an understatement. We bought an affordable, sprawling, yet humdrum, ranch home on a lake. It was pretty enough, but isolated. After having been there for a short time, I realized I was probably the youngest person for about 15 miles around. I knew no one in the area, and those whom I did know lived in Austin, 50 miles away. To make matters worse, I loved being outside, but in Texas, it was too hot! I grieved the loss of my beautiful mountain lifestyle and fell into a dark place.

After six months of isolation, I decided to spend more time in Austin, where I met a successful businessman in the real estate industry. I started hanging around him to gain a better understanding of the business. Eventually, I ended up working for him, running his entire operation. While I learned a lot about the business of owning real estate, I often panicked about my decision-making abilities. Sometimes I fell flat on my face, but was determined to keep moving forward. I began purchasing and managing my personal investment properties, and eventually, experiencing some success. However, I was still feeling quite unhappy "having" to live in this remote area, driving back and forth to Austin. At the time, the speed limit was only 55 mph, so the commute was arduous.

In the process of being honest with myself, it dawned on me one day that I had been collecting "evidence" that I was right, and Terry was wrong. Our friends in Aspen were shocked that we left and couldn't believe my husband would *do* this to me. It added fuel to my fire, and I grew angry. It was taking a toll on my health, as I was eating poorly to comfort myself. Then, I thought of the adage, "Would you rather be right or happy?"

I decided a change in attitude was needed and began my research. How was I going to do this? My situation seemed impossible—it felt like I was in prison. Still, I knew deep inside I had become a victim of my circumstances. It was not a pretty picture, and I didn't like who I had become. I was treating my sweet husband poorly, blaming him for this nightmare in which I had found myself. I started reading books about how to create a better reality, drawn to Napoleon Hill's book, *Think and Grow Rich*. I realized it was time for me to take responsibility for my life. The most important lesson I garnered from this book was, "Nobody is coming to save me." It was a revelation and a daily reminder that propelled me into a more positive future.

But what was the future I envisioned? With the clear understanding that we would not be moving back to Aspen, finding a home in Austin became a priority. I visualized a respite, a sacred space, and a gathering place for our friends and family. I wanted to be close to downtown, but didn't want it to be too urban. I cut pictures out of magazines and pasted them on a vision board. I created a timeline as to when I wanted this to happen. I was consistently grateful for the love I had in my life, as well as the home we were about to find. I knew it was coming our way—I could feel it and trusted that the house was waiting for us to find it.

One day, we were driving to a friend's home to visit and were early. I asked Terry to drive around the neighborhood, as we had never seen this part of town before. I saw a man putting a for sale sign in the yard of a beautiful home. We stopped, walked up to the front door, and said, "We'll take it!" Terry was a bit shocked, but he understood it immediately.

I have been in this home for 25 years and have loved every party, every dinner, every concert and every bit of love that has blessed us here. Though Terry has passed, I have remained in our home. It was difficult at first, but fortunately, I found another love—my darling Tom—and we now share it with a blended family and dear friends. It is still my respite and my sacred space for which I am wholly grateful every day. The welcome mat is always there!

# Finding Joy
# By Amanda Long

I t is a story you have heard before, likely as an after school special. A 16-year-old runaway, in a sketchy rental suite, skips school often, but works at a local restaurant to get by. She dates the wrong people, makes poor decisions, and is at risk of all types of trouble. You think you know how this story goes. But this is my story, and it might surprise you.

I was a smart kid who didn't apply myself. Some teachers said I was a negative influence and distraction to others. I was forced to work multiple part-time jobs to get by, which kept me from attending classes regularly, but somehow, I managed to graduate.

Not only did I graduate, but I was also awarded a small scholarship to a local college, so I took a writing program that interested me. As the only recent high school graduate in a class of older, mid-career students upgrading their resume, I certainly didn't fit in. I did well in my classes, but it didn't spark joy.

Afterward, I started to take general courses while juggling two jobs. Unlike high school, I loved going to classes, learning, socializing, and being in an educational setting.

Then, I met a boy. I stopped going to college for a couple of years, got pregnant, and the boy left me. Sure, there was more to the story, but essentially, that's the plotline. I decided I needed to go back to school to get university transfer credits, and I needed to do it before I had my baby.

And I did.

It was hard—attending classes while extremely pregnant and working. I did well in my classes and even tutored some classmates. But then, it was baby time.

I missed classes that first week of April while at the hospital, but the next week, my instructor looked at me shocked as I marched into the classroom, a week postpartum, to write my final exam. I passed all my classes and had enough credits to transfer to a university to pursue my degree.

I enjoyed that summer with my baby before I had to return to work and school. Now reliant on student loans, I hadn't worked enough hours as a student to qualify for maternity benefits, so I was broke. I had to go back to work and back to school. It was the only way I'd ever get ahead.

I worked the bare minimum to afford what we needed while a friend watched my daughter. I went to university and got my first degree. It was then that I realized I wanted to be a teacher, and so I applied to continue my university learning and got a second degree in education.

I met my first husband at that time. He was kind, treated my daughter well, and we had ten years together. Though our relationship was not terrible, it felt like a marriage of convenience over time. He watched my daughter while I finished school and pursued my career goals, creating a stable life for us. I was thankful for his support, but fell out of love with him.

I didn't leave right away. I had convinced myself that true love was only for the movies, and I was foolish to believe in fairy tales. I didn't want to be another divorce statistic, and my life was *fine*. And so, I stayed. I stayed for too long, and it sucked the joy out of me. I noticed my entire personality change and knew I couldn't continue living like this.

I had so many dreams. I had promised my grandfather before he passed that I would get a master's degree, something I had never imagined possible for someone like me. I had come from poverty and struggled so much as a teen, only to overcome those obstacles. I had wanted to travel the world and see different places and cultures, but never had the time or money. I realized I wasn't living my best life, and my husband had no desire to grow with me and help me reach my goals, worse—he had no goals. We were both crawling through life in a loveless marriage. And so, we divorced.

It was a difficult transition. He moved out, and while my daughter was upset at first, I explained honestly that we were not happy anymore. I told her that she was getting to an age where she would be dating, and I wanted to model healthy romantic relationships. Although it was tough in the beginning, the divorce was ultimately the best decision for everyone.

I enjoyed my new freedom. I applied for and finished my master's degree, and started to go out more with friends. I embraced adventures that came my way with excitement. I went to painting nights at local pubs, sporting events, and escape rooms. My daughter and I went camping with friends, and found joy in everyday living. As I began to find happiness in my life, positivity radiated off me.

While I was busy enjoying life, and when I least expected it, I found love again. The kind of love that changes your life for the better. We had known each other for a few years through mutual friends, and one day, it simply clicked. Suddenly, I discovered that fairy tales are real. We dated, he proposed, and we were married on the beach, a childhood dream of mine. My husband loves me as no one has ever loved me, and I truly believe it is because I learned to love myself so fiercely and live life so passionately that it attracted the right person.

I look back at my life, even the challenges, with fond memories. The hardships I overcame built resilience in me. From living alone at 16 to my happily ever after, our blended family moved across the country last summer and lives every day fully, doing things that spark joy.

# Guys Love Trucks
# By Kit Cabaniss Macy

A trusted friend and colleague once said to me, "Your success in the feelings category determines your success in all other categories." She was quoting Napoleon Hill. I didn't realize it at the time, but these words changed my life forever. Beyond that, they shed light on what I had unconsciously known for most of my life, but I had never brought it to the surface and stared it down.

As the only girl in a family of six kids, I grew up in what could loosely be called a fraternity house. I know about boys, and boys know trucks. They dig them. Their attraction to and fondness for trucks is something I have tried to understand for years. Is it because these powerful motorized vehicles make them feel that way, too? Or is it because they can be tinkered with, making the beast within, the conqueror? Is it the sense of independence they provide when you climb aboard and drive away? Is it the pride of ownership that wells up, especially after your truck has recently been washed and waxed? Or is it perhaps the feeling of paternal protection, when you've washed and waxed your "baby?" Trucks represent more than merely a mode of transportation. Beginning with Tonka trucks as children, I believe the mystique continues throughout the life of a man. Guys love trucks.

Recently, my husband said to me, "Since we're semi-retired now, how about we pare down to one vehicle? I'll sell the truck, and we'll both use your car." After a moment of my silent foreboding, it seemed like a reasonable idea. No truck payment. Less expense on fuel, maintenance, insurance. Additional room in the garage for storage. Less liability. I thought, why not? I temporarily abandoned and betrayed the sage wisdom given to me so long ago, that my success in the feelings category would determine my success in all other categories.

It took approximately five weeks before I noticed my husband shopping online for trucks. I didn't say anything, because after all, I was guilty, too. The difference is, I don't shop for vehicles. But, guys love trucks. My online window shopping is for books, clothes, and other sensible items.

After an adjustment period of subsisting with one vehicle, I felt as though I had gained a sense of accomplishment in achieving peace in the daily negotiations about the use of the car. It wasn't hard to compromise, after all. My fears of feeling trapped at home without a vehicle were imaginary and with no basis in reality. It felt like he was comfortable with the arrangement, too. Peace in the land.

One day, out of the blue, he stated that he had found a truck he wanted to take a look at and probably buy. We'd go tomorrow. I was surprised to learn that his truck lust online was more than idle stalking. But the truck of his dreams was located two and a half hours out of town. It would take an entire day of driving to look at it, test-drive it, negotiate the deal, and return home with two vehicles (probably during rush hour). The shopping trip was not my idea of how to spend the day. In my heart and my "feelings category," I knew there must be a truck for sale in our local vicinity. There simply had to be!

As we were settling into bed for the night, I found myself wanting to check the "trucks for sale" ads, if only to see for myself. Amazingly, there it was. A beautiful, four-wheel-drive truck that seemed exactly right. I tapped my husband on the shoulder and woke him from a semi-sleep to show him what I had found. This truck had fewer miles and was selling for less than the one scheduled for consideration tomorrow morning. It was the color and style he wanted, and the best part for me is that it was located less than 20 miles from our house. After he examined the ad and photos of this adoptive truck, he said, "That might work. How'd you find it?" I told him I had searched for pickup trucks in our vicinity. He swore he'd checked every ad, and this truck did not appear in any of his searches. After looking to see how long the advertisement had been running, we learned that it had come online less than an hour before we saw it.

Did we manifest this truck? It's hard to know, for sure. But I do know that it was my earnest and heartfelt desire that my husband has the monster vehicle he desires because, after all, men love trucks. It was also my strong desire to not drive six hours to get it and bring it home.

I believe that because I had an earnest and persistent request for a great truck for the person I love, close to home, manifesting it became easy. My intention was clear. After finding that ad, it felt like the situation was in alignment. He was happy, and I was delighted. My willingness to take the focus off my objections and refocus on what was best for the greater good provided providence to lead. We were assisted in the situation. I felt great knowing he would have his truck, and that it was closer than we had imagined. By surrendering and being willing to drive all day, even though I had other tasks scheduled, opened the way for me to find his truck. I know this to be true, because, the success in my feelings category had determined the success in all our other categories. Importantly, Napoleon Hill also said, "The mastermind principle consists of an alliance of two or more minds working in perfect harmony for the attainment of a common definite objective. Success does not come without the cooperation of others." For knowing this, I am grateful.

## Manifesting Your Career
## By Stef Mann

When I was entering the workforce beyond my first fast-food job, I followed the local masses and got a job at a call center.

It sucked, and I hated every minute of it.

I remember calling home to my mom multiple times and being frustrated with the job and everything that came along with it. She would wait until Wednesday to say, "It's okay, you're already halfway through the week," and give me any encouragement she could fabricate. At the time, I wasn't aware of my heightened sensitivity to other people's energy, so I seemed to have a more difficult time than most.

I did know that "work your butt off for five days a week to desperately reach the weekend and then repeat it all over again" was not the life for me.

After moving on, I imagined life in a career where I'd be happy. I had been designing web sites since I was twelve years old and I was studying communications at university, so I planned to work in marketing. I began to picture myself working with marketing clients and having a fully creative job.

Back then, I had no idea what manifesting was, but I did know that if I started acting in the position that I wanted to be in, I would get there. I wasn't sure how I was going to get a job in marketing, or where I would end up, but I spent all my free time designing logos for friends and continuing to build websites for personal interests, all the while knowing that in one way or another something would appear. I was determined not to hate going to work every day strictly for money. I would have a career where I would call the shots one day.

Even if the vision in my head wasn't where I ended up, the most important thing was living with a vision—being able to picture something the current me would be happy with.

Because of that set intention, I ended up in a computer course with a friend of a friend. After completing the course, he offered me my first web design job with his startup company. He had to teach me a lot, and I was incredibly thankful to have a perfectly aligned job for that time; something I knew I wouldn't be doing forever, but I'd gain what I needed to move forward. Doing what I loved had turned into doing what I was paid to do, and it wouldn't be the only time.

I never doubted it though. Since I had quit that call center job and vowed to myself to follow a positive path, I have always kept that promise, and I believe that has always been my biggest asset in creating the reality that I desired, later learning the energetic term: manifesting.

I kept up that mentality as I worked through jobs. With each position I have had, I have been able to imagine myself closer to something bigger, while still gaining the knowledge and tools that I needed. At my longest graphic design job, I built relationships, learned about business, and grew to understand clients from a creative perspective. I've also been able to easily figure out when something wasn't working for me, and even with a job that anyone would essentially dream of, I got to the point where I realized I didn't want to follow someone else's vision and moved on. While it was an amazing job, something was still missing—my freedom.

From that point, I had already developed a new hobby: photography. I knew that I wanted to be an entrepreneur, and with this new direction and clear vision in my mind, moving forward, I was able to structure the next few jobs in order to manifest it.

Yes, a few jobs. Each one a step closer. Each teaching me something about being an entrepreneur and how to get there.

I worked at a city job, learning about managing my overstretched time and being in charge of designing everything within a single brand.

Then, a tech job where the environment wasn't ideal, but I learned skills to make me a better problem solver. I also negotiated from day one to only work four days a week—another step closer to having time for my business. Even some interoffice friction taught me to stand up for my beliefs and gain greater confidence in my abilities.

Finally, I moved into a job that was close to home and provided me with the freedom to run their online marketing however I wanted, including adding photography to the position. This job was also only four days a week, and once I had been there for a while, I proved it could be done in two days a week and, eventually, I quit to run my photography business full time. If I had not gone in with the intention of having this transition job and seeing an end picture, I would not have had an easy move to full-time self-employment.

Now I've run a successful full-time photography business for four years in an extremely competitive industry, and I'm already manifesting (and living) my next career of being an image coach who helps others visualize what they need in their personal and business lives. Every job has contributed to this manifested career.

Every step of the way, I have always acted two moves ahead, visualizing what my next point would be. It's not hoping, it's knowing. That has been my key to manifesting. Knowing you will be where you want to be and being able to see ahead on the timeline to do so and what pieces you will need to take from your current spot in life to launch yourself forward. Use every step to your advantage as a piece of the puzzle you're working towards and manifest that dream career!

# What Lies Beneath The Skin
# By Maria McGonigal

We are closing another decade, and even though we know time is an illusion, we have learned how to give meaning to time.

Sometimes, we wish that time could erase the painful memories that our hearts can barely whisper. But that is not so. Human beings are soft and permeable, and memories sink deeply into the bones.

When my mother informed me that her left arm would need to be amputated, the feelings were excruciating. Those feelings are always only a breath away and a memory I dread to revisit.

The pain I felt was like a sword's blade piercing my heart, and an unrecognizable mist instantly descended in my world. I felt utterly lost as if my body had disintegrated into the mist. It was surreal and so cruelly real at the same time.

My mother's life, and our family's lives, changed when her left arm was amputated. A rare and extremely aggressive cancer was ravaging inside. Still, for an imaginative and courageous woman who had learned how to survive circumstances that would drown most, that was just the beginning of a new life.

But who is Olinda? My mother, Olinda, was a little girl who grew up in Portugal during a fascist regime that lasted fifty years. Her family knew the rotten, sour taste of poverty all too well. Still, they knew even better about the power of imagination to dress their life in gold.

My youngest sister's anthropology paper begins, "The Story of Olinda: Mater at Matrix: The creation of memory and forgetfulness in the space between us. Once upon a time, there was a girl who played with her sister, pretending to be 'ladies,' simulating with her bare and raised feet ethereal high heels. The 'ladies' in torn clothing covered themselves in imagined costumes made of silk and fur, adorned with pearls and jewels. The 'ladies,' raised in poor homes, believed they owned the bright stores of the streets they walked with their dirty little feet." (Noronha, 2001)

Our mother always had a grand imagination!

I believe the quality of imagination gave her the resilience and grace to endure the unspeakable challenges life threw at her.

She inherited that from her father, a storyteller who read for the family when TV was only a dream. He was the only one in the household who could read and write. The children would gather at his feet in bed to feed their souls with rich stories of magic and wonder.

My mother's bedtime stories were filled with grandiosity, beauty, and magic. They were simple universal stories that have been passed down for thousands of years, but she crafted them with diamonds and gold.

My mother would use a lamp to project shadows on the wall. Her hands skillfully danced from one mudra to the next, bringing to life the king, a magical tree, or a horse that carried the valiant prince on his conquest for the princess' heart.

Moreover, she brought another layer of reality when she mesmerized us with the creation of sounds that catapulted the story into a magical reality.

She created the sound of the castle door opening, horses trotting, a waterfall, and a wolf howling in the moonlight. Each character had a distinct voice and personality.

Even as I write today, my entire body feels ecstatic. I transport myself to long-forgotten lands of unimaginable beauty. Emerald forests embrace magnificent castles, honorable kings' rule, dreams manifest, and magic floats in the air, permeating everyone and everything. I believe these kingdoms exist, and their characters come whisper in my ear when I merge with a sunset.

From her mother, the family shaman, or medicine woman, she inherited the faith and wisdom to know that Mother Nature always has a cure.

Her brother, David, was sent home from the hospital, gravely ill. Her mother fed him fruit and olive oil, the only food they had available. But with lots of love and prayer, he survived and lived a long life.

This was the rich background of my mother's childhood, filled with stories, faith, prayer, and magic.

After her arm was amputated, she returned to daily life with a fierce determination to accomplish everything she loved to do.

The amputation didn't break her strong spirit and imagination. The doctors showed her how to cut onions, but her imagination provided alternatives. The day she returned home from the hospital, she went into the kitchen to cut onions the way she saw in her mind. She was going to do it her way. "This is the way," she said, "it's so much better than the way the doctors told me."

She held a long-time dream of drawing. Her grandfather was a ceramist and painter, and her brother followed in his footsteps.

After she lost her arm, she expressed her desire to draw. She felt like art would fill a hole that would otherwise be impossible to fill.

On Christmas of 2009, my husband Rian and I gifted her with paper, crayons, and a drawing desk. Two months later, she had over fifty drawings, including self-portraits, family portraits, and some of her favorite subjects.

She has done hundreds of drawings, and every day, she improves her ability to express her imagination through colors and lines.

Drawing with one hand has become a healing meditation. It is her saving grace as she deals with constant phantom pain and the daily challenges of living life with one arm.

When we choose to use our imagination, we can turn the darkest times around and allow them to shine the brightest light in our lives. In my mother's story, the amputation brought forth the gift of healing.

Olinda is my hero and an inspiration to all of us. May the courage, patience, determination, dedication, and grace reflected in her drawings inspire you never to give up!

Citation:

Noronha, Susana de (2001) Mater et Matrix: A produção da memória e do esquecimento no espaço entre nós, Author Edition, Coimbra

# It's About Thyme For Tiny Dancers
# By Rian McGonigal

My first experience with healing music came unexpectedly in the mid-'70s. I was playing classical guitar in a French restaurant named It's About Thyme, when a party of five adults came in with a little girl about four years old.

I was playing guitar transcriptions of Cello Suite No.1 by J.S. Bach. The Suite has seven movements: a Prelude, and six dances of the time: Allemande, Courante, Sarabande, Minuet I and II, and Gigue.

Touched by the magnificent Prelude, the little girl got up and started dancing to the remaining movements. Her joy captivated the entire restaurant. She created new dances for each movement, observing the tempo changes. She was a natural!

During the slow Sarabande, the little dancer approached me. She was fascinated by the sound, reaching for the strings. I glanced at the family, their eyes fixed on her. She came so near, I had to pull the guitar back. Then, her mother came forward, picked her up, looked at me intently, and said, "Thank you, thank you!" The adults at the table were beaming. The little girl danced to the end. Sid, their waiter, was watching in amazement. The entire restaurant was glowing.

The family finished. As they left, each adult shook my hand with both hands, repeating, "Thank you, thank you!" I felt so deeply appreciated, but I was also vaguely puzzled.

I took my break. Sid came over to me, looking like he knew something I didn't. Then he said those five memorable words: "That little girl is deaf!"

I was stunned.

Sid continued, "I know the family! She is deaf! Everyone at that table felt like they had witnessed a miracle!" He stared at me, wide-eyed. I stared back, as the significance sank in.

I went home profoundly affected, and shifted my attitude toward music. I would now perform with the belief that music can heal, and at times, create miracles. I had witnessed "The Miracle of the Tiny Dancer" and needed to take action.

My manager had been booking me on college circuits, local radio, TV. I informed him about the little deaf girl dancing, and my intention to pursue therapeutic music. He began booking me at nursing homes, drug rehab centers, homes for criminal teens, and similar places.

The feedback received was that the performances had a therapeutic effect. Troubled teens were more respectful. Drug rehab patients experienced better moods, needing less medication. The elderly population was more enthusiastic and slept better through the night. I was extremely pleased with the results of the performances, which motivated me to expand.

I wanted to offer authentic musical experiences without the steep learning curve. I started weekly drumming workshops; the results were amazing. One young man said that drumming, using both hands equally, reduced his dyslexia symptoms. Another woman said her therapist recommended drumming to vent anger positively, and it was working! Introverted people said drumming was an effective way to bond quickly with others, with no need for words!

A child therapist, familiar with the workshops, contacted a center for abused children. They requested to video a workshop with the kids to use to train their staff. I agreed. They informed me, "Adults close to the children commit most of the abuse. Trusting adults is difficult for them and takes time." I hoped I could gain their trust in one workshop!

I provided the drums. The kids responded extremely well. In a short time, we created a cohesive group, learning different rhythms, blending with a group, and soloing. Before we knew it, the session was over. One kid said, "This was the most fun day of my life!" Others agreed. All were happy! The workshop was a meaningful success, one of the most rewarding of my life.

My next opportunity to further this work came from my second bout with cancer. Synchronistic events connected me with a cancer treatment center, offering both medical and holistic treatment. I would go through an intense chemotherapy protocol for three months, and wanted my physical, mental, emotional, nutritional, and spiritual needs addressed.

I had done extensive research on cancer treatments and clinical trials, both in and out of the USA. I also got along well with staff and patients and even mediated a few situations. The hospital saw value in that and offered me a position consulting with prospective patients, and as an ombudsman between patients and staff. Most significantly, they supported my request to start a Therapeutic Music and Sound Department. I now had a patient population to work with!

To supervise their counseling program, the hospital invited Dr. O. Carl Simonton, the legendary pioneer of mind-body medicine. When I met Dr. Simonton, we felt like kindred spirits. Carl was a medical oncologist who researched mind-body medicine in the 1960s. He designed the first clinical study considering attitude as a factor in the outcome of disease. He also started visualization in pediatric cancer by having kids imagine their cancer cells being gobbled up by Pac-Man.

When I shared my experiences with music, rhythm, and sound as healing modalities, Carl was delighted. He confided, "I recently received guidance in a dream to use more music in my work. Would you also direct a therapeutic music and sound program for the Simonton Cancer Center?"

The stark contrast of my circumstances made me dizzy! I was an emaciated cancer patient, enduring months of sickening and exhaustive chemotherapy; and, I had become the first director of therapeutic music for two of the most progressive cancer treatment centers in the world!

Cancer manifested one additional gift. Chemotherapy shrank the six-inch diameter tumor. I then required major abdo-thoracic surgery to remove anything remaining. The 22-inch scar sealed the successful results inside but put me in bed for over two months. When I recovered, my mom arranged a Six Star Mediterranean cruise to celebrate my remission, recuperation, and birthday.

On September 13, 1993,

Aboard the Crystal Harmony,

While floating on the azure sea—

I met my wife, Maria.

# Altruistic Alchemy In Action
# By Paula Meyer

I had this amazing experience of seemingly creating money out of thin air, and it happened in a way that I didn't expect.

Back in 2012, I had been remarried for many years and was raising two children from my first marriage with my current husband. We had been struggling financially due to my ex-husband's failure to pay child support for many months, to the tune of about $12,000. I did everything I could to get him to pay, and finally, I had to resign myself to the fact that it was never going to happen and instead stewed in the anger and bitterness about the unfairness of life.

At the time, I was working for an author who taught about mind over matter and how your thoughts create your reality. I knew the truth of my powers of creation, but my emotional addiction to being angry and bitter at my ex-husband for failing to pay was no match for the knowledge of my true power. I tried positive affirmations by sending love to my ex, forgiving my ex, and forgiving myself, but nothing worked to unlock the chains that held this reality together.

One weekend, we were in beautiful Vancouver, Canada hosting a workshop at the University of British Columbia, which my boss taught. It was an advanced meditation workshop, and typically, during these types of workshops the staff didn't participate in the meditations. Rather, we held the space in the room for our attendees and made sure everyone was comfortable and safe. On the last day, which was Sunday, my boss graciously suggested that I participate in the meditation so that I could experience the power of group meditation. The group we worked with was experienced in meditation and mindfulness, and given that I know a lot of the people well, I thoroughly enjoyed supporting them throughout the workshop. So, I found a place to sit within the group and began.

When the meditation started, I was grateful for the gift of being with these people, and rather than focusing my attention on myself and something I needed to improve on, I chose to ask the Universe for abundance for everyone in the room. I am not a visual person, so I don't see vivid colors and real life images when I visualize in my mind, but what I did see in my mind's eye was like looking at the sunrise in a cloudless sky, and everything was tinged with gold. It was a beautiful, simple, and calming image, and I simply kept requesting abundance for all. When the meditation ended, I felt calm, happy, and golden!

When the workshop was over, we packed everything up and said our goodbyes to our amazing organizers. My boss and I began the long drive back home from Vancouver, Canada to Rainier, Washington, which was about a five-hour drive. While driving back home, I got a call from my husband telling me that our small website business was going crazy with orders due to an ad campaign we ran, and he asked me if he should shut it down. I laughed and said, "No, let's see how many we would get." I was excited to get home and jump on my computer to see what kind of craziness was happening! To my surprise and amazement, we received over $10,000 in orders that day!

On Monday, I went back to work at the office and began my usual busy post-event week, playing catch up with emails and projects that had taken a back seat to the event preparations for Vancouver. On Tuesday, I received a phone call from my child support case manager with some incredible news that my ex-husband had paid off his entire amount owed for child support! She said I would see that in my bank account in the next few days. I laughed and said, "I'll believe it when I see it in my account!" I was skeptical but hopeful, and guess what? The money showed up in my account a few days later!

Amazingly, in a span of 48 hours, from the time of that meditation on Sunday until that call on Tuesday, I received a total of over $22,000!

My boss wrote about it in one of his books in which he explained that when I chose to ask for the greater good of everyone rather than myself, that released the energy between my ex-husband and me. This exact energy could then be used to create a new reality where we were both free from the negative energy that was supporting, endorsing, and keeping the negative situation in place.

My boss and others in his field have also learned that when you use your energy to support others in the form of healing groups, intention groups, or prayer groups, the altruistic act of giving your healing energy to others has a rebound effect on those that are giving it! There are so many fascinating stories about healers who heal themselves in this way if they participate in these kinds of groups.

Years later, I had a much better understanding of how that happened during my meditation experience in 2012. Although this wasn't exactly a group healing meditation, we were in a large group of people who were all meditating for the good of themselves or others. My simple altruistic act of sending my energy to all in the room for their abundance, in turn, created abundance for me! And I didn't have to beg, weep, or attempt to negotiate with the Universe!

What a fun and lucrative two days!

Remember, we all have this ability to create! Give it a try!

# When I Look Into The Deepest Parts Of Myself, I Find You There
## By Kardiia Milan

*"Find yourself, and you will find your soulmate."*

A story of manifestation, and a love that transcends lifetimes. Throughout the brief interlude presented here are italicized actual messages expressed from one to another and captured as loving exchanges while the flower of our love blossomed.

*"It's amazing how little anything matters—anything like in regular life—once you've seen what's possible and perfect."*

Beyond all odds and in the most unlikely of circumstances, I found my true partner. Through truths that came to us in deep meditation and in unquestionable knowing, we realized that our energetic ties to each other began somewhere in time that was somehow separate from the plane we now live on. It is unclear how the weavings of time coexist. It would seem, however, that lifetimes upon lifetimes on planets near and distant overlap in ripples of emotion like handfuls of pebbles thrown into a still pond.

*"I feel I've known you for millennia—crossing dimensions to find each other again in space to again re-live our archetype stronger together."*

One night, separated by distance but soulfully connected and fully in love, my partner and I entered a calm meditative state together after talking on the phone for hours. After moments of silence, a packet of emotion was delivered. A standing wave of information was downloaded into our shared consciousness. These packets of sacred information are capable of defying physics as we understand it. These divine offerings are packets of information transmitted by some unknown force in the universe and can only be translated by our third eye—also called our pineal gland. This lens that peers into the fabric of manifested existence, if properly tuned, can decipher energy, emotion, and thought from other dimensions into a viable, visible, palpable, re-living, and re-telling of lives lived separately from us now. These can be thought of as past lives, but in actuality, we have no way of knowing if these experiences are past, future, or coexisting.

> *"I have a feeling we've done this before.*
> *Or maybe that's me remembering the future.*
> *Or a different reality.*
> *Or the fact that it feels so familiar, like home."*

All at once we saw ourselves as different people in a different plane of existence; our genders reversed, and our ages greatly advanced. We saw our life together in this distant time and place—growing old together, nurturing the land and plant life around us. Our partnership was clear and long and strong and undeniable. Our life together on this plane was as real as you sitting here today reading this, and is eternally etched into the annals of time, unweathered as the light that illuminates this present moment.

> *"Undeniable,*
> *a feeling like no other,*
> *and that was incredible, everything turned off*
> *and an overwhelming,*
> *yet perfect amount*
> *of pure bliss, happiness, and love took over"*

The barriers in this three dimensional existence that separated my partner and myself were seemingly impassable. Manifestation however, is not without a sense of the miraculous.

> *"When I make the transformation within me, the transformation goes out to all of life—to all of life and all of consciousness and all of creation."*

We had manifested a partnership, the roots of which were as ethereal as angels descending onto fields of wounded mankind. All odds were against this union that we knew to be the truth. By convention, there was nothing that would allow us to be together, however by belief, there was nothing that could be more true.

*"I think you are activating every cell in my body and transforming it back to perfection. I love what we allow each other to experience. It's like I feel through you, within you, I feel you within me. I feel every ounce of perfection, peace, purity, love, joy all at once."*

Never before had either of us trusted so blissfully and wholly in the power of the universe and creation. Piece by piece, struggle by struggle, time after time, and no matter the price, we relentlessly chose each other above all else, and by the nature of what this book calls manifestation, we now preside in our heaven on earth together.

*"This—this is the future. This is the emotion that ripples through our existences time after time after time. This is the beauty in all things. This is the beauty that rides through every timeline in existence, elevating and teaching and vibrating. This is the deep exhale of the universe loving itself, and this—comes from your heart."*

# Practical Manifestation: Dreaming, Declaration, Reality
# By Meaghan Miller Lopez

In this moment, I am present to peace, wonder, and potency. I'm sitting in my art studio, on a blue velvet cushion in a golden chair, leaning back on pillows made from a series of paintings that documented my recovery from traumatic brain injury (TBI). All my life, I've been dreaming this right-now reality into existence. My life is a conscious manifestation, the fulfillment of a childhood dream that's now coincided with reality.

My studio is small and not my final expression, but it's one of the spaces that's been opened and filled with light, healing, and creativity. Every part of my life that's been tended to with awareness and intentional practice gleams with potency. The messy parts, and there are a few, have not yet had their turn at being spun into gold.

Manifestation is practical. It's a practice. Simply put, it's the act of bringing an idea, dream, or desire into the material world as an object, experience, or shared reality that others agree exists.

When we talk about manifestation, we're pointing to the awareness that we're the creators of our reality. We're the ones who say what we want. We're responsible for opening the energetic space to receive the match for our desires.

Three years ago, I was a sales director for an online publisher. Fifteen years before then, I'd scrawled out a manifestation list of what I wanted to achieve—my personal and professional goals. The last of the items had been checked off. I saw no path for growth in my workplace. I'd lost heart for tolerating the dysfunction of the environment. It was time to create something new.

While on a retreat about wonder and poetry, I made a declaration.

"I surrender my life to being an artist," I said. "I allow art-making to take over my life."

When I shared at the retreat, people were inspired and cheered me on. But when I came back to work, the statement occurred as ridiculous. There was no evidence for this being possible, but I didn't give up.

Looking back, I see the old reality was already breaking apart. As it seemed to worsen, I kept on creating. Every breakdown was a sign that this chapter was ending. Instead of reacting with frustration and anger, I made my declaration again, then again, and again.

"I surrender my life to being an artist. I allow art-making to take over my life."

How this would come into form was unpredictable, but making the declaration amused me, which raised my vibration. Every time I said it was a confirmation of my commitment to creating this new reality, despite the reality around me showing no evidence or agreement.

I kept on creating, letting the universe know I was serious, unshakable, surrendering, allowing. I took actions consistent with the reality I was creating. At home, I claimed this room as my art studio. I began making art for an hour a week. I invested in an out-of-town painting workshop, bought all the supplies, the plane ticket, and secured a place to stay. I never made it to the workshop.

The created life appears when we clear the space, step into the unknown, and let the universe deliver. One day I pulled down the hatch of my car, and the bike rack I'd forgotten was attached struck my head with exponential force.

Because of what I'd been creating for my life, despite the challenges from my injury, I saw my TBI as a gift from the universe, enhancing and elevating my consciousness. In the darkness of the early days, I saw what my life was for, and once seen, I couldn't turn away. I'd lost cognitive capacities, but gained awareness of myself as an infinite being.

Over the first year of my recovery, my career and previous life fell away. In the space that opened up, I painted the awareness I had no words for. I curated what I listened to, and the energy of people in my life. I used Instagram to document my progress, and as a tool for self-discovery. I intentionally nurtured new neural networks, the foundation of my new reality.

Today I'm an artist and creative advisor. My purpose is bringing potency and magic to day to day life. My life is filled with what I love, and the evidence for this reality is now easy to recognize. Art and consciousness are everywhere—at home, I walk past stacks of paintings and supplies. My days are filled with co-creative conversations. Manifestations happen fast, with ease and velocity.

Good morning, my love, it's time to wake up.

We are here for each other.

What would you like to create?

**Recommendations**

Please don't wait for injury or bad circumstances to begin tending to the manifestation of your dream life. Having the life you want leads to sharing the unique gift you are with the world. Every action you take towards having the life you want expands your capacity for potency, magic and manifestation in day to day life. Aligning yourself to live on purpose is worth the risk, and contributes to the greater good.

In lieu of a brain injury, I recommend the following for getting clear about who you are and what you're here for:

1. Human Design: Based on birth time, this system reveals the energetic coding of your soul, where negative conditioning

gets stuck, and the ideal strategy for you to co-create reality with the universe.

2. Akashic Records: Access to the vibrational record of your soul where you receive wisdom, love and guidance from your personal masters, teachers, and loved ones. You can learn to access your individual record, or find a certified Akashic Records practitioner (like me) to give you a reading.

3. Flower Essence Remedies: A vibrational healing modality that gently clears energetic blocks and conditioning stuck in the subtle energy system.

4. Transformation: The Landmark Forum and Wisdom Unlimited Course by Landmark Worldwide provides distinctions and conversations for creating a life you love.

# I Haven't Re-Tired, I've Just Repotted: Rediscovering Mission And Purpose In The Second Half Of Life
## By Claudio Morelli

Alexander Graham Bell profoundly stated, "When one door closes, another opens; but we often look so long and so regretfully upon the closed door, that we do not see the one which has opened for us."

Little did I know that when a significant door closed for me, another would unexpectedly open a few months later.

After spending thirty-five plus years as an educator, something I loved and was passionate about, I was faced with a dilemma. What do I do now that retirement from my full-time job as a superintendent of schools has potentially closed the door to leading, influencing and impacting?

When the door did close, I enjoyed an initial couple of months of rest and relaxation. I did not have any specific plans following retirement. I felt I deserved some time away from leading, contributing, and influencing. I was tired and thought I deserved a break.

After a while, growing unrest settled in, followed by sadness, grief, and regret. I began to miss that buzz and energy from being around people and doing something with and for a purpose. I wondered if I would ever be able to recapture the zest of helping someone or influencing people in an organization. I started to wonder, "What's next?"

Then, as my good friend, Barry, shared, "Claudio got a call. Not a telephone call. Not a margin call. A call from God."

I had no idea this call was coming my way. I was not aware that God was orchestrating an open and unique pathway to purpose and influence when two life-long friends delivered a message. Gerry and Shirley planted a seed that helped me to commit to serving with the Wellspring Foundation for Education in Rwanda. A new-found door of transformation and joy opened up for me, although I did not recognize it at the time.

Initially, I internally slammed that door shut. I was reluctant to seize this unique opportunity when Gerry asked me to consider a job as the Educational Advisor at the Wellspring Academy in Kigali, Rwanda.

My initial response was, "There is no way that I am going to do this." Negatives regarding the position flooded my mind. The job was in Rwanda and meant that I would be far away from my wife and family for long periods. I would have to leave the safety and comfort of our home and life in Vancouver. My mind never even considered the positives of this potential opportunity. Anxiety and fear kicked in, and I spun into a negative downward spiral that happens to me when doubt arises. I tend to avoid and bury these worrisome situations and quickly move to denial.

At that moment, I also knew a voice was preparing something different for me. My concern about what to do following retirement was being answered. I did not understand why I was asked to consider this task. I felt unprepared and unsure about how this journey was going to unfold. I was confronted by a critical decision and was not convinced it was the right one, even though it would provide me with a means of continuing to lead, influence, and impact. Something I definitely wanted to pursue.

Although this call to lead was unexpected, I finally acted with conviction to listen and answer the call. For over six years, I have volunteered and consulted with Wellspring. I have discovered a real passion for serving with and supporting educators in Rwanda. I never imagined this challenge and experience for myself. I never dreamed that I would be learning and leading in Rwanda, a beautiful country with resilient, resourceful, and courageous people. A country that suffered so much during the genocide against the Tutsi people.

This invitation to serve in Rwanda brought about tremendous discovery and abundant joy as I visited and interacted with my colleagues at the Wellspring Foundation for Education. My time in Rwanda has had a profound impact on my personal transformation. I have experienced unexpected and uplifting benefits as a result of my journey to Rwanda. Beyond being able to continue to serve, lead, and influence, this life-changing experience has given me a new mission in life.

Because I took this step of faith, I have been able to share my experiences and inspire others to move out of their comfort zones. My journey in Rwanda has given me so many opportunities to share my story with friends, colleagues, and family, who have communicated how my journey has led them to think about their individual contributions and service.

I also discovered that retirement should not put up any roadblocks to maintaining a purpose and mission in the second half of life. My service in Rwanda made me realize that your age or stage of life does not matter. You can still contribute, serve, lead, and influence. There is no reason why you cannot revitalize your sense of worth, contribution, or value. It is not about having the right qualifications—it is about your willingness to serve and to be available to help. It's about preparing and then offering your heart. All of us have value and abilities that can contribute and influence. I have become a strong proponent of seniors and elders, advocating that their purpose in life is not over.

I am so thankful that Gerry and Shirley came calling on behalf of Wellspring, and I am grateful for the encouraging voices of my wife and family.

Today as an elder, I continue to have a sense of purpose, worth, and value. I am committed to helping others, organizations, communities, and countries. I am very much alive, and as Craig Groeschel definitively stated, and I echo, "You're not dead, so you're not done!"

Don't regret the closing of a door! Be alert to that voice that beckons you to what potentially could be a surprising outcome.

Citations

Groeschel, Craig, @craiggroeschel. "You're not dead, so you're not done!" June 16, 2013, Twitter.

Morelli, Claudio. *Learning and Leading in the Land of a Thousand Hill: An Unexpected Mission of Transformation and Joy* (Vancouver: Fireside Parliament Books, 2019), pg.xii.

# Let's Make A Vision Board
# By Aerin Morgan

One of the first things I learned when I started to genuinely "study" metaphysics was how to make a vision board. I loved that it involved poster board, glue sticks, and cutting things out of magazines. I never actually expected it would work—but it did.

When I made that first vision board, I was living in a small apartment. I decided to dream big and found a photo intended to represent my future home. The building in the picture was a sprawling Spanish-style mansion with an open veranda, wide staircase, and a lush garden filled with colorful flowers and tropical plants. Compared to my tiny apartment, it seemed like a heavenly place to call home.

I meditated with my board every night for a month, as my teacher had instructed, and then set it on my dresser so it would be visible whenever I walked into my bedroom. Time passed, I got a roommate, and my vision board was relegated to the back of my closet.

Fast forward a few years. My roommate was now my husband, and soon after we married, he won a trip to a resort in Playacar, Mexico. As we were escorted to our room, I looked around to admire the hotel's lush gardens. We strolled down a long staircase, and I almost fainted when I realized that it was the same staircase in the photo on my vision board. I may not have gotten my "dream house," but I did get an all-expenses-paid visit.

### What is a vision board?

A vision board is a pictorial representation of what you want in life. Today you can make one digitally, but I still prefer to create mine by hand.

**What you'll need:**

- Poster board, foam core, or some other surface to serve as your background.

- Images of what you'd like to have in your life. I prefer dividing my space into sections that represent the different areas of my life: personal, career, money/finance, travel, health, relationships, and so on. You can cut images from magazines or simply Google and print them.

If you have trouble getting started, begin with larger categories, and narrow down from there.

Wealth and financial prosperity: Find images that contain money and people who are enjoying their financial freedom.

New job, promotion, success in school: Look for images that focus on the desired outcome, not the details of how you're going to get there. Graduation caps, A+ report cards, smiling faces around a conference table are good choices. Remember not to include real-life images—you may *think* you want to work for ABC Electronics, but the universe may have a better plan, and you don't want to limit yourself.

New or improved relationship, friendship, passion: Find images of happy couples. Don't get hung up on physical characteristics—a perfect relationship should be the main focus. This works for friendships too. When I first moved to Dallas, I found an image of several people sitting around a table laughing and enjoying dinner together.

Success in quitting an addiction or making life changes: A vision board is a great way to start the journey towards quitting a bad habit and making meaningful life changes. If there are things in your life that you no longer need or want, try finding images that illustrate what your life would be like without these negative influences. Also, be sure to include images of encouragement to remind yourself that you're on the right path and have the strength to see your way to the finish line.

Improving your health and fitness: When you're thinking about adding images that inspire you to lead a healthier life, find ones that represent how you want to *feel*, not only how you want to look. Also, be sure to include pictures that illustrate a sense of accomplishment and joy. If there's a part of your body that needs healing, find an image that represents a perfectly healthy example of that organ/gland/bone/body part. Never use a picture of an injury and then try to work backward.

Spiritual growth and protection: A deeper sense of peace, a connection to your angels or guides, a firmer understanding of your place in the world, and a desire to expand your psychic or healing abilities could all fall into this category. When searching for a deeper connection to the divine, look for pictures that elicit a feeling of love and protection.

**Putting it all together**

Once you've gathered all your pictures, it's time to put them on your board. Your board can be any size or shape, and once you've laid out your images, you should have a good idea of how large your background needs to be. I prefer foam core and map pins because it gives me the freedom to add, subtract, and rearrange things as needed, but you should choose whatever is easiest and most convenient for you.

I like to arrange images by category. This way, I can see certain areas of my life as a whole. You, however, can place your images in whatever configuration feels best to you. There is no right or wrong way. Don't over-think it. When you're done, your board should be visually pleasing to *you*. That's the point—to have something inspiring that *you* enjoy looking at!

**So, you've finished your vision board—now what?**

To have success with your new creation, you need to work with it. Again, there are no rules on how to do this. Some people simply hang it in a place where they'll see it every day, some make a daily routine of meditating on the images, others slip it under their bed so it can subliminally transmit their desires while they sleep. Whatever you chose, remember to see the items on your board as already being a part of your life.

To learn more about vision boards, see sample affirmations, get presentation ideas, and read more about putting your board to work, visit my blog: www.aerinmorgan.com.

# Tumbling Into My Purpose
# By Dr. Fred Moss

A quiet acceptance and resignation were to follow.

1. *Will my two children be okay when I'm gone? Yes, I bought life insurance.*

2. *Damn, I thought there was something else for me to do here.*

I awaited the obvious and inevitable final *boom* while careening freely into helpless abandonment, finding some perverse peace in this culminating magnum opus of a joy ride. But I guess it didn't happen like that, although occasionally I still wonder what actually did. No, something else more impactful happened instead.

I deduced that I was right side up. Whirr, whirr, my dying engine purred. I checked to make sure my face was still on. Wiggling my hands and feet seemed to prove that I was generally still in one piece. Yay!

Oh, I get it. My car is going to explode now! I better eject. Nudging the driver's side door open, there was enough room for me to exit. Getting my duffle bag from the trunk, which had been moved into the back seat upon impact, I left the pretzelled automobile behind and began to mosey up the hill that was now representing my somehow averted certain demise, on my way back to the highway.

Two gawking vans had found their way to the spectacle that was now becoming a harrowing experience. Stunned to now see me, they were sure they had seen a UFO when the rotating headlights seemed to come out of nowhere during the half gainer that my free-floating vehicle gracefully displayed. They probably considered me to have been an extraterrestrial alien. Well, I sometimes do too!

I was not extremely injured, given the extent of what was left of my dear vehicle. A cut on my left earlobe and a bruise on my belly from the seatbelt were noticed. Overall, I was in remarkable shape. The police had arrived and were now interviewing the man. He had fallen asleep at the wheel before our lives collided, and he would be charged with DUI. I reflexively recalled that I, too, had fallen asleep while driving in 2002. After my head-on collision and subsequent DUI charge, my life has transformed in beautiful ways. I have 17 years of sobriety from that date as I write this.

My first intentional move was to accompany my co-collider in the back of the squad car, and immediately and completely forgive him for what had occurred. In that act, I quietly and karmically forgave myself for my recklessness committed eight years prior.

I had looked destruction in the eye and was somehow allowed to stay here on Earth for another chapter. A new level of respect for living was joined by a new sense of levity. Life is precious and should be lived with reverence because it ends before we think we are done.

As the days, months, and years since that fateful September 25, 2010 date click forward, I have looked at the impact that it has had on me and my relationship with all of humanity and life. What did happen, and how has my course been affected?

I have lived a life packed with miracles. I have become much more spiritually aware and have been to Israel many times, including obtaining a passport upon my making Aliyah in 2017. I have had many beautiful relationships and been completely devoted to a lifetime of growth and development as a way of being. It seems that I manifest my world almost too simply, something like "if I say so," being the only factor necessary to make any and all things happen (within a broad range of reason). I seem to get the exact life that I call for and call "so" with some freakish degree of miraculous frequency.

And as these "accidents" fade further and further into my rearview mirror of life, I recall a feature of the experience that definitely took place, which somehow helps to put it into cosmic perspective.

You see, as I was in free-falling trajectory mode that evening, I had a conversation with God, and He answered both of my questions:

1. Your children are well and will be taken care of from this point forward.

2. Yes, you have other things to do, so I am going to leave you here to have another chance to do that.

And then he gave me a caveat that has been my experience as I look back retrospectively from here towards that day, "I am going to give you *everything* you want when you ask for it. Good luck with that! I will be watching."

I have great friends, and my family is healthy. I have a great partner, and we are exploring everything that is here to discover in the world of man and woman playing and working together.

I am committed to altering the narrative of mental illness on a global scale, and to each and every person having a life for which they know that they matter. I am living that world now and making a difference every day.

I manifest the life that I declare to be so. I am the poster child for "word creating world." My life is a dream, even including all the pain and suffering that naturally come as an intricate component of the human experience.

Sometimes I think that I am especially chosen for this role, but frequently, I am left with the possible reality that we *all* get the life we ask for to some degree. Trials and tribulations within one's life can appear to be numerous and unfair or unjust, and the tests that these experiences allow us to face more often than not lead to miraculous results.

Declare and manifest.
Then manifest and declare.
Then repeat the process.
*And watch the miracles unfold.*

# You Deserve Better
# By Astrid Navarrete

W e all want more. We all want better. We all wish for an easy life, a successful career, A good looking partner, and lastly, to eat without gaining weight. Oh, come on. You know you do, there's absolutely nothing wrong with that. There's absolutely nothing wrong with you at all. You dream because all you want is meant to be yours.

Five-year-olds have no problem dreaming, even though the doctor diagnosed them with an overactive imagination. Children are often a couple of steps ahead of the adult version of who we are today. Our inner child recognizes our deepest desires; it needs convincing; you may have been convinced in the past that good things are only for special, lucky ones or the wealthy ones.

You may feel unworthy, incapable, and almost wrong. Doubt is a slow killer. Like our inner child, doubt recognizes our deepest desires and acts against us. Doubt has a teammate, lack. Doubt and lack are both on a mission to murder your wildest dreams. How silly is that! It's like putting our life on hold until we shake other people's diagnoses.

Scary, isn't it? The idea that other people can significantly influence our whole life even though we still have the power of choice. The way we think, speak, dress and the choices we make are highly influenced by the closest people around us. It is common to emulate people who aren't good for us. The need to gain others' approval may cause us to reach rock bottom and decide to make necessary changes and improve our lives. Practicing self influence is essential. How do we get out of the jail cell of the mind? How do we get money without a job? How do we give our children a supportive lifestyle? How do we release depression and take care of ourselves? By choosing better. Choosing better is the first step to manifesting more of what you deserve. Just like the law of gravity, everything is all happening naturally. If life has been a struggle, it may be true that it will continue to be, unless you decided you want to see and experience it differently. Because you choose better, you then deserve better and are open to obtaining better, more comfortable and faster.

My life has always been a by-product; it was already happening right in front of me. Being victimized by a family member at the age of four only attracted more serious abuse into my life. I was only four and that was unfair. Yet again, life doesn't have to be fair, because life will only give us what we focus on. Years of abuse that led to future abuse caused me to spiral. I couldn't choose better simply because I didn't know better. I could still feel the dark energy like an angry shadow that followed me around as its prey. As a teenager, I experienced love the way I wished it to be until the shadow of my past caught up to me. It wasn't my fault you see. There was already ancient energy, a cellular model. The lingering shadow I'd wish never to see showed up beside me in the form of a new lover. I don't want to share about it further; know that I was forced to choose better. I found myself influenced by this old dark shadow that loves to feature in my life movie by playing different characters in my script with a similar climax every time. Then I remembered that I was the original writer of my story. I can choose to write a better ending — one where the light shines through the cracks.

Your thoughts create your reality; I'm sure you must have heard of this by now. You get to choose the frequency that brightens up your life. You choose the people in your life, careers, partners, and lifestyle. After years of learning social conditioning, I'm still not done. Having difficult experiences has caused me to look further inside and to dream of an easy lifestyle. I can choose the colors of my life and decorate my creation any way I choose. If you are looking at the shadows in your life, you can choose new colors, new facets and new light to shine through the darkness. I nor you need to be desperate for what you want because it's already ours. We don't need it. It is already here for you and for me. We can choose better because we deserve better.

# Divorce Is Never Easy
# By Janet Grace Nelson

anifesting a fairytale ending of a 22-year marriage that fell out of love. No one ever gets married without the hopes of staying together "until death do us part." We were no different. We had a whirlwind courtship that brought us down the aisle within five months of our first meeting. We had dreams of having a family together, pursuing our careers, and having it all. On our first anniversary, our daughter was born, and less than two years later, our son toddled after. Living in the Midwest, we loved being close to our extended families and sharing our love, as our siblings and dear friends were also growing their families.

My husband's career was escalating, and a job offer from Disney had us making a huge decision. Do we want to leave our families and everyone we know and love? Should we move out to California to help advance his career? It was a difficult decision to surrender my desire for family over his desire for the advancement of his career; however, I did. His dedication to his career, along with being 3,000 miles away from family and friends, created a wedge in our relationship, which later grew to a "Grand Canyon."

Over the next 15 years, we worked diligently together to find new ways to communicate our needs and also feel connected. Our dedication to our children and the new tribe we had created seemed to be the anchor that brought us back together each time.

We sought relationship counsel with many different advisors over the course of those tumultuous years, and each time, we unveiled layers of who we were. It became clearer that we processed life differently. He was focused on achieving the goals he had set for himself, while I was focused on family and my dedicated pursuit of keeping us together. It felt like a roller coaster—emotionally, mentally, spiritually, and physically—until the fateful day when we knew it was time to get off.

Two months of enduring his complete silence had left me feeling totally alone and alienated. I had never felt so dishonored and disrespected by someone I deeply loved. I kept trying new ways to communicate and connect us back to the love we once shared, but none ever worked.

As I listened to my heart's deepest desire for love and peace, I knew it was time to move on. Although I was scared, I knew God's plans for my next chapter would reveal itself in divine timing.

At that time, I had been practicing manifestation techniques, and I knew the power of belief and visualization. I used my imagination to paint images of us having a loving conversation in a peaceful environment and connecting at the heart.

What followed next was shocking, and I never saw it coming. As the divorce proceedings began, our lawyers entered a five-year battle. His lawyer was determined that I receive nothing for what was accumulated over our 22 years of marriage, while my lawyer was trying to ensure that a fair deal was made.

My former husband's greed and anger brought out a forceful monster who had decided that my contribution to our marriage was of no value. My heart was broken again and again, as I couldn't believe this was the man I loved and shared my life with.

I knew that all I wanted was to have a "heart to heart" with the man who I once loved, and I felt a deep sense of purpose for our time together. I knew that if I could envision this possibility, I could manifest it. I spent many months focusing on my vision of us connecting on a heart level and having a peaceful resolution.

As we entered our final court-ordered mediation, all the lawyers and forensic accountants were present with their stacks of files and subpoenas.

My former husband was seated directly across from me as the lawyers began arguing. To my surprise, he glanced up at me and asked me if I'd like to have a private conversation in the next room. I accepted his invitation, and we walked across the hall to his lawyer's empty office. After several minutes of awkward silence, he spoke. Clearing his throat, with a look of remorse on his face, he pointed to the conference room and said, "I don't know where to begin to apologize for this horrific circus that I alone have created, you don't deserve this." I was taken aback by his apology, but I also knew I was watching my manifested vision come to life before my eyes. He continued to open his heart and speak lovingly about the amazing children we brought into the world, and that our marriage was filled with many beautiful memories that we should always cherish. It felt as if time stood still as we returned to the love we both knew had been there.

I knew that God had gifted us with this precious time to reminisce and finalize this chapter of our lives that felt lovingly aligned with my heart's desire.

I understand now that connecting to your heart's deepest desires will help you navigate through life's most challenging and difficult times. My hope is that we will all take the time to open our hearts and listen to what we would love to create. See it in your mind's eye and allow yourself to believe it is achievable to manifest more good in your life than you ever dreamed was possible.

# Island Magic
## By Nicole Newsom-James

My brother, Remington, had been transferred from the mainland directly to Hawaii by the creative healing forces of the Universe. How excited I was to visit and explore his new home!

My first trip was in 1990. I stepped off the plane, and Remington placed a beautiful necklace of flowers around my shoulders. I deeply inhaled the beauty of them. He had taken some time off from work to take me to Diamond Head on Oahu to gather green peridot from the volcanic stone walls. After collecting a handful of these little pea-sized beauties, Remington had me look at the sky, and asked if I knew of those 3D pictures that you stare at until all the lines and splashes of color formed some sort of picture, which then pops out at you. I had seen them and enjoyed discovering the design within. While I was staring at the baby blue sky, he asked me to blur my eyes and focus on the space between the sky and me, like I did with those pictures. I followed his instructions, and something started to take shape. Then pop! It was there. I looked around in amazement. The space between me and the outreaches of the sky was now filled with huge bubbles of gas. I kept looking at them, fascinated. They would not go away. As I spun around, I continued to see them everywhere. My big kahuna brother told me that these bubbles were the life energy of the planet. I could not be blinded to them anymore. They were everywhere. This vision of magic rocked the rhythm of my world. I was out of sync with all I knew and understood life to be. You could call this the "big bang" in my little universe. Because of this experience, I knew that my mystical life was only at the beginning of the wave, and I needed to ride it.

After two weeks of bliss, I returned to the metropolitan city of Houston, Texas, with all of its hustle and bustle, and headed back to my corporate job and waited. I waited in anticipation for my next vacation.

On my next trip to the islands, my friend Karen joined in the adventure. She had never been to Hawaii. We stayed with my brother, and the following day took off to Maui. As we drove the winding road to Hana, our eyes were taking in the sights of mountainous waterfalls to the right of us, while the ocean glistened to the left. I thought that this must be what heaven looked like.

We decided to stop to hike one of the trails to a popular waterfall. It took a rocky mile to get there, but it was well worth the trip. Karen stepped closer to the waterfall to get a better camera angle. I hung back and admired the view. Out of the silence, I heard a tiny voice say, "I'm down here." I looked down, but nothing was there except a rock. I heard the voice say, "Dig me up." I complied. This seemed the normal thing to do when you hear a rock tell you to dig it up, you do it. I was in Hawaii, after all. So, I dug it up.

Upon examination, I discovered that this natural rock was in the shape of a turtle's head. What luck! I had recently been reading about these little rock carvings in the shape of animals, called fetishes. It is said that a little earth spirit lives in each one and carries a special power. The turtle image is said to carry the spirit of protection, fertility, and mother earth. My little rock animal had not been carved by any human being. It was carved through time by the wind and water of nature herself. It was a treasure.

In 2009, I landed on the Garden Isle of Kauai and found myself staring at the oldest Catholic church in the Pacific Islands. I walked around back to the church's grotto. I was on a mission. I had brought gifts for the Blessed Virgin Mary on the center altar where two Archangel Raphael statues resided on either side of her. I was praying for guidance in my new work as a spiritual healer. I left my turtle fetish, and a beautiful clear Herkimer crystal at the feet of the Madonna and prayed. I was given the knowledge that I was to help those drawn to me to reconnect with and respect their feminine energy. Prayer answered. Yet, this was one of my less than magical visits to Hawaii. It could have been my company. But once home, vacation pictures printed, I started going through them. A friend had taken pictures of the grotto; at the entrance, you could see the four bench pews leading up to the bowed head of the Virgin Mary along with the Raphael angels to each side of her. I searched for my pictures of the grotto, pondering that moment of prayer, wondering if I understood my mission correctly. I found my exact picture of the Virgin Mary and gasped. Mary's head was bowed in every picture I had seen of her—but mine. In my picture, Mary's eyes were looking directly into mine.

This was more than a coincidence; my message was confirmed, and I immediately moved in the direction I had been given. I opened a healing center called Spirit Sense in Highland Village, where I began sharing my intuitive gifts. Spirit Sense bloomed into a place of healing the body and its spirit. My special gift was in locating blocks within a person's energy and removing them. These blocks held them back from their life path. They were normally an issue or trauma from their past. But no matter what the issue, once the spirit was healed, the body naturally found its way back too.

Spirit Sense became my little piece of Hawaii.

# Humanifestor
## By Sophia Olivas

"If they remove you from the home, you'll live on the streets and become a whore and get pregnant or become a druggy and be killed."

Words from my mother, spoken to me after Child Protective Services (CPS) was called to our home to investigate years of abuse at the hand of my father. Mom was warning me what would happen if I did not lie to CPS about the abuse.

At the age of 14, having disagreed with how my father was raising me, I thought I could do better, so I left and did way better. I chose the streets, homelessness, and hunger over the material comforts that masked the darkness. During the years that followed my departure from the family unit, I devoured books on self-development. I knew that educating my mind was key to healing and thriving. The internet was not yet around, so I spent hours in the library, asking questions, and seeking teachers. My actions attracted mentors that saw something in me, and they, in turn, directed my studies.

What happens to you does not define you—it fuels you. It can illuminate your purpose. "Watch your thoughts as they lead to feelings. Feelings lead to actions, and actions lead to results." (T. Harv Eker).

I spent years in therapy dissecting my childhood trauma and healing the impact of what I had made it all mean. Despite all of that work, it was when I discovered manifestation that I began thriving. The moment I gave up my past and stopped using it as an excuse, its hold on me dissipated. Manifestation allowed me to co-create with the Universe, free from the constraints of the past, as creation lies in the present.

The most important lesson about thriving is to become aware of and master manifesting. It's the secret behind the success of those that we hold in esteem. Manifestation is a universal truth, a law, that when applied, is a leveling tool, as it does not recognize social, educational, geographical, gender, or financial status. Anyone, at any time, can call upon it.

The first thing I learned about manifestation is to hold a thought as if it was already so, or "fake it until you make it." Visualization and vision boards are also excellent tools for this. Create vision boards for New Years, and watch how many things come true by the following year. Who would you be, and how would you act if you had "X?" Do that—be that.

Everything is energy. The Universe cannot tell the difference between positive and negative, real or imagined. It only hears what is being said. For example, if you are late for an important appointment, and you have plenty of time, you get all green lights and traffic moves in your favor. The opposite is true when you are running late. It even has a name, "Murphy's Law."

Words matter. They shape and create your world, so choose them wisely. Pay attention to your external and internal dialogues. If you don't like the fruits, look at the roots. If the results you are producing are at odds with what you want, look to your thoughts. Look at what you say about what is occurring. Pay special attention to what you make things mean. What happened can easily be overwritten by what you say about what happened. Humans are "meaning-making machines" (Landmark Education). The meaning we give things is an automatic human response, it's always happening. What can be controlled is the narrative. "Change your brain, change your life" (Dr. Daniel Amen). If you want instant change, change your perspective, and do so by changing the narrative. What you say about the world, about others, and about yourself shapes your world and provides marching orders for the Universe to carry out on your behalf. Once spoken or thought, the Universe will work to conspire and provide evidence, because "thoughts are things" (Mike Dooley).

What's my superpower? I am a *humanifestor*. I say "chair," and it falls out of my mouth. I set an intention for the end results and then let go of the lap bar, put my hands up in the air, and enjoy the ride— mouth open in a wide Cheshire grin with my hair blowing. Manifestation requires two things: uncertainty and chaos. It's for the brave. It's for those who want it badly. It's for those who have been beaten down by life, who have known loss and doubt, and who are willing to get up one more time, hearts open, trusting their path, and the path of others. You have to surrender blame and fault in others and in yourself. You have to be willing to give up the specifics, the details, the *hows*. That's letting go of control.

I solo backpack in foreign countries, traversing places rarely visited. I land without knowing anyone or the language, and some do not have lodging. I go, trusting that when I land, the perfect person, resource, or opportunity will appear. That's inner strength. That's belief in humanity and in my path. That takes more courage and grit than it does to prep, control, and force outcomes. Thirty-plus countries later, I have a wealth of connections and incredible memories of all the beautiful people that have opened their homes and hearts to me. Have a clear outcome and insist on *un*certainty about how it will come about.

For those that may be currently experiencing a challenge, "Embrace the suck. Don't shrink. Don't puff up. Stand your sacred ground" (Brené Brown). Focus on the outcome.

The future has not yet been born, you are co-creating it. Have the courage to ask for your heart's desire and then take action, any action, from right where you are, that moment, with what you have. You are needed and *now* is your time.

230

# The Manifestation Queen
# By Terry Om

As a young child, what I wanted most in life was to be a witch.

I wanted to have special powers—to be able to move objects with my mind, to be able to remove myself from scary situations with the blink of my eyes. I spent countless hours staring at a fork or a pencil on the table, summoning them to move; even a slight twitch would have satisfied me.

I grew up in the era of *Bewitched* and *I Dream of Jeannie*. My idols were skinny, white women with puffy blonde hair who could make magic happen at a moment's notice. It was a devastating day when I realized I was a witch devoid of the special powers my mentors possessed.

I eventually turned my focus onto a career path that did indeed take a miracle to succeed. I longed to be a singer—to be a famous, successful one at that. One big problem was that I lacked self-confidence; perhaps my failure at becoming a witch had taken a toll on me. Still, I pursued my dream as diligently as humanly possible. Alas, as a lowly human, my career path had to be painstakingly trodden, mortal footstep by footstep at a time. No time travel or magical transporting made my efforts any easier. After years of attempting to manifest a singing career, I succumbed to the realization that my goal had not come to fruition in the way I had always hoped. Now I had failed at two of my long-lost dreams.

What I didn't realize then is that my attempt to manifest these goals was made in complete fear. I longed for these dreams passionately, yet always in dread and fear that they would not come true for me. My sights were then forced to change into manifesting a family for myself. I must not have been clear on what I wanted, because the husband who appeared was not right for me, yet I persevered in having the family I had envisioned. I gave birth to a beautiful son, followed by a second miraculous boy.

Having no mother, sisters, female cousins, or aunts, I longed for a daughter. So, to manifest a daughter, I began to eat, sleep, and breathe the mantra, "I have a daughter." Then, my affirmation doubled to double my chances! I used the mantra, "I have two daughters." I prayed it, recited it, mumbled it, dreamed it—it was always there. Low and behold, my daughter was born, healthy and happy, into an extremely unhappy marriage. Having a daughter and my two sons definitely made staying in the relationship doable. I can recall one of the saddest quotes I've ever heard delivered from my five-year-old daughter, "Mommy, why did you marry such a mean man?"

As the years passed, the day came when my daughter made a big plan for the two of us. When it was time for her to pack and go off to college, I would also make my move out of the house. Eight months before the big plan was to take place, the relationship with my husband became even more toxic. I knew I had to manifest a way out and fast. I manifested, envisioned, dreamed, recited, and lived and breathed a safe, affordable place to live in. Staying all those years in a loveless, hostile marriage was partly the result of a lack of funds that would allow me to live in a place of my own. Although I was trying my best to hang in there as long as possible, I started searching online for rooms for rent.

Then, out with friends one night, an acquaintance started talking to me about her verbally abusive ex-husband. We began to compare notes. Soon after, she offered me a room in her apartment at no cost. She wanted to give back because of the help she received when she had to leave her marriage. This was a game-changer, allowing me to finally leave a bad situation. I had manifested a safe, affordable place—where my husband couldn't find me. A now-angry husband began to harass me for leaving, and I had to get my manifestation powers up and running once again. My friend suggested that we send him love. I began to manifest that love would come to him soon so that he could be distracted from his anger towards me. Within a few days, I discovered my soon-to-be-ex-husband had begun online dating, and the women were stacking up. I had become a virtual manifestation queen—far better than being a witch.

Sometime later, I recalled other times I had manifested important matters in my life. A few years earlier, while teaching my high school class in downtown Phoenix, one with students from all over the area, mostly traveled by public bus and light rail to come to our small, all-girl, Title 1 charter school. Many of my students lived in poverty, many with one parent, or perhaps a parent in jail, a majority of them living with moderate to severe anxiety and depression. I loved my students with great empathy and devotion. Nearly all day long, I answered to my students calling me "Mom."

My a-ha moment came when I discovered an anonymous post-it placed on a gratitude bulletin board that said, "I'm grateful for Miss Terry because she treats all of us as if we were her daughters." It was then I realized that some manifestations take a little longer than others. All the mantras, affirmations, prayers, and constant visualization for a daughter had resulted in 130 of them!

# Happiness Comes In Very Unexpected Ways
## By Karen Weigand Oschmann

L ife with John wasn't easy. We were together for seven years, but honestly, I never felt like his girlfriend. John was a recovering addict when I met him and was active in Cocaine Anonymous (CA). He had a good support system and was living with friends who were also active in CA. John and I both joined Match.com about the same time, and not long after, we were matched and went on a date. We hit it off, and John moved in with me several months later. About a year later, we bought a house together.

Several years later, our friend, Krista, and her baby were temporarily staying with us because her husband was abusive. After several months of them living with us, John finally confessed to me that he was the baby's father. I was devastated and kicked Krista out, but not John. Because, in my mind, a bad boyfriend was better than no boyfriend.

Six months later, John went to visit his son in Ohio. He couldn't afford a hotel, so he stayed with Krista. I bet you can guess what happened next! Nine months later, Krista gave birth to a baby girl. Yes, John had cheated on me again, but I stayed with him. He convinced me that Krista was back on drugs, and if we got married, we could get custody of his children.

A year later, John started having horrible stomach pain every time he ate. After no help from countless doctors, tests, and ER trips, a friend mentioned gluten intolerance. Once John started on a gluten-free diet, he was finally pain-free, which was an immense relief.

What I didn't know was that John was coping with his stomach pain by using heroin, and he quickly became addicted. Thus began my nightmare of living with a heroin addict. Coming home from work to catch him nodding off on the sofa became a regular occurrence. I also found him unconscious on the floor with a syringe next to him several times. We fought all the time. He was lying to me, disappearing for periods of time, and basically treating me like crap.

During this time, I started attending services at a local Center for Spiritual Living. I enjoyed what I learned there, and the people were amazing—so nice, open, and accepting. I learned that our thoughts create our lives and that with focused intention, I could change my life.

Lezli, a church friend, told me her manifestation story. She was having dinner at a friend's house, and the friend's husband, Bob, was so gracious, loving, and attentive, that Lezli was impressed, and said, "Why don't I have a Bob? I need my own Bob!" Not long after that, she met the perfect man and the love of her life, whose name is, of course, Bobby. Bobby is a wonderful person who loves Lezli completely and never hesitates to express it. Their relationship became my example to follow—I wanted that!

After one horrendous fight with John, I was overcome with emotion and begged the Universe for someone who would be to me what Bobby is to Lezli. I wanted to be with someone who would love me completely, as I am, who would treat me and others with respect and kindness, who was intelligent and funny, and who thought I was the most beautiful person in the world, inside and out. I was sobbing and hopeless, but I was heard.

John left again to visit his kids, and amazingly, did not impregnate anyone this time. When he got back, he told me he had quit heroin and wanted to improve his life. The next weekend, we attended an investment seminar. John was excited about this opportunity, so we signed up for the program. That was on Sunday, July 20, 2014. The next day, four days before my birthday, I came home from work and found John dead in our bedroom of a heroin overdose.

As the shock of his death lessened, I began feeling incredibly guilty—had my prayer somehow made this happen? One day, I was sobbing in the shower, asking over and over, "Why did you do this to me?" At that moment, I felt and heard the words, "I did this *for* you." A few days later, I spoke with a psychic medium who told me that John and I, while still in spirit, had agreed to experience this situation together as a way for both of us to learn and grow. That gave me a great deal of comfort.

One day, not long after John died, I received a Facebook message from Bill, a friend I hadn't talked to in many years. We had connected on Facebook in 2009, but never had a lot of interaction, other than the occasional "poke." Bill and I had worked together back in the 80s and had flirted around with each other a bit. Back then, Bill had a reputation at work for being a flirt and liking the ladies, so, of course, I was attracted to him. However, he was engaged, so it never went further than flirting, and we drifted apart after he got married and I got a different job.

After John died, Bill and I started messaging each other, then calling each other and talking for hours. He told me that he had been in love with me since we worked together. Because I remembered Bill as a flirt, I was sure that he was only playing around. He was not. He came to visit me, then again, then again. Then I visited him. Finally, he moved his entire life across the country to be with me, and I accepted that he truly loved me.

Bill and I have been happily married for almost four years. I couldn't have picked a better mate for myself, because, believe me, I tried! My manifestation certainly didn't come in a way that I had ever thought of, but it was perfect nonetheless.

# Unnamed
# By Josef Peters

It started when I climbed down. A carpenter on a roof in the winter of 2013 in central Ontario, Canada, I felt a slam in my chest and passed out. When I woke up, an ambulance had been called. I tried walking to it, but was forced to lay on a stretcher. I remember the ride to the hospital and the tests. It was decided that I should fly to a specialist for further testing. The diagnosis was that my aortic valve had dissected, which normally kills 90 percent instantly. I needed surgery—which took place five days later. My aortic valve and ascending aorta were replaced with mechanical prostheses. At home were my wife, and my two-year-old, and two-month-old sons, and I came home shortly before Christmas.

After time off, I returned to carpentry. Fast forward to summer 2016. Around my eldest son's birthday, I felt flu-like symptoms and, being stubborn, decided to stay home until they passed. I insisted they would. I realize now that I was neglecting my left side and stubbing my toes. After four days, I had my father-in-law drive me to the hospital. Walking into the ER at the nearest hospital, I had the first of several out-of-body experiences. It was a stroke, which is blood pushing on the brain causing damage often resulting in paralysis or death. I was flown to a neurological hospital. Unbeknownst to me, I had a craniectomy (a piece of skull removed), with a ten percent chance of survival. The craniectomy allowed my brain to swell and reduce damage. The cause was an Arteriovenous Malformation (AVM).

It is unclear to me when I woke up. I was told the mechanical prosthesis in my chest was infected and needed to be replaced. I wasn't strong enough to endure another major surgery, so we waited two weeks, then I was transferred to a cardiac hospital. It was a dangerous procedure with a less than five percent survival rate, and there was only one donor left in the organ bank. My family was told to say goodbye. After the procedure, I woke up! I stayed one week in the ICU before I stabilized and returned to the neurological hospital's ICU. During all of this, I experienced terrifying, nightmarish hallucinations that I had to follow through with to live. I was attached to machines, feeding tubes, catheters, and IVs of sedatives and antibiotics. There was an army of doctors and specialists visiting me daily, including neurologists, cardiologists, interns, resident doctors, physiotherapists, nurse practitioners, nurses, and geneticists, as I was now suspected of having Marfan Syndrome (a rare genetic condition affecting connective tissue in the body).

I was told I'd never walk again. I couldn't eat, drink, use the washroom, sit up, or breathe by myself. I could barely move my right side and had no movement on my left side. I slowly regained some of these abilities that I had taken previously for granted. It took a month for me to realize that half my skull was missing. After a few weeks, I could move my right arm, left foot, and some of my left arm. When I could sit up, eat and drink alone, I was transferred to inpatient physiotherapy, where I learned to walk again, as well as recovered more movement in my paralyzed arm. I spent another six weeks in physio before I went home. One and a half weeks later, I had a stomachache that turned out to be appendicitis, which put me in the hospital for another week I still had the piece of skull missing. It was confirmed that I have Marfan Syndrome, and by the end of that year, I was ready to have my skull repaired. Called a cranioplasty, the surgery was a success, and I went home the next day.

Approximately one week, later the neurosurgeon who saved my life murdered his wife. Another week later, I had my first seizure in my sleep (a normal side effect of the surgery), and I went to the hospital. Roughly two weeks later, the new skull became infected and was removed again. I was quarantined in the hospital because it was thought I had a "superbug" that was resistant to antibiotics. Anybody entering my room was required to be in full protective outfits, including gowns, boots, masks, hairnets, and gloves. I did not see my children during this time—I was at the lowest point of my life. Over a week later, it was dismissed as a false test result. Having seizures suspended my driver's license automatically for six months, so I started a regimen of anticonvulsants. I went home and had to wait almost another year while the hospital reallocated all of my former neurosurgeon's patients, and during that time, my wife and I separated. I continued to suffer seizures sporadically until January of 2019.

I began attending outpatient physiotherapy—slowly, but steadily, regaining movement in my paralyzed arm. I made a habit of walking and exercising an hour or two per day. I started a daily journal with three headings: what I am thankful for, my goals, and what makes me happy. I was reading self-help and psychology books every day. In the spring of 2018, I had my skull replaced again. This time no complications. By summer, I was riding my bicycle ten kilometers per day, until I was run off the road and fractured the collarbone on my weak side. As of writing this, I'm attending physiotherapy and a chiropractor to treat the fracture and for stroke recovery. I see a psychologist to help process all of the emotional trauma. I have also returned to school for civil engineering. It has now been confirmed that both my sons have Marfan Syndrome, as well as my dad, sister, uncle, aunt, and at least one cousin. Rather than focus on those negative results, I look at the fact that my family now knows and can monitor their symptoms.

# Manifesting My Dream Home
# By Kim Purcell

Manifesting has become a buzz word in spiritual circles, even the mainstream. But I wonder if we all mean the same thing. Let's clarify. For me, *manifesting* means dreaming something into being. Setting an intention and making it happen. Making a wish come true. Visions become reality. We can dream the life we want to live into being.

I learned something about manifesting that might seem trite, but for me, it was a big revelation. Maybe you remember the childhood game of imagining walking into your dream life. Close your eyes; envision your future. For me, it was my dream home—walk into the hallway, what did I see? Keep walking into the kitchen, what did I see? Walk into the garage, what car was there? Walk outside, what do you see? A brook, a stream, a meadow? One day, flash forward 30 years, I was in my home, and mind you, this was my dream home. I happened to be pausing for a moment to enjoy the table-scape I had created—a lavish bouquet and a big, luscious bowl of fruit. As I stood admiring, I remembered this was *exactly* what I had envisioned when I played that game as a little girl. I could hear my friend say, "What do you see on your table? Is it flowers or fruit?" And, I could hear my tiny answer, disregarding the instructions limiting me to one choice or the other. I said, "Both!" And, there it was, both flowers and fruit divinely decorating that table in my real-life dream home. The 'a-ha' was that some of the magic in manifesting begins in our imagination. When we go into the future of possibility without any attachments or judgments, whether it's right or wrong, feasible or not, what we are doing is articulating a vision of what could be. Setting our intention.

In the quantum conversation of manifestation, simply noticing what we want can help to make it be. That may sound too esoteric. Let me try again. When we focus our attention on something without limitation, the universe supports us in making that happen. Manifesting then becomes mastering the art of co-creation.

When we imagine creating anything, in this case, my dream home, we can invent a vision of a dream so palpable, so vivid, that we literally draw it into us. We create for ourselves possibility so real we can taste, touch, and feel it. By crystalizing the intention, the universe is already beginning to manifest it. The wind is at our back, so to speak. To quote Nobel laureate, Tagor, "The stronger the imagination, the less imaginary the results."

Circle back to my dream home, sometime after that epiphany about the flowers and the fruit. I had recently learned we needed to sell our home. We had bought at the height of the market, and the market had crashed. My husband and I reluctantly agreed that we had lost enough money; it was time to stop the bleeding and sell. I was forlorn. Somewhere in the midst of my agony over leaving, I thought, "How could I possibly be devastated when I hardly ever truly appreciated it?" So, I made a pact that I would express my gratitude daily.

So began my daily gratitude practice. One day, I sat on the dock giving gratitude for the land, for the waterway we lived on, for the breeze that brushed gently on my face, for the birds that were singing and thriving in the preserve across the way, for all the divine creatures that lived beneath the sea. And like magic, it was like everything in the universe in that small little snapshot of my world, arose and spoke to me to let me know that my gratitude was felt. A school of baitfish started jumping under the dock, a dolphin arched up out of the water right in front of me, a dragonfly soared in front of me for minutes on end, nearly landing on my nose. The universe spoke back. Loud and clear. As if on some sort of divine movie screen. Gratitude itself was giving back—as if to say, "You're welcome. Thank you for noticing."

As I floated back toward the house in awe, delighting in the dolphin and everything, I noticed a flower I had never seen before, growing alone next to a big hearty oak. Miniscule next to the massive trunk, but exceptionally vibrant, generously offering its beauty to me for the first time. Somehow in my noticing it in that moment, I could feel its divine connection to all that was, to the fish, the birds, the neighboring tree, the land, the sky, and me, in that moment and my gratitude. It was all part of the same magical moment when the manifestation of my true dream home began.

I did adore that home, but it was never about those walls. It was our beautiful family itself that filled that space with a vitality and a vibrancy that would follow us wherever we went. So when we moved into the rental, which was half the size, on a quarter of the land, with no waterway in sight, it was still somehow dreamy. The gratitude I practiced there on the dock of our old home stayed with me. And, like magic, the yard came alive, and birds became our friends, and the home became *our* home. With gratitude, every home can be a dream home.

Now, don't get me wrong. We were building a new home. The rental became smaller as we set our sights on being in the new home. It even became stifling the more our attention shifted to our new, bigger home. Where we put our focus and our gratitude is where the dream is most alive. So, yes, again, we are in our new dream home. But, I am no longer attached. I am grateful. And, so it is.

# Manifesting A Life You Love
## By Grace Redman

I sat on the sidewalk, crying hysterically. The boy I was dating had lost his temper over something trivial and exploded in rage, grabbing my car keys from me as I tried to get away, and throwing them on the roof of a nearby office building. He then proceeded to punch me straight in the head.

As I sat there bawling, I felt utterly ashamed, embarrassed, and disgusting. The pain that radiated through my head, soul, and heart was unbearable. I felt like lying down and never waking up again.

This was not a new situation. From my teens to my 20s, I consistently attracted abusive, toxic interactions. It resulted from the fact that I had little self-esteem and simply didn't feel worthy of love, especially from a male figure. I felt this way because it was all I'd seen growing up—women close to me being emotionally and physically abused by the men in their lives. It happened to me countless times too.

I knew in my heart and soul that what I was experiencing was toxic and unhealthy. It was not normal behavior, although many in my circle viewed it this way. It also wasn't something I wanted to continue to accept. I knew for damn sure I wanted better for myself.

I started to pay more attention to my small inner voice, the one that whispered quietly to me that there was hope—that I could find a better way. Reflecting back on those dark times, I now know it was God who planted that vital voice of hope and reason in my mind; to push me to make a change.

That punch to the head from that boy was my catalyst for change. At that moment, I had an intuitive feeling that I needed professional support and guidance. I couldn't reach out to anyone around me because that wasn't the way we did things in my circle—it would be utterly humiliating to speak about your emotional challenges. You sucked it up, put on a happy face, and pretended all was perfect.

At 19, I also didn't have much money for a therapist. But through the grace of God, I stumbled on Catholic Charities in my neighborhood. They had a student therapy program and only charged eight dollars for each session! I mustered up the courage and called the phone number to make my first therapy appointment of many.

At my first session, I met Rebekah, a young therapist right out of school. It was the beginning of a relationship that would last 25 years! I would spend all those years working hard to overcome various mental ills, including depression, anxiety, low self-esteem, co-dependency, a horrible body image and relationship with food, a desire to always people-please, and workaholism. I learned how to set boundaries, love myself, walk away from toxic situations, and most importantly, find my worth, and step into my power!

A lot of this came about through my love of reading and learning. At only 15, I stumbled upon the works of Tony Robbins and was fascinated by his thoughts on how to achieve success in life. Rebekah also recommended a few stand-out books, and I always headed straight down to the bookstore to buy them. Forget the library—I wanted copies so I could highlight and re-read.

I also looked to the movies in an attempt to create a life I loved. Yes, I know it's the movies, but at least it was a somewhat positive example to have. I wanted to emulate those I saw on screen who were smart, successful, loved, respected, and financially independent. That last one was extremely important, as I knew if I could look after myself financially, I wouldn't have to depend on a man to do so. And of course, I also wanted a partner who would love and respect me.

I never gave up hope that I would find these things. I absorbed all I read like a sponge. Books from overcoming co-dependency, to how to excel and succeed in business. And today, 30 years after the first time I walked into Rebekah's office, I am excited and so happy to say that I have broken the cycle I thought I was destined to remain in.

I now own and manage one of the most successful staffing companies in the Bay area. I'm also a certified personal transformation coach working directly with women to help them break their negative cycle; I've been married to a loving and kind man for 21 years, and together, we have two healthy teenage boys; and I've managed to diminish my negative self-sabotaging behavior. It's taken time, commitment, and discipline, plus a firm devotion to self-love and self-care, but I've manifested a life I love.

A few years ago, I found out my therapist, Rebekah, was retiring, so I went to see her for what would be the last time. At this session, she admitted to me that the first day we met, she believed there was no hope for me. She felt I would continue to walk down the same path of abuse, low self-esteem, depression, and anxiety, like the generations before me. She profusely apologized for thinking this way, saying she was a new therapist at that time and didn't know any better.

I wasn't offended by Rebekah's words. In fact, I felt a tremendous sense of accomplishment. I had broken a number of unhealthy cycles, and had manifested and created an incredible life. Granted, it was *not* easy. But I did it!

I hope my story shows you that no matter what your experience or background, we all have it within us to create and manifest a life of happiness—in fact, it's our birthright to do so. So I say to you: you've got this! Go out there and create that life you love!

# Imagine New Perceptions On Being Human
## By Suzanne Rochon

A s far back as I can remember, I have held a deep desire to impact the world by inviting people to discover their true potential as I realized mine. While I have been able to recognize the inherent value and potential in others, I have conversely questioned and discounted my similar significance. A career in social work helped realize the dream of making a difference in the world and provided the honor of witnessing the growth and healing of others firsthand, yet I remained in the shadows of my evolution and expansion until I discovered personal change through manifestation.

"Likes attract" is an idiom that I have always subscribed to and, as my life and career unfolded over the years, I have experienced varying degrees of this as people, events, and experiences came in and out of focus. It is this *attractive* force that brought three of us together, orbiting a shared sense of purpose that would be further defined and refined every day. Like many unique moments in our lives, the conjunction of a number of sympathetic factors led to opportunities that I continue to explore and describe in the following story.

The tendrils of a shared vision were palpable when we were colleagues in a common workplace, but the timing was off. We enjoyed brief encounters in the hallway or the lunchroom, recounting the occasional story of the weekend past and sharing laughs to shed light on the darkness of human suffering as we made our way to the next client or the next task. It was the beginning of realizing the power of conscious decision in manifesting a desired reality.

Each of us, for unique reasons, needed and were willing to step out of our comfortable and stable environment to explore what lies in the anxiety-provoking and fearful unknown. That moment when you leap into the chasm, magic is created, yet few choose to gather the courage and give themselves permission to leave the comfort of the secure in favor of the potential for a raw, risky and real journey that may completely redefine every aspect of the paradigm of living that we have followed. First to take the leap was the feisty, spontaneous redhead, with her *let's wing this* fearless attitude. The successful private practice, Being Human, is the result of her approach, inspiration, and energy. The second colleague to orbit the growing energy and concept of a collective was the hot-pink-lipstick-wearing, soft-spoken, and fun-loving risk-taker who conceived her practice, named New Perceptions, with an approach to therapy as bold and exciting as the name. The third of the three, guided by a relentless desire to discover her truths and to share the insights of a 25-year journey of self-development, was the more cautious and subdued of the triad, who eventually created the burgeoning counseling practice named Imagine Life Solutions.

As we first came together on a cold winter's evening, we began to feel a synergy and a connection too strong to suppress. The flow of energy was unmistakably present as we began to build and co-create a collective vision for ourselves. Our drive to shift our inner and outer worlds from the mediocre to infinite potential, which we believe exists in all of us, supported the movement of energy from the realm of the mundane to the creative space where authenticity and freedom reside. The excitement of what was possible was growing exponentially as each of us rhymed off what we envisioned as our future: podcasts, groups, retreats, books, speaking engagements, and tours. As we continued to share tales of our respective private psychotherapy practices, the realization that the combination of our three business names was the manifestation of our life's passion took our breath away! *Imagine New Perceptions on Being Human* was created.

The sisterhood that gave birth to our new collective was made possible by the mutual respect of each other's unique abilities and strengths, the tears we allow each other as we continue to grow and heal ourselves, and the support and acceptance we extend to each other. The laughter and excitement we share and the knowing that, while we are successful in our individual pursuits together, the collective of empowered, soulful, passion-driven women is greater than we can imagine, which is immensely satisfying. We recognize in each other an unlimited potential and value, which further propels us in our dream of impacting the world through connection, love, and healing. The joy and excitement we feel when we come together to create the next project and the next vision, is what drives turning the imagined into reality.

Manifesting is a misunderstood notion that can be mistaken for hard work and luck. While action and work are required, the setting of clear intentions from the perspective of infinite possibilities rather than lack of is a useful starting point. Humans are naturally hardwired to focus on the negative, as it served an important purpose in protecting us from real threats in our early existence. Like most people, the three of us experienced years of apprehension and anxiety towards stepping out of the darkness and into our light, yet held the vision that we are so much more than what we have allowed ourselves to be. It was our individual quest to connect with our deeper selves that created the space to awaken our purpose. Ironically, the work of accompanying our clients through confusion, pain, and suffering to completeness, acceptance of their worth, and embracing the light within, is what we have had to do for ourselves. Believing in ourselves, in our potential, and in our purpose, is the wind that propelled our sails to support our growth and expansion. The key to manifesting is the belief of our unlimited value.

We have entered the space of conscious creating, and can now truly *imagine new perceptions on being human.*

# The Beholder's Share Of Angels
# By Julia Ross

The Beholder's Share reveals deep truths about the human experience as it invites the viewer to engage in self-awareness and the acknowledgment of biological and sociocultural influences that can alter perception.

"The artist gives the beholder more to do, drawing the viewer into the magic circle of creation, to experience the thrill of making, which had once been the privilege of only the artist."
~ E.H. Gombrich (1909-2001).

Born to a family of artists, painters, and sculptors, my fondest memories involve creative works of art. Until a couple of years ago, I believed real artists were classically trained. My perception was that all gifts were not given, but rather taken, with great work ethic and persistence.

I woke up realizing the blessings of our family, love beyond comprehension. Twenty-eight years of marriage; our two children, now adults, both graduates of The University of Texas (UT). Our son was five years into his career in private equity and commercial real estate, and a business owner. Our daughter was graduating in three years from UT—we were so proud.

We would celebrate in Miami Beach and Key Biscayne, then back in Dallas for Father's Day. We would cook together, swim in the pool, and stay up late in conversations outside around the table. We would reminisce about family trips and those we had taken alone, sharing experiences and discoveries, plans for the future. We cherish those conversations.

June 29, 2018, I woke up at 6:00 a.m., made coffee, and checked email. I then checked client ad campaigns, updated a couple of marketing reports, dressed, and headed to the Dallas office, listening to NPR. I arrived at the office, made more coffee, and reviewed social media campaigns. At 9:50 a.m., I received a call that would forever change our lives.

249

Time would stand still. It was a Friday that I wished I could turn back to Wednesday. On my way home Wednesday, I had talked with my son, Cameron. Being stuck in traffic from my office to the major freeway for at least 20 minutes allowed us time to catch up on the last couple of days. He came home from work and worked out, looking forward to having dinner with a friend. He told me he loved me. We made plans to talk later that night, but never connected again.

A morning call informed me that our son's life ended unexpectedly.

By Friday, friends and family would begin a celebration of his life that would last through the week. My husband, daughter, and I were present, but only a shell of existence as we floated above the scene to view the service at the Oasis in Austin, where family and friends gathered to share memories and watch the sunset in his honor. We stayed a few days, drove back to Dallas to a quiet house, which seemed much quieter than the empty nester threshold we embarked upon only a few years prior.

There was a new energy about the home. Physically visible at times, visions in twilight and during meditation, I knew we had angels among us.

I began painting often, as a form of healing, to relax and in an effort to dissolve time, which was as painful as the minute he left, if not more each day. Still of the mindset that any true artist is classically trained, I did not credit the product of these creative sessions to anything other than a progression of time and effort.

I thought we had everything accomplished, all in its perfect place, but found myself flat on my back. Meditation would help me move forward. A couple of weeks after our return, I pulled myself off the floor and began painting. The product would lead me to a solo exhibit with the painting as a showcase piece, calm waters flowing on a beach to be followed by a crashing wave. The 60x60-inch painting was completed in two days, no doubt with the help of angels.

Painting would become an extension of meditation. During early sessions, guided communication would become clear after hours of painting in silence. The body of work displayed in the exhibits to follow would include various impressionistic qualities, with differences in style, to include visions of angels physically manifesting within the paintings.

My work lends itself to the fate of angels, at times due to the mediums I use. Encaustic wax dries with many forms, uncontrolled by the artist. Part of the healing process, the lessons of angels demonstrate that end success is not always determined by persistent activity. In fact, my best work seems to be defined by unplanned elements.

Colors of twilight began showing up during meditation, which I continue to work to recreate. Currently on an art tour throughout the country, I have the opportunity to include others as an extension of my work, completing the circle of the gifts received. Full circle, The Beholder's Share begins with great artists of the past, gifted through meditation, by the beautifully talented Art Angels, to me and others we come across.

Upon every sunset, we know he is still with us, as we press forward to live and laugh, hand-in-hand with our angels. We continue to share memories of our son with others and do our best to make sure others realize they are loved, valued, and cherished for their contributions to this world.

I am blessed to live the artist's life, receiving and contributing great gifts, no man could recreate. This is not the path I expected, but it has provided insight and understanding into my purpose in life. Art enables a channel to my higher self, to experience and cope with the twists and turns of life, providing a light to progress upwards. Lessons learned; the art of life is a masterpiece.

# Manifesting Mr. Right
## By GG Rush

**M**y heart was a shattered, broken mess: a thousand little shards of broken love. The person that I loved with that once-full heart had hit it with a sledgehammer. For two decades, I thought I knew that person and the person I was. Now nearly two decades later, my heart is finally healed and all mine. My love is available to give again. Of course, I loved my daughters and my parents and my pets through all of that, but there is a missing love in my life. My soul mate is out there; of this, I am certain. Now comes the time for me to begin to find that particular someone. I will start to manifest "Mr. Right."

In my first entry in this book, I spoke of manifesting my authentic self, and that did happen and continues to happen as I grow and breathe. I am a different person than I was with "Mr. Wrong." Where do I begin in my manifestation of Mr. Right? Once I started thinking about this, some signs started to appear. My dear friend, Susan, sent me a package the other day. I opened it, and there was a brass frog holding a weird looking stone. It frankly looked a little phallic. I called her, and she told me it was a Shiva Lingham stone from India. It is a fertility stone used in ancient rituals. But for me, she felt I was ready for love and that this would help me manifest my mate! I started thinking about this story and sat down and wrote it.

The way manifestation works for me is I start seeing myself living the dream I have. Sometimes I make a vision board—sometimes a list of what I want. I made a list of qualifications for Mr. Right:

- Loves my daughters
- Kindness
- Romantic
- Loves animals
- Loves travel

- Patient
- Loyal
- Not too handsome (no vanity please)
- Likes to dance
- Loves film noir
- Great kisser
- Treats me like a queen
- Finds me interesting and attractive
- Narcissists need not apply

Now I am starting to see this man appear in my life. We start spending time together. Dating and flirting. The first time we kiss, it sends an electrical current all the way down to my toes. We spend hours talking and listening to each other. We begin anticipating being together and enjoy our hours together. He buys me flowers and small gifts. We go to movies and dancing and sit together, at times saying nothing at all. He holds my hand when we walk, and puts his arm around me protectively and makes me feel safe. We travel the world and share all its wonders and treasures. We are soul mates destined to be together and share our golden years. I see this happening. I believe in manifestation and destiny. And I believe in true love.

# Finding GG: Manifesting My Authentic Self
## By GG Rush

I was born Sandra Gail Rush. My mother was told by the nurses that I could not be called Sandy because of my dark hair. And so I was Gail—which caused confusion every new school year when I was enrolled as Sandra Gail Rush. Over the years, I became Gail Rush Gould after marriage. Then I became Mommy, Mom, & Mother. That name stuck and always will. When I was divorced, I kept Gail Rush Gould as my legal name. A young co-worker who became a good friend called me GG. And this is the story of how I manifested my authentic self, GG.

During my 30s and 40s, my life was defined by being a wife and mother. I had a part-time career in real estate, dabbling in a life outside the home. But I was primarily a homemaker and mother. I raised two beautiful daughters who grew into independent and amazing young women. I spent my days volunteering at the school bookstore, baking classroom goodies, chaperoning field trips, and being a Girl Scout cookie mom. In the summer, I was a leader at Girl Scout Day Camp. I was pretty darn good at those things.

When I turned 50, my already struggling marriage crashed and burned. The divorce was painful and heartbreaking. I wasn't my best self. I wasn't feeling proud or good or confident. I lost faith in myself, I gained weight, and I drank. I wallowed in self-pity. But I got a great job, one I have kept for 11 years. I managed to hang on to our home. And I went along, not truly living, but getting by. I was broke most of the time. The house began to need repairs. My youngest daughter wanted to go to college. I started to want more out of my life. I started to imagine a life where I would not be struggling so hard. A life doing things I wanted to do. I learned to manage my finances, save money, and improve my credit. My daughter got scholarships and grants, and I took out a parent loan. Because I had paid bills on time, I was approved for the loan. So four years later, my daughter graduated from a private women's college. It was an extremely proud day for both of us.

But I wanted more. I wanted to travel and to write and to make a difference in the world. I started seeing myself doing those things. I made my first vision board. On it was a beautiful bedroom with rich Moroccan colors—oranges and purples. A picture of a woman walking on an exotic beach. My favorite author Elizabeth Gilbert's book "Eat, Pray, Love." A dancer. The word *travel* pasted in several spots on the board. I dreamed of these things.

That week I got an email about an upcoming show that Oprah was putting together called Super Soul Sessions in Los Angeles. It was free. And Elizabeth-freaking-Gilbert was a headliner! I found cheap airfare and a great rate at a hotel, so I went. It was a life-changing experience. Not only did I hear Liz Gilbert speak, but I also heard Brene Brown, Deepak Chopra, Marianne Williamson, Michael Beckwith, Tim Story, and many others, including an inspiring speech by Oprah herself on setting your intention. And right then, I set my intention. I wanted more of this. And I would make it happen. And I did. I've been to many events, and each time I learned more and kept envisioning myself on those stages, saying something that would make a difference.

I started thinking of my goal to travel the world and began looking at maps and watching travel shows. Once again, an email popped up in my inbox from Groupon Getaways. Affordable trips that included airfare and hotels and trains. I checked it out and signed up. I have gone to Spain, Bali, Iceland, and Italy on Groupon. It was happening—and on my budget!

At one of the events I attended, Liz Gilbert was speaking, along with Martha Beck. I was fascinated by Martha's brilliance and wit. I started reading her books and taking her life coaching classes online. I was seeing myself fulfilling yet another dream of doing something worthwhile with my life. Martha spoke of her African Star program.

I envisioned myself there, learning firsthand from Martha Beck. You have to apply to the program and be accepted to attend. So I applied, and I told myself I was already accepted. And I was accepted. And this past May, I attended the program at a magical place called Londolozi Game Reserve. I met a group of people who have become my lifelong friends. It was a dream come true.

At the beginning of 2019, I made my annual vision board. Two of the words I glued on six times were *inspiration* or *inspired*. The word *writer* was on there too. In the spring, I attended the International Women's Summit. I met many wonderful women. One of them, Kyra Schaefer, was a publisher. She was putting together a book called—wait for it—*Inspirations*. What?? I signed up. I couldn't not sign up since the Universe had given me the opportunity. I submitted a story *Silence* by GG Rush. It was about going on a silent game drive in Africa. It was published, along with 100 other stories by a group of fabulous authors, and the book shot straight to number one on Amazon!

Now I am GG: world traveler, life coach-in-training, published writer. I'm still Mother. But I have been living my authentic life. I dreamed it once upon a time. I *manifested* it!

# Design Your Life Through Manifestation
# By April Sanchez

I remember first hearing about manifestation and having the ability to create the life that I truly wanted over ten years ago. Admittedly, I was a bit skeptical at first, but the dreamer in me wanted to give it a try. I did my best to remain positive and tried putting good out into the world, hoping that what I put out would come back. I even made my first vision board to help me visualize all my desires. Over time I noticed some of these things showing up in my life, and I felt so empowered knowing that I had attracted this new job that paid well and was close to home. As time went on, I started to feel let down when other desires I had on my vision board weren't happening for me. Doubt began to creep in, and I started to search everywhere for all the things I was trying to manifest, becoming more impatient and doubtful. What I didn't realize then was that my doubt, inner beliefs, and negative thoughts were energetically blocking all the desires that I had put out to the universe to attract into my life. My trial and error led me down a road of wanting to understand how this gift of manifestation worked. Through research and self-discovery, I uncovered that to manifest my desires, it first had to start with me.

I believed then that life was happening *to* me, and what I uncovered over time was that life was happening *through* me. I put together my first vision board with all the places I wanted to travel to, a car that I had always wanted, pictures of couples holding hands, and of course, pictures of money. What I later learned, was that all the effort that I had put into what I saw as the perfect vision board did not have as much of an impact as what lay within me, and my inner relationship to these things. The combination of my thoughts, inner beliefs, energetic vibrations, and views of myself and the world is what was blocking all of these wonderful people and elements that I was trying to attract into my life. I had a desire to attract the partner of my dreams, but deep within me, there was a part of me that felt scared and wondered if it was ever attainable. I wanted to manifest all this prosperity and income, but deep down, I would still wonder where it was going to come from. I was treating manifesting more like wishing, and I learned that wishing is different from believing. I began to realize that some of my life experiences had created these limiting beliefs that lived deep within me. These limiting beliefs kept me vibrationally disconnected from my true desires because I didn't truly believe.

Manifestation is first attracted to energy and energetic vibrations. This is where I had to start to align myself and my belief system with what I desired to attract into my life. At first, I struggled with how I was going to do this, but I knew I had to try. I wanted not only to be able to attract all these wonderful physical elements into my life, but I also wanted to *feel* better about my life. I discovered that being nice and positive around and to my friends and co-workers mattered less than how I truly felt inside. My inner-feelings and how I felt about myself are what was connected to my energetic vibration. My energetic vibration is how and what I was attracting into my life.

I took some time to understand what steps I had to take to align with the universal vibrations to manifest my true desires.

1.  I started by redesigning my belief system to align my beliefs with my desires. I started with committing to journaling every day an entire page of "I am" statements. These I am statements were focused in a positive light. By doing this, I was able to re-write my truth. At first, I struggled to find the positive attributes about myself, but as time went on, it flowed much easier. I would write down attributes that I wanted to embody when I first started to shift my mindset. My journal entries would look like this:

I am worthy
I am whole
I am loveable
I am beautiful
I am able

2. I learned to practice gratitude by focusing on what I already had and being thankful for all that I had. Being in a place of gratitude also vibrates with the energy and feeling of having enough. I did this by setting a task on my phone that would pop up as a daily reminder that said, "Name three things that you are grateful for." I also created a gratitude board as a visual tool to show what I was grateful for—shifting from the vibration of lack and of not having enough to the vibration of gratitude and growth.

3. I focused on the feelings that were attached to the physical and material things that I desired. This practice helped me to connect on a deeper level, and it allowed me to sit in those feelings and feel them deeply, as if I already had what I was attracting into my life. For example, "In this loving relationship that I desire, I feel safe, I feel respected, I feel appreciated, and I feel joy."

4. Then, I created a new vision board with all of my physical desires, and incorporated pictures of my 'I am' statements, along with the feelings that connected with what I was attracting and manifesting into my life.

I am grateful that I took on the pursuit of understanding the ability to manifest all my heart's desires. These steps helped me to change the trajectory of my life. I am an author in this book through the art of manifestation and the steps that I took to become energetically aligned.

## After The Apocalypse: Miracles, Magic And Manifesting
## By Dr. Carra S. Sergeant, LPC-S

L ife happens! Things are moving along fine, and then before you know it, boom, your life is suddenly turned completely upside down. Standing squarely in the middle of your personal apocalypse, you find yourself in a position where life, as you know it goes on full pause for four years. Your past is a blur, your present is hell, and your future is destroyed beyond repair—or so you think.

The details of my apocalyptic event are not pertinent to this story; suffice it to say that what happened was caused by my faulty thinking and my poor decision making. While I refer to the event throughout this story as my "mistake," the word mistake is truly an understatement. When I stepped out of the "eye of the storm" on December 15, 2014, I was left with the reality that the career I had spent an entire life developing was gone, and I was in financial ruin. On that day, I found myself standing, at the age of 62, on that post-apocalyptic fork in the road where I had two choices: retreat or rebuild. This was when magic entered my life.

I was told that due to my mistake, I would probably be unemployable. I allowed that belief to take root in my soul. Short of divine intervention, I thought that the rest of my life would be doomed. I needed a miracle! In the metaphysical sense, a miracle is defined simply as a change in perception. For me, that meant I had to facilitate the miracle that I needed. I had to change the self-perception of being unemployable. I actively worked to reject that belief, telling myself every day, "I am not my mistake," and "I am worthy of another chance." Eventually, my survival instinct kicked in, and I began to accept those affirmations as my truth. The miracle had started: my perception was changing.

"Okay, good job; now what?" I thought. What did I need to do next? I am a big believer in the law of attraction and a longtime proponent of the magic of manifestation. It was obvious to me what my next step should be. It was time to put my magic into action. "My new job starts in January," I said to myself and to anyone who would listen. Everyone was excited for me. They would ask, "What is your new job?" It was embarrassing to shrug my shoulders and admit that I had no clue what that job would be, but I was sure it would start in January. On January 5th, I walked into my new job at a local fitness center. I had spoken a new reality into existence.

As I mention in my biography, I am a Licensed Professional Counselor. Being a therapist is not what I am; it is who I am. After two years, I began to miss that part of me, but my license was no longer valid. In January of 2017, I once again turned to God, the universe, my guides, and angels for help. My new mantra became, "I am a reinstated Licensed Professional Counselor." The universe responded quickly this time because, within a month, I was given an opportunity and a path to follow, which would culminate with the full reinstatement of my license. I would need a counselor supervisor and an office. Who would possibly supervise a now 64-year-old woman getting reestablished as a counselor? How could someone in my financial state possibly find a decent office? Cue the magic: "I am a provisional counselor, under supervision, and my office opens, July 1, 2017," became my new siren call. Every day I repeated this, believing it with all my heart, speaking it with all my power, and being grateful, *in advance*, with every cell in my body.

The counselor supervisor who eventually accepted me turned out to be someone I had supervised when she was a counseling intern. I found an office during a random social media search, and they took a chance on me in spite of my financial issues. It seemed so random for these two events to fall exactly into place when they did, but I truly believe that there are no coincidences. I was granted a provisional license and officially saw my first client on July 5th. "Wow, this manifesting stuff is magic," I thought. With renewed faith and a deeper belief, I started manifesting the real prize: "In 2018, I am a counselor with a fully reinstated license." Once again, the universe responded: my license was fully reinstated on December 28, 2017.

As I write this, it is November 2019, and I stand fully on the other side. Through manifestation, I now have a thriving private practice, I completed work on my Ph.D. in May 2018, and so much more. I learned that:

- Being able to manifest is not magic. It is a gift, and it is not specifically unique to me.
- Manifesting is a gift bestowed on each and every one of us by a powerful universal force.
- It does take some practice, and it requires a strong sense of self-worth because the universe only gives us what we *truly* believe we deserve.

Surround yourself with like-minded, supportive people. The universe blessed me with people who unconditionally supported me, so thank you: Nannelle Noland; Glenn Sergeant and my entire family; Sandra Castille; Margaret "MeMe" McKerley and the entire Noland/McKerley family; Charles and Karen Woodard; Tim Trant; Andrea Vidrine; Candase Martel; John and Allie Davis; Sara Ezell; Brenda Hill; and Sarah Brink.

God and the universe want us to have great abundance in life, but we must know how to access it. State your desire in the present tense to send a message to the universe that you expect your request will be granted. State your gratitude, in advance, and of course, after. Ask, believe, and expect! I promise that the universe will respond for your highest good. Happy manifesting!

# The Redirected Call
# By Felicia Shaviri

"Planning is not always necessary; our most powerful life-changing experiences come when we jump in and simply ride the wave."~ Shaviri

I remember it like it was yesterday. I found myself reaching into my back pocket for my cell phone, and thought I would call my sister Debbie. We talked on the phone daily, even if only for a brief hello. This call was different, though. For one, I don't recall dialing my sister's number, and two, the voice on the other end definitely wasn't a woman. Instead, it was the voice of my old coach David "Dr. Buff" Patterson. Here's a blurt from that convo:

David: Hello

Me: Hello? Deb?

David: Falisha?

Me: David?

David: Yeah? What's up, girl?

Me: Umm, I was calling my sister Deb, how did you end up on the phone? I'm a little confused.

David: I don't know. You called me.

Not that it was a bad thing. I hadn't spoken to David in a while; he had been my personal training coach back in '99, was an incredible mentor, and basically became like a big brother to me. During the conversation, David shared that he would be retiring from the sport of bodybuilding, which was a passion he had stumbled upon decades ago. After reminding me of the time I came into his office and shared with him how I'd always wanted to compete in a bodybuilding show, he invited me to join him at his final competition at the Emerald Cup in Bellevue, Washington. Without hesitation, I asked him the date, and he said April 26th next year. I immediately said, "I'm in," and David, being David, responded with, "Now you know me, Falisha, talk is cheap." Yep, that was exactly something David would do—remind me of what I had said I wanted to do fourteen years earlier during our initial consultation.

I told David I needed to get off the phone so I could run it by my family. I needed to know what their thoughts were, as I knew what I was about to take on was not going to be a cakewalk by any means. I could feel my heart pounding and the butterflies floating about in my stomach due to all of the excitement I was feeling. I asked my family to have a seat at the dining room table so that I could speak to them about something important. My younger two were eager to hear, but my oldest wasn't sure what to expect. All were seated except for my husband, who insisted that he was good standing and could hear me clearly.

I could feel it trying to creep in—you know, the negative talk and self-doubt attempting to steal my joy. But there was something else there, a still small voice that was heard within me and would not let me back down or run away, not this time. She said, "You stand up, you stand tall, and share your dream!" I shared the "accidental" call, the conversation I had with David, and his offer to have me join him as a competitor. I asked them their thoughts about me being in a bodybuilding competition, and let them know that, although it was important to me, I didn't think I could do it without their support.

My son was the first to shout out with glee, and the other two joined him. The kids were immediately supportive and excited about the venture that I was about to take on. I think they were more excited about being a part of the process, willing and ready to stand and help their mom reach a long-awaited personal goal, and that made me even happier. As I struggled not to tear up in the presence of my children, I took a deep breath, smiled at my children, gave them hugs and high fives, and said let's do this!

> "Be you. Be such a strong, distinct you that you don't long for anyone or anything outside of you."~ S. Classon

After receiving the green light from my family, I began to take steps towards fulfilling a wish I'd had since I was about six or seven years old, after seeing Pamela Grier in action. She played the role of "Coffy," who was a drop-dead gorgeous vigilante who kicked butt and took names.

I began to meet with my trainer and several other competitors weekly where we would share our progress, moods, foods, the good, bad and the ugly. The training was intense, cardio twice daily for nearly six months, along with free weight training. Often I would go into the gym, pull the hood over my head, bury my face in my hand towel, and cry nearly the entire session. Yet through it all, I never thought about quitting, and trust me, there were many opportunities that I could have. I was working full-time, my children were nine, thirteen, and seventeen, there were two dogs, and not only did I have to make meals for my family, but I made my meals separately. I don't think I have ever taken on something that was as challenging as my first competition ever.

The coolest part of this experience was realizing that it wasn't about the show, winning a trophy, weight loss, or placing; it was about a journey to discovering the power of thought. Sometimes we grow impatient or give up on a wish, goal, or dream far too soon due to some of the obstacles, challenges, or self-doubt. When we ask for something regardless of how long ago it may have been, that thought, request, or wish patiently waits for us to navigate our way to it one step at a time.

# Finally A Master Manifestor
# By YuSon Shin

Growing up and into adulthood, I had a hard time imagining that I had any control over my life, much less the power to magnetize good things to me. I did not have the magical ability to manifest whatever I wanted. In fact, I was sure the Universe was actively working against me. As an Asian American trying to assimilate, I was repeatedly told not to voice my opinions or desires. "Be quiet." "Don't draw attention to yourself or your family." I was told many versions of "Life is hard, then you die," "Only the rich get richer," and "Who are you to think you can do/be whatever?" I learned not to want or ask for anything and also that feelings should be suppressed.

When *The Secret* by Rhonda Byrne came out in 2006, the Law of Attraction concept of using thoughts and feelings to create your reality was mind-blowing. Those exact things I was told to shut down were the secret to success and abundance. I felt betrayed and cheated by my parents and the Universe. I imagined my life would be completely different had I been taught this as a kid. *The Secret*, I was sure, was going to change my life. However, it only took me halfway to the goal line.

Even after *The Secret,* I struggled. I manifested sporadically, and it felt awkward. I had inner struggles of self-confidence. Years of growing up in scarcity and negative programming had taken a toll. I didn't feel worthy. I didn't feel I was enough.

Big shifts in manifesting didn't happen for me until I learned the Bengston Energy Healing Method, a potent healing and manifesting technique. It is so powerful, it does double duty. Although I knew almost a dozen healing modalities, I had never heard of this one, but as a healer, I was eager to learn.

One morning while walking my dog, a neighbor mentioned the Bengston Method in conversation. She said it was the only technique she knew of that was scientifically tested and shown to cure cancer in mice, and she told me about the book, *The Energy Cure* by William Bengston, Ph.D., and about his upcoming workshop in Santa Barbara. Curiosity had me read this book in one weekend. Afterward, I still needed additional information. This technique seemed too good to be true. My brain didn't quite grasp the concept of Image Cycling, which is the core practice within the method, so I attended the workshop.

The cycling technique involves making 20 or more mental images of things you want in your life. I call this my wish list. Nothing is too big or too small. I imagine taking a snapshot of myself experiencing each of those 20-plus specific desires. When I imagine taking each picture, I experience having that thing with great detail and use all my senses to create a real experience.

For example, one of the items that I have put on my list is taking my mom on an Alaskan luxury cruise. First, I asked her permission by asking if she would like to go on a cruise with me. Her consent was in the form of a yes to vacationing with me. She didn't need to know about the list. Then I sat for about 5-10 minutes "experiencing" this cruise with my mom using all my senses. So, in my snapshot of this vacation, we are on the top level of the cruise ship on our private balcony. We can both feel the snappy, cold air of Alaska and the wind whipping our faces with our hair. We can hear pieces of a nearby iceberg falling into the ocean that is surprisingly loud. I feel so much love as I am giving my mom a hug. Because we don't typically vacation in our family, I am feeling immensely grateful to have an amazing vacation with her and to still have her living. I can feel the softness of the faux fur coat she is wearing. And I can still taste the lobster dipped in melted butter and molten chocolate cake that we had for lunch with the captain.

Then I take each of the pictures of the 20-plus things I want and put them on a Rolodex, or the giant Price is Right wheel, and spin it super-fast until it's a blur. It requires memorization of the list. And at first, I needed to focus, concentrate, and cycle consciously, but as I have been cycling for a while, it is now something I can do on autopilot.

Image Cycling is a strange healing technique that still doesn't make complete sense to me, but I have helped humans and animals with a variety of physical and emotional issues, including depression, digestive disorders, stroke, and cancer. Image Cycling is also instrumental in making many of the items on my wish list a reality, and having it be an effective manifestation technique makes a little more sense to me than healing. I am cycling so fast that I cannot sabotage or doubt myself. It's the process of putting an order for what you want into the Universe, but on steroids.

I have manifested little things like free lunch or parking spots in busy areas. I've also manifested big things like a promotion after I was told that wasn't possible. I have manifested trips to Kona to swim with wild dolphins. I wanted to be a speaker, and someone I met over a year ago invited me to speak at her event. I wanted to be an international teacher of intuition and healing, and I recently returned from Thailand, where I taught women entrepreneurs the art of intuition. Also, I was invited to teach again in Thailand, and also in Italy next year. I wanted to be an author, and this will be my second collaborative book.

The Bengston Method made all this and so many more wishes a reality. It made me a master manifestor.

## Courageous Curiosity
## By Josie Smith

Ihere I was sitting in the lotus position, an irritated, part-time athletic store employee in her mid-twenties. I was surrounded by a group of young, stressed women worried about declaring a major in college and depressed about leaving their high school sweethearts. It was the retail holiday season, and my manager had planned a Life Visioning Meditation exercise. As I sat in the lotus position trying to stop my monkey mind from racing, I had constant thoughts of, "What the heck are you doing?" I had recently quit my full-time corporate job that had paid me to manage people, eat wherever I wanted, stay in beautiful hotels, and purchase free gas. All I could hear was, "You idiot, you sure screwed up this time!" But the truth was that I was only using that job for a paycheck. I was dying slowly and had no integrity as I spent eight hours a day wishing I were doing something more fulfilling.

We started the exercise by creating a written life plan for ourselves ten years in the future. We then worked back and envisioned ourselves at five, and then three years in the future. I found the exercise to be fun and exciting; in a single moment, I found myself lost in the fantasy of the Josie ten years from now. I was a multi-millionaire real estate sales professional, managing my fitness empire on the side as I lived in a big city. Yes, this was it, I had it all figured out! This was my future.

Once the writing portion was complete, we started a guided meditation. I was new to meditation and was trying to follow my breath as instructed, but the commentary in my mind was running the show. When I finally fell into a meditative state, I was met with a vision, but it was not the one I had written about. I saw myself beside a black SUV with a handsome man holding a baby girl; we were all dressed in winter gear in what appeared to be a family photo in front of our family mountain home. Sounds amazing, right? Not for me! I found myself struggling against this vision. Where were my money and businesses? My homes? I am a Southern girl, and I had no desire to live somewhere cold. Additionally, I have always wanted my first child to be a boy—why was I holding this little girl? All I could think about was how God got this wrong.

At this point in the meditation, the leader must have seen the perplexed expression on my face. "Whatever you see is perfect. Do not resist it; simply allow it," she said. Once the mediation was over, I ran to the leader to contest what I had seen. I asked how I could fix this vision, which had shown me a life that I did not want for myself. She then gave me the best advice I have ever received—she told me to become invested in my vision. What if my consciousness was hinting at what could become my best life, and I had no idea how good it could get? Through my frustration, I became curious, and I went on a quest to find the place of my future in my meditation. I prayed to God every day, asking to send me signs, clues, miracles, people, and conversations that would lead me to the place I saw in the vision.

A few days later, I found myself sitting in a self-transformation seminar with a good friend. I shared with her my vision and the new possibility I had set for my life, and how I wanted to relocate to the place I saw in my vision. Baffled, she asked how I would find this place. I told her that I had no idea, but God gave me the vision, and I trusted him to make the provisions. As we were getting ready to leave the seminar, a man walked up to me and asked if I liked to take photos. In my mind, I thought to myself that this was a terrible pick-up line. When he saw that the expression on my face was one of confusion and disappointment, he quickly followed up with "I'm a new photographer, and I need to build my portfolio." I agreed to help him and asked for his number so that I could reach out to him. As he read off his number with an area code of 303, I stopped him to ask where this area code was from. He responded, "Denver,

Colorado." I immediately looked at my friend and said, "I'm moving to Denver."

Two months later, I packed my car and made the journey from Houston, Texas, to Denver, Colorado. I had no money, no job, and no place to stay. I had complete faith that God would reveal the vision and provide clarity.

A manifestation delivered to me in meditation while I was a broke, part-time sales associate has unfolded in ways I could have never imagined. Denver has become my home, where I have established friendships with extraordinary people who I consider to be my family. I now enjoy a career in a field that chose me, where I was the top sales producer in my region within the first three months of employment. I live in a top floor apartment with a fabulous resort-style pool view, and have had fun experiences with lovers from all over the world. It's amazing what can manifest in your life when you take on a spirit of courageous curiosity. My story is far from complete, but a lot of soul searching has led my vision to become a reality. Once a city lover with dreams of being a mogul, I now yearn for a fantastic family full of love and appreciation.

# When The Universe Responds
## By Alica Souza

Only a year ago, my life was in complete chaos. I was bound in an unhealthy marriage spiraling out of control that led to a divorce. I was now a single mother of four children. I was a stay-at-home mom for two years. I had no career, no direction, and had lost all sight of who I was. This was my rock bottom. Initially, I asked God, why me? How am I going to do this by myself? However, I chose to take responsibility for my choices and begin making changes. "God grant me the serenity to accept the things I cannot change, the courage to change the things I can, and the wisdom to know the difference." This prayer helped me release what no longer served me and strengthened my faith.

Once I detached my identity with failure, the Universe began unfolding before my eyes. I decided my circumstances weren't going to define me. I chose to be grateful exactly where I was. I could finally create the life I wanted. The healing process began, and my inner wounds were exposed. It was as though layers were being peeled away each day.

I immersed myself in self-care. Each day I would go on an hour run listening to music. This was a special time for me to pray and receive divine answers. My spiritual eyes were opening, and my gifts were revealing. I knew that all the pain I encountered was necessary to transform me into what God intended me to be. On one of these blissful days, I asked the Universe to put someone in my life to direct me. That's when I met my spiritual life coach. The timing was impeccable—I needed healing, and I was on fire for manifesting my new life. I had to start small, but with my energy matching the Universe, I became aware of endless opportunities.

I started working at a convenience store to get back on my feet. It was quite humbling. I was extremely grateful for this first step in my process. While I was at work, I would mindfully be thankful so that

I would receive a better job. I did my best to stay positive at my place of work because I knew that a better opportunity would come to me. I began noticing a beautiful woman coming in during the evenings. I even complimented her on her beauty. I had no idea who she was. One day, as I was working, the phone rang, and I answered it. A woman on the other end asked for the blonde who had worked the night before. I knew she was referring to me, but I hesitated, unsure of what she'd say next. After a brief pause, I told her my name. She then said she had been coming into the store and noticed that I was a good worker and that I presented myself well, and that she was a manager at National Bank. She offered me a job. I was blown away! A few weeks later, I had a job at the bank.

In the midst of me transitioning into my new job, I decided a new car would benefit my family. Even though I was newly divorced with limited work experience, I didn't waver in my mind. I knew I would get a car. I would picture myself driving in a new car for two weeks straight. Then, that day came! As I was driving my car home for the first time, I was exhilarated. I was intrigued by how my needs were being met by me being in alignment with the Universe.

I took it a step further. I wanted a better place for my children and me to start over. I imagined the home having three rooms and enough space. I wanted it in a particular town where my kids preferred to go to school. So I claimed it. I had no doubt I would get this place. One day I decided to start looking. The first place I found was exactly everything I imagined. I eagerly filled out the application and waited a few days for the response. Meanwhile, I was in a state of thankfulness, and I got it.

I now leave my new home in my new car and go to work at National Bank. For me, this is only the beginning of my new life, but I have come so far in only one year. It is beautiful to witness your true self shine after a period of darkness.

I have obtained wisdom through my suffering and miracles through my faith. I choose to become a conscious creator of my reality.

I believe in the Seven Universal Principles of Manifestation:

1. The law of attraction or vibration
2. The law of perpetual transmutation
3. The law of rhythm
4. The law of relativity
5. The law of polarity
6. The law of cause and effect
7. The law of gender

# First Deserve, Then Desire
## By David Stevens

Seeing yourself as being deserving is an often-overlooked part of manifesting. It is the missing element that is needed for true and long-lasting results. Let's explore the three levels of manifesting: intention, attention, and this deep level of being deserving.

Much of the thinking around manifestation is concerned with the first level, which is clarity of intention. It is the *what* of our manifestation focus. This is certainly important because when we are clear and energetically aligned with our intention, we are fully committed and focused on what we are creating. Intention is on the level of thinking.

The second and deeper level is the *how* of manifestation: using our attention to harness the magnetic power of positive emotions such as gratitude and appreciation. Doing this energizes the fulfillment of our desires. Attention is on the level of feeling.

There is a third level, which is deeper than thinking and feeling. This level is that of *being deserving*. No matter how clear we are in our thinking or how powerfully we attend to positive emotions, unless we can fully see ourselves being in the achievement of our goal, we will not have long-lasting and fulfilling success. Do we see ourselves as someone who can have our goal? If we truly feel we deserve something, we will have no tension about it because we know that we are worthy of it. With this deep vibration on the level of being deserving, successful manifestation is inevitable.

In the 80s, I worked at a luxury hotel in San Francisco. I became friends with a Vietnamese woman named Sue. Sue grew up in a wealthy family in South Vietnam with servants and tutors. Her father was a high-ranking government official. He had been brought up poor, but became educated and rose up the ranks. One day he came home and informed the whole family that they had to leave South Vietnam because the conflict with the North was heating up, and it was no longer safe for them to remain. Sue was in her early teens and did not grasp the gravity of the situation. She thought they were only leaving for a few days. She even took the equivalent of a few South Vietnamese thousand-dollar bills to use when she returned.

The reality and permanence of their move began to dawn on her, as they were sent to a small, desolate Pacific island inhabited by other refugees who had left South Vietnam. They were instructed on how to build a lean-to shelter and how to catch fish to supplement the one bowl of rice they were given daily.

The family used some jewels they had brought with them to pay for Sue's older brother to travel to San Francisco. He immediately started working as a janitor and soon started a janitorial company. As he accumulated money, he sent it for each of his other family members to travel to San Francisco.

The whole family lived in a small two-bedroom apartment south of Golden Gate Park. They all started working various jobs. Sue started working as a cashier at the luxury hotel and was saving money to open a sewing factory. The family pooled their resources and started buying real estate in one of the most expensive cities in the world. Over the next few years, they bought three quick-oil-change franchise locations and were well on their way to being wealthy again.

There was never any question that they would regain what they had lost. They deeply knew they deserved wealth, and that made it easy to take whatever steps necessary to fulfill that desire.

Now we will explore a technique for activating and applying the vibration of being deserving.

Willpower-driven thinking about goal achievement creates intermittent results because it works against this fundamental truth of our being: that we are always fully deserving and worthy.

"Winning isn't everything, it's the only thing!" is a famous quote from legendary football coach, Vincent Lombardi. For some, this phrase may be inspirational, but it also has a dark side. The dark side is that if "winning is the only thing," and we don't win, then we are nothing. Feeling we are nothing is the opposite of being worthy. The idea that we are worthless because we failed is an insult to our deepest nature. The over-emphasis on the achievement of a goal by a specific time can limit us to picking sure-thing goals that do not require us to stretch and grow.

An antidote to this self-limiting thinking is the magical phrase, "Wouldn't it be nice if…?" The reason this phrase works so well is that it does not invalidate our worthiness. There is a sub-text to this phrase, that "I am whole, perfect, and complete as I am." This affirms the truth of who we are as capable souls and creators.

Close your eyes for a moment and think of some change or goal you want to see manifested. Then say that phrase "Wouldn't it be nice if…?" completing it with a statement of your goal as already achieved.

This practice allows us to fully have our *being deserving* and be fully adventurous in pursuing truly inspiring goals, because we are first affirming that we are whole, perfect, and complete, and then affirming our desire. First deserve, then desire!

# Living My Dreams
## By Janice Story

I was so excited when I first learned of the opportunity to contribute to this book. Over the last few years, I have been able to manifest some amazing things, and I could not wait to write about them. So why, when I sat before the computer, was I struggling so much? I'd had months to write my chapter, and now here I was with only two weeks left to write, edit and submit! I had my content and plenty of it, but I had yet to write one word. But, as the saying goes, there are no accidents. It wasn't until this past weekend, while I was driving home from an incredible experience that I understood the reason for my writer's block—that experience was meant to become part of this story.

In recent years I have been so fortunate to work with some amazing teachers like Sunny Dawn Johnston, Kate Shipp, and Melissa Corter, each of whom helped me with my self-esteem, confidence, and finding my voice. But one of the most valuable things they taught me was about manifesting what I desired. Melissa, in particular, teaches amazing classes focused on manifestation and releasing blocks that are holding you back.

Without a doubt, the healing room on the side of my house has been one of my most incredible manifestations to date. I won't write too much about that here, because the full story is included in another book, *Healer: 22 Expert Healers Share Their Wisdom To Help You Transform*. I will say though, that I brought it into existence by constantly thinking about it as if I already had it. I saw myself with clients and teaching classes in it. I told everyone about it and journaled my vision consistently. And guess what? My room looks and feels exactly like I imagined it to be.

I was also able to step down from my toxic corporate job and manifest a business doing what I love the most—helping others—and in my backyard! And that was only the beginning. I connected with an amazing man who was in the process of creating "Soberman's Estate," a facility to help men through their recovery from alcohol and substance abuse. We spoke several times over the course of seven months, and although he had not hired me yet, I could see myself working there and told everyone that I would be. I would journal about my days working with the clients and how they interacted with my horses. I could see my horses in the stalls, and could feel myself in the barn and discussing with other staff whatever experiences that had come up that day.

The scenes in my head were so real that I knew they would become a reality. All I had to do was let go of the "when" and the "how." In March of 2019, I signed the contract to become their equine and meditation coach. It has truly been an honor to be able to support the clients in their recovery efforts and to create such a safe space for them to help heal their lives. I literally ride my horses or walk them over. I have manifested the most amazing job!

Becoming a published author was another dream I manifested into reality. I had loved to write poems and such when I was younger but always hated English classes. I particularly recall receiving a terrible grade and some negative comments on a paper I had written. I became so discouraged that I completely quit writing my poems. Yet somewhere inside, the dream of writing remained, and last year, when I was asked to contribute to a collaborative book, I jumped at the chance. It felt great to write that first story and be able to share experiences with others in the hope that they would find some inspiration to heal their lives. I started seeing myself writing more and noticed that once I stepped into feeling like an author, more opportunities started showing up for me to write. Now here I am, contributing to my sixth collaborative book. I am a published author!

The first time I thought about becoming a speaker, I was working at a Celebrate Your Life event at The International Women's Summit. I was standing in the back of the room when Lisa Nichols began to speak, and I was mesmerized. She told the story about the first time she spoke in front of a crowd. She was the only woman in a group of men, all of whom were dressed in black suits. Trying to fit in with them, Lisa had dressed similarly, rather than like her colorful self, and found it was difficult to speak. She was talking about authenticity, and as I listened to her, I couldn't help but wonder, "What everyone will think when I am standing up there in my jeans and cowboy boots?"

Though I could feel what it would be like to be a speaker, it seemed as if it would never be more than a dream—until this past weekend, when I was invited to speak and hold a workshop with my horses at Celebrate Your Life in Sedona! Indeed, my pipe dream felt like a dream come true as I stood there in my boots and jeans, sharing my horses with forty amazing attendees. The feedback I received was so heartfelt, and it was such an honor to be able to hold a sacred space for their experience as they opened up to some healing. It was truly one of the most incredible experiences of my life!

You can manifest that which you desire, but you must live it, visualize it, breathe it, and, most importantly, feel into it. Put it out there, but let go of the expectations and be open to receiving it, however, and whenever it shows up! You'll often find that when it does, it is even better than you imagined.

# Intention
# By Erin Talbot

The fall of 1988 is a moment I have frozen in time. That is the day I told my school counselor what was happening at home. It is the day I hid behind one of those chalkboards—the type that slides down, where children hang their coats and keep their lunches. It is the day that I was interviewed by two social workers, and the day I, as an eight-year-old child, confronted my mother alongside two police cars. It was also the day I was removed from my biological mother and put into government care. For the next 10 years, I would be a *foster kid*. Even as an adult, I still feel like a foster kid.

I can still remember the abruptness of aging out of foster care. On my 19th birthday, I was suddenly viewed as an adult. A tidal wave of shock struck. I was suddenly responsible for everything. I aged out early, as I was considered to be "mature," but nothing could prepare me for what was in store. To cover rent, groceries, and bills, I had to work three part-time jobs. I had day, evening, and late evening jobs. I spent my days at the front desk, my late afternoons selling work-boots, and late nights slinging drinks. I would close down the bar and wake up early to get back to my day job—and repeat. I was socially isolated, as every moment was spent working. I lost connection with friends who had the privilege to cling onto childhood a little longer.

Despite working three part-time jobs, there was never enough for even the most basic items. I can still remember the $16.00 per week I had for groceries. A 34-cent can of no-name vegetable soup was the only vegetables I could afford for many weeks. I'd add an extra can of water and stretch it to three servings. Bulk oatmeal, a loaf of bread, peanut butter, a gallon of milk, and sometimes a bunch of bananas. That grocery list, the agony over each penny, is permanently etched in my mind. The last few days, meals would be only glasses of milk. I was 25 years old before I could afford groceries.

I look back at those years and wonder how I worked so many hours a day on such inadequate nutrition? I wonder how I managed the isolation and loneliness? At times I've wondered why had all that intervention been done—only to be "set free" at 19 with no support and no guidance. I had the misfortune of aging out of government care as a new government came in, and as they saved for the pending Olympics, many foster kids (wards of the province), including me, watched the supports we were promised as children dismantled.

It was that promise of support that had given me hope. I'd been told by my social worker that I could attend university, that I had a future to look forward to, that I was smart, and that I had potential. The past was traumatic, abusive, and filled with neglect, but I had a future to look forward to—and that was what got me through those difficult years. The notion that I could attend post-secondary school and create a life for myself became my mantra, so when the supports melted away, I was adamant that I would find another way. I gave trust to the universe and went one day at a time. I moved to the lower mainland and started at Douglas College. I found three new part-time jobs and worked around the clock. If I ever looked at my budget, it was so far in the red that things—tuition, books, rent, groceries, sundries, gas, insurance— seemed impossible. I continued to work three, four, and sometimes five part-time jobs. The majority of my papers were written after long 16-hour days. I was given grace by many of my professors who understood the circumstances I was up against and offered flexibility on deadlines. I only encountered one professor who refused, and I guess he never fully understood my story and the systemic barriers I was up against. Poverty is a powerful tool of oppression and is the only opportunity for students aging out of care.

Somehow I managed my way through university, and for the past 10 years, I have taught in the province of British Columbia. I am filled with wonder and gratitude for the fortitude, resolve, and grit my young self portrayed. I am in awe at the pace and steadfastness, and feel exhausted thinking about those long days during my toughest years. It is usually in the moments when the sun hits my face, that I take pause, inhale, and reflect on all the things I am grateful for:

- Breaking the cycle of abuse. I knew the second she was laid on my chest that the cycle was broken.
- A healthy, inquisitive daughter who brings so much joy each day.
- The sound of her infectious laugh echoing throughout our home. Is there any better sound than that of a child laughing?
- The wet nose of an excited golden retriever as I arrive home.
- A beautiful home on a hill in a small, close-knit community surrounded by lakes.

All the things I've longed for have come into reality. The things I envisioned, prayed for, and willed into existence. It is these moments where I look around, take inventory, and am in awe at the life I have built. The life I have imagined. Goals set with intention and whole-hearted belief that there was a way. The grit of getting up each day in the face of extreme hardship and poverty—believing and knowing that there was a better future. Impossible days somehow blended together. Had I known what I was up against, I might not have done it, and in hindsight, I'm so relieved that I didn't give up. I have so much gratitude to the universe that has my back!

# How I Created A Six-Figure Income Using Manifestation Techniques
## By Lisa Thompson, Ph.D.

Growing up, I was equally split in my passion for creative endeavors and for more analytical topics, including science. I loved my creative side, but I didn't believe I could have a steady career as a creative. All I had known were "starving" and "struggling" artists. I decided early on that my creativity would be relegated as a hobby when I wasn't doing my real job.

I graduated from college and continued straight to graduate school to obtain my Ph.D. in science. However, my love of art and design continued as a hobby through my schooling, and I spent my spare time making and selling jewelry. I also helped friends space plan and design their apartments, and dressed them for their new careers as professors.

After my second year in graduate school, I seriously considered quitting science to attend art school, as I kept being pulled in an artistic direction. My parents convinced me to continue my degree, saying I could change careers once I had my doctorate. I took their advice and finished my degree.

At the end of graduate school, I reacquainted myself with the spiritual school I had attended as a teenager. In that school, we learned about the concepts and quantum mechanics of consciously creating our reality. This included processes of meditative visualization and creating our day, later made famous by Dr. Joe Dispenza in the movie, *What the Bleep Do We Know?* Having knowledge of these tools would prove invaluable as I went through my adult life.

Early seeds were planted for my future creative business. As a professor, I had students who introduced me to the television show,

*Trading Spaces*. Later, after leaving academia, I was in the mortgage industry, and I became fascinated with watching the home-staging TV show, *Designed to Sell*. I thought the concept was brilliant, and I wondered if home staging was a real career or something only for television. I continued spending my spare time making jewelry, as well as painting and decorating wood furniture and décor.

Fast forward several years later. I left the mortgage industry and met my second husband. I got pregnant, and I needed a break from working to have a healthy pregnancy. Although my husband wanted me to stay home with the kids, I knew I was not meant to be a stay at home mom. With HGTV on in the background all day long, the idea of home staging became more interesting and possible. I researched how to start a business and got trained in the industry. When my son was six months old, I took the plunge and opened my home staging and interior design business.

My husband initially supported me starting a business because he thought it would be a hobby and assumed I would fail, keeping me dependent on him. He did not know who he was married to and how powerful I am.

Using the skills and knowledge I learned owning my first business in the mortgage industry and at a year-long job working for a business management consulting firm, I put together a business and marketing plan. My goal was to be the premier home staging company in my county, earning a six-figure income, to prove to myself it could be done. I chose to overcome my childhood belief I could not be financially successful in a creative field.

As a business owner, I used traditional methods of generating business, including joining networking and business groups I knew about. In addition, I formed a mastermind group with other business owners who had the same goal of being six-figure earners in their respective industries. When we started, none of us were even close to this level.

I implemented all of the manifestation tools I knew from my spiritual school and other sources I had learned over the years. I wrote out my long term goals. Harvard Business School had done a study where they followed a particular graduating class and their income achievements after finishing business school. They found those students who wrote their goals on a piece of paper earned twice of those having goals but were not written down.

I wrote out my income desire daily, at least 20 times as if it were already true. This particular exercise was done in incremental steps. I started with an income I thought I could achieve, but which was slightly outside my comfort zone. As I achieved each level, I gradually increased the amount until I reached my goal of being a six-figure earner. This took some time, but I did not give up. I saw how I achieved the smaller goals, which eventually led to achieving the bigger goal. Baby steps were one key to my success.

I regularly visualized my success in meditations. I created my day by calling forth new business. I made lists of specific real estate agents I wanted to work with and let my networking partners know who I wanted to meet. I created vision boards. I actively engaged with present-tense affirmations to rewire my brain for acceptance. I hired a business coach to keep me accountable and on track with my goals. I was intentional in my business, and I was actively engaging in the world, thus creating my reality. Opportunities flooded in.

By year five in business, I achieved my goal of earning six figures, with my company being known as the top home staging company in my area. I am now at the end of my eleventh year in business, still going strong.

Although there were moments of tears and frustration, I didn't give up when it would have been easy to do so. Despite competition in my industry, I knew I would be successful. I stayed consistent in my activities. It all started with a passion for design, a dream of success in creativity, and continued focus and trust in the Universe to co-create my reality.

# The Power Of Healing
# By Katie Tryba

As a child, I experienced ten years of sexual abuse from a family member.

Luckily, my mom realized the importance of counseling, and when she found out what was happening to me, she got me into counseling right away. I was thankful to have someone unbiased to talk to, someone who I couldn't hurt when I remembered things. Even as a child, I understood how painful it was to share certain memories with a parent. I went through eight years of counseling with a magnificent therapist. I appreciated her honesty when I asked about the side effects of the long-term sexual abuse I had experienced. She shared that it might be easy for me to turn to drugs and alcohol to cope. Plus, she warned that I might want to submit to men, as my brain and body were programmed to do after so many years of sexual abuse. That's what I needed at that time—*truth*. I decided then that my body was a temple, and only those who worshipped it would touch it again with my permission.

Six of those eight years of counseling were spent battling a long court case against my predator. During those years, as a child going into my teens, I had to sit on the stand in front of my predator multiple times, with his lawyer trying to trick and confuse me. I'll never forget when, as a ten-year-old child, the lawyer said, "If you can't remember what color socks you wore, are you sure you remember him touching you there?" I remember wanting to cry and not understanding why an adult would talk to me that way. Despite the multiple victims, and new victims that emerged during the court case, he was let off. I always remembered feeling a lot of guilt for that loss, since memories became a little more clear later. As I got older and I finally had a better understanding of what sexual touch was, I had a better understanding of what I should have said when I was ten. My last time on the stand for the case was when I was sixteen, and I could only use my testimony from when I was ten years old.

After the devastating loss in the courtroom, I felt let down by the courts and felt that they wouldn't protect me. I struggled with night terrors for a while and was afraid to sleep, as he was coming after me in every dream. My predator tried to contact my school to get private information about me after the case was done, and I had to get a restraining order. I learned that life doesn't always play by the rules, but in the long run, things got better. After two more years of counseling, I left for college, thinking I was healed and I could move on. Unfortunately, a few years into college, I was the victim of attempted rape in my home. I was able to fight them off, but it messed me up emotionally and caused a lot of anxiety. I didn't go back to counseling, and for years I swept it all under the rug. Even though I wanted to believe I was over the childhood stuff, I still had so much shame I couldn't talk to anyone about it.

Something changed in my late twenties. I felt safe sharing my past, and in return, others felt safe sharing with me. I wanted to help other survivors, so I started volunteering as a sexual assault advocate for my area, quit teaching, and went back to school for my master's in counseling. I was surrounded by strong women and men willing to share their stories. My shame was gone, but my anxiety of the dark, sleeping in new places, and not being able to sleep without locked doors remained. My brain and body still believed I needed all of these things to be safe to be able to go to bed, no matter how many years had passed. My body was constantly flooded with adrenaline from going into fight, flight, or freeze mode. I truly believe this added to or is the cause of some health issues I have. Also, after all the counseling, we never reached or processed all the years of memories my brain had disassociated to protect myself. I figured I would have to live and deal with these after-effects.

In my journey to help heal others, I learned about *brainspotting*. Brainspotting is using the visual field to find trauma or any negative experiences stored in our brain. Talk therapy only reaches the front of our brain in the prefrontal cortex, but trauma is held in the back of the brain in the amygdala. Brainspotting can reach the trauma, process it, and resolve it. The research for brainspotting was promising for those with PTSD, and if I were to get trained in the technique, it seemed only ethical that I experience it for myself. I was afraid it might make me remember, and that it would be too painful. After learning more about it, I understood that my brain and body would heal at their individual pace, knowing how much I could handle. I took the leap and did multiple sessions, thinking this would be a learning experience to help me learn the technique before getting trained. To my surprise, it tapped into my childhood trauma, decreasing my fears and anxiety to a point I didn't know was possible. In my attempt to help others heal by exposing myself to other types of non-invasive counseling techniques, something in me changed, and I was finally at peace with my past.

Having a difficult past does not mean you are sentenced to a bleak future. Your presence in the world can be positive and used for good, and you will have a bigger heart filled with empathy and the wisdom of hard times. Always bet on yourself and keep believing.

# The Checklist
# By Katie Tryba

I was getting ready to move into our first home with my husband and two dogs. As we were packing, I came across a checklist I wrote in college about things I had hoped and dreamed for in my life. Some hopes were simple, maybe even silly, like bungee jumping. *Check.*

Some had specific detail like *marry a loving husband who loves his job.* Maybe I don't give myself enough credit, but I was surprised in college that I had enough insight on how important it is to like what you do. Looking back now, I think of how a wise person once shared with me that everyone wants three things in their job: high pay, a flexible schedule, and to love what they do. They said that about 80% of us get none of these things. Most people have jobs that are not rewarding, they don't enjoy the work, and they do not have any flexibility. They said that if you get one of those values, you should feel fortunate and maybe stick with that job. If you get two of those things, that is uncommon, and you probably have a better job than 90% of the population. They said that if you have all three of those things, you should feel extremely blessed. However, within a few years, you may grow unhappy with the work that you do, and you'll try to find something that you like better. The value of loving what you do is subjective and fleeting; for most of us, we get bored or impatient after a year or two (even in a job that we love), and we start to want more, making it less satisfying. However, my husband is fortunate, as his job does check a lot of those boxes, and even when he gets restless at his job, we think of this advice, because he does love his job. *Check.*

Let's rewind back to *marry a loving husband.* As a little girl, I have no idea why I prayed so hard to fall in love someday. I blame Disney because, after a trip to Disney World as a child, I wanted to marry Mickey Mouse or Eric from *The Little Mermaid.* Mickey was so nice

290

to Minnie and would do anything for her. I didn't truly care about Eric, I just liked that Ariel was so kind, adventurous, and strong. I mean, she did save Eric from drowning, and I didn't need or want to be saved. I got a glass wind-up music trinket of Mickey and Minnie Mouse holding flowers that plays the song "Someday My Prince Will Come." I used to obsess over it, sing along with it, and daydream about marrying my true love. As the years went by, the list of qualities became a little more important, but kindness was still key for me.

I met my husband, Travis, in college. We were acquaintances with a similar circle of friends. We were both in relationships with other people when we met as friends. I graduated two years ahead of him and moved out of town. When Travis graduated from college, he got a job and needed a place to live. By a stroke of luck, he moved in with one of my best guy friends, Tim, and the week he moved in, Tim invited Travis to come on our annual camping trip with a group of about twenty friends. Right away, Travis and I hit it off, laughing until we cried, giving each other nicknames, pranking each other like school kids, and singing songs around the fire while making up the words. This was the first time hanging out that we were both single, since we both had broken up with our exes the same day six months prior. We teased each other that it was meant to be. After that camping trip, we became inseparable, and two weeks later, I introduced Tim to his future wife, Sarah. We started double-dating, and three years later we all got married and stood in each other's weddings within two weeks of one another.

Qualities I wanted in a husband: kind, generous, heart of gold, funny, makes me laugh every day, trustworthy, reliable, and responsible. Travis is my best friend, and he checks all the qualities listed and more. He makes me feel like the most important person in the world. What I value the most is that he loves me for me. Oh, and by the way, that Mickey and Minnie trinket is still in our bedroom on the headboard to remind me that some dreams do come true. *Marry a loving husband. Check.*

There are still things on the list that are not checked yet. We have been trying for children for over four years, and in that time, had our hearts broken with a miscarriage. I started to worry that there was something wrong with me, and I started to feel not good enough to be a mother. I also worried: what if Travis thinks this about me, resents me, or wants to have children with someone else? I shared these fears with him, and this is what he had to say: "I only want to have kids with you because I want mini-Katies someday, I don't care about mini-Travises. So if they aren't like you, I wouldn't want kids with anyone else. If we can't have kids, then let's have a long and happy life growing old together." In this moment I fell even more in love with him than I thought possible. I don't know in what form yet, but I know we'll be parents someday because I can envision it.

It's been two years since we found that list, and I'm still trying to make that 18-year-old girl proud of me, and no joke, the last thing on the list was to *be published in a book. Check.*

# The Back Of The Beer Label
# By Chantalle Ullett

I spent most of my youth looking and searching for the one person who I thought would complete my life. My youth was a trivial and tumultuous one. Feeling neglected, unloved, unwanted, and unneeded at home, I kept searching for someone to love me for me—a person who would accept, honor, and support who I thought I was. You see, I have been involved in many relationships from a young age, the majority of them being unhealthy and full of drama. Out of the many guys I dated through the years, there was only one person who broke my heart. It was excruciating. I couldn't eat or sleep, I avoided going home, and I worked nonstop to avoid feeling empty and alone. The Universe knew better.

I spent the better part of two years trying to fill the void. I was in terrible rebound relationships and dated meaninglessly for a little over a year, continuously repeating the pattern of previous relationships. Whenever someone asked me why I wasn't in a serious relationship, my phrase of choice was, "I have yet to meet a good man."

Thursday, March 17, 1994, my life changed. That's the day I met my husband in a bar called O'Toole's in Ottawa, Ontario. How we met was, in essence, divine intervention. Every Thursday night was when my girlfriends and I would go dancing without fail. However, on this particular night, no one wanted to go. I had this undeniable urge to go out. It was as though I had a voice telling me to go out. The search was on. I called so many different friends to go out. Everyone kept saying no, except for one, a former female coworker whom I hadn't talked to in over a year. It took some convincing on my part for her to come out with me, but nonetheless, she said yes, so off we went to O'Toole's.

As we got to the bar, I met up with some current coworkers and danced the night away. It was almost time to go, so I went in search of my girlfriend who had accompanied me. She was talking with a group of guys I didn't know. And there he was: six feet two inches tall, jet-black hair, clean-shaven, jeans, cowboy boots, with a killer smile, who happened to be one of my coworker's friends. She walked away with their mutual friends, leaving me alone with him. We introduced ourselves, his name was Jim. We spent the rest of the evening talking, laughing, and enjoying ourselves.

As the evening came to a close, Jim asked me to dance the last song of the evening, which happened to be a slow song. He was such a gentleman. He escorted me onto the dance floor, held my hand, and gently wrapped his arm around my waist, pulling me in close. For the first time since I was a little girl, I truly felt safe and secure in someone's arms. As the song came to an end, he kissed my forehead then asked for my telephone number. Seeing as it was before cellular phones, the only item he could find to write on was the back of a beer label. How Canadian!

After giving him my telephone number, we parted ways. The following evening, my phone rang. It was him, asking if I had plans for the evening. Unfortunately, prior commitments had been made on my part. I called him the next day. We spent endless hours talking on the phone about a variety of topics and getting to know each other. We set a date to see a movie the following week.

We went to the movie premiere of *Guarding Tess* on Tuesday. We made plans to go out again on Thursday. During our meal, our conversation revolved around our previous relationships. Afterward, we headed back to his house to talk some more, where he continued to bewilder me with his charm, poise, and gentleness. That evening, we mutually agreed to be exclusive.

Back then, I naively thought a relationship meant the person you were with simply accepted you for who you are. Who knew 25 years ago that writing my phone number on the back of a beer label would forever enhance the rest of my life? Jim and I have learned and grown through the years, understanding and guiding, while supporting the dreams we have for each other and as individuals.

# Manifesting The Imperfect
## By Breyen Wee

I have strived to be perfect since before I can remember. No more.

For many years in my journey to stop being a perfectionist, I have kept myself pigeonholed as exactly that: a perfectionist. I have consciously, and probably subconsciously, been calling myself a perfectionist all my life. A childhood memory that stands out for me is one from first grade. While practicing printing, I remember that if a letter on my printing page didn't look "perfect," I would erase and redo it as many times as I thought necessary in hopes of printing the best, most perfect letters. This got me so much praise. The teacher would hold up my work as an example and tell the other students that they should try to print as neatly as I did. Some children would have been mortified by this kind of attention, but I liked it. I was a quiet and shy student who kept to herself, and it felt good to be recognized. It also felt good to look at the finished product I had created. Teachers would write in my report cards that I was a perfectionist, but it never truly had any negative connotations to it. Nobody told me to stop trying so hard or to be okay with handing in messier, less thorough work. This is the first of many times during childhood that I can remember wanting to be perfect.

I have always felt that I needed to live up to everyone's expectations of me. What would they think if I didn't? I had certain standards that I felt I had to live up to. I didn't realize, though, that feeling like I had to live up to certain standards took a toll on me. This continued throughout high school, university, at my jobs, and at home. At some point, after having children, I began to realize that these expectations were almost always self-imposed.

After I became a parent, I still found myself striving for perfection and telling the universe I was a perfectionist, even though it was becoming clearer that perfection was simply not possible. My children had to be well-dressed and well-groomed. They had to be quiet, calm, and well-behaved. I had to look put-together. If people came to visit, my home had to be clean. I had to try hard to get my pre-baby body back. If all of these pieces weren't in place, wouldn't I be judged? What would people think of me? When my children were both in their toddlerhood, I began to recognize that I was putting most of this pressure on myself. Ed Mylett says that "People aren't thinking about you; they are thinking about what you are thinking about them," and his words resonate so deeply within me.

I know that no matter how hard I try, I will never be perfect. Families are imperfect. Motherhood is imperfect. Womanhood is imperfect. Imperfection is beautiful. I am grateful for everything in my life, and I know that it isn't perfect. I have a soft belly that folds where it never used to. While it is not perfect, it carried my babies, and for that, I am grateful. My home isn't perfect. There are pieces of blue sand from my children's sensory bin on the floor, dirty dishes in the sink, and a mountain of laundry to be folded, but this is where my children learn and grow, and for that, I am grateful. My lifestyle isn't perfect. Sometimes I have the greatest intentions of waking up early and exercising or meditating because that would provide me with the elusive "life balance." Right? Let's be real here. Occasionally, I also press snooze seventeen times, throw my hair in a messy bun, and do the day. Sometimes I skip exercising altogether, bake a batch of cookies, and eat them all on the same day. This is not glamorous, but it is real life.

My health isn't perfect. I take medication every day and am learning to manage depression and anxiety when they rear their ugly faces. I have fantastic doctors and amazing family support and, for them, I am grateful. I am also hopeful.

I am not a perfect parent. At times, I feel like all of the tasks involved in parenting are piling up, and I feel overwhelmed. However, I know that my children are loved and cared for, and for that, I am grateful. I believe that it is healthy to accept that life is not always perfect. Besides, our kids don't want to look back at pictures of a perfect mama. They will look back at photos and remember how you made them feel: loved and cherished even during all of the "imperfect" moments.

To be perfectly honest, I often still feel like I need to perform up to my self-imposed standards, but I am making a concerted effort to stop, because striving for the impossible doesn't feel good at all. It feels crappy. I no longer put it out into the universe that I am a perfectionist. I tell myself that I am imperfect, and that's okay. I am learning that gratitude, mindset, and manifestation all need to work hand-in-hand. When we are feeling grateful, our mindset becomes more positive, and this positivity helps us to manifest all of the amazing things we want to attract into our lives. Most evenings, I write out a list of parts of my life I am grateful for and another list of what I am manifesting for myself and my family. I write them in the present tense and truly believe that these events and things already exist for me in the future. I invite you to join me in putting less pressure on yourself, practicing gratitude, and manifesting the imperfect.

# My Greatest Teacher
# By Dorothy Welty

In July of 2011, no longer did it seem a choice of whether or not to leave my husband. Aside from the frustration, anger, and resentment that had overtaken me as a result of being married to an alcoholic for 22 years, was the realization that I had lost myself in the years of desperate attempt to control the uncontrollable. I woke up one morning that July with a sense of urgency and the courage to leave. Rather than trying to control everything around me that was beyond my control, I thought regaining control over my life by leaving my husband would bring me control. Little did I know it would take me several more years to realize that leaving my husband was only the beginning of the lesson I was to learn.

After leaving my husband, I entered a five-year nightmare beyond anything I could have ever imagined. My son, who came with me when I left the marriage, was already exhibiting unimaginable rage for the years of neglect brought by a father who was ruled by his addiction and a mother who was ruled by her need for control. As out of control as life with an alcoholic had been, it wouldn't hold a candle to the chaos that was to follow. My 12-year-old son was already shaving and towered over me at six feet tall. His rage and rebellion, along with his more mature appearance, would draw him to a much older group of peers immersed in the local drug culture. One by one, most of these teens would either drop out or get expelled from school. Over five years, several of his peers would die, and nearly all the others would wind up in prison before the age of 20. This five-year nightmare with my son would be full of truancy, in-school suspensions, out-of-school suspensions, hospital visits, break-ins to my residence, frequent calls both to and from the local police, and a constant fear that one or both of us would not survive. On almost a daily basis, I would sit in the car in the parking lot at work to dry my tears and pull myself together before heading into my job. Upon arriving home, I would weep uncontrollably while the car idled in the garage as I contemplated allowing the exhaust fumes to rescue me from the pain and fear.

Life had brought me to my knees. I was in a spiritual crisis. I was experiencing my dark night of the soul. I couldn't stand my life, my circumstances, or the person I had become. The choice now was to either cop out of life or surrender to life and the lessons it was here to teach me.

I needed to shift my consciousness from the law of cause and effect to the law of attraction. I had to shift from reacting to everything around me to responding from my heart and bringing forth love in my approach to living. Using the law of attraction to manifest a new life for myself was a gradual process. Looking back, it began with choosing to redefine my relationship with my son. Rather than labeling him my greatest nightmare, I decided to view him as my greatest teacher. Rather than reacting to his disrespect and rebellion, I learned to state my boundaries, declare my truth, and remove myself from playing interference in an attempt to protect him from the consequences of his actions. One of the consequences that followed was kicking him out of the house upon graduation from high school when he, yet again, had brought drugs into the home.

Now completely alone for the first time in 30 years, I embraced all of the pain of the past three decades. I cried for my wounded inner child. I mourned the many losses and disappointments. I allowed myself to fully experience the hurt, the pain, and the fear so that it might pass through me. I came out the other side with a determination to embrace the opportunity to manifest a whole new life. I meditated and envisioned myself living in joy, peace, and love despite my circumstances.

I began envisioning the life I had always longed for. I longed to live in a residential neighborhood instead of a complex. I longed to live near the mountains. I envisioned a home where I could enjoy the outdoors, entertain friends, and have a creative space for writing and other artistic pursuits without all the maintenance of home-ownership. I envisioned myself in a job that valued people, relationships, and the opportunity for professional growth. These visions were not of the mind or designed in detail. These visions were of my heart and the longings of my soul that had been drowned out by all the hurt and fear of the past three decades.

In July of 2017, I accepted a new job and moved from St. Louis to a suburb of Denver. I now live in a residential neighborhood with a homeowner's association that takes care of exterior maintenance. I have a view of green space and the Front Range. I can enjoy the outdoors year-round. I have two guest rooms and room for my creative pursuits. I work for a college that values people, relationships, and opportunities for professional growth.

I had left my son behind in Missouri until he called and pleaded with me for a second chance. He drove out to Colorado and lived up to his promise to respect my rules. He turned his life around. He enrolled in school, found a job, and pays me rent. He graduated from community college this past spring and is continuing his education.

I continue to meditate as a daily practice. I believe I am worthy of abundance. I respond from a place of love rather than react from fear. I see life from an infinite rather than limited view. I am full of gratitude and love for my son, my greatest teacher.

# Ten Steps To Manifesting Your Soul's Purpose
## By Blyss Young

I first learned about manifestation in my 20s. I was a single mother making ends meet as a waitress. My first introduction was *not* a spiritual one, but more a positive way of viewing life. Your words and thoughts are powerful; if you can envision something, you can create it. The term "anything is possible" became part of my new mindset. This idea that your words and mental state create your opportunities transformed me from being someone who was at the effect of life circumstances to someone who is the creator of my life circumstances. However, as I've learned over the years, this is merely the beginning, and manifestation is a constant evolution. You expand, stretch, push, envision, clear away the mental brush, raise your vibration to meet that which you desire, and voila! Only to begin the cycle again with the next expansion.

As I write this, I have recently completed an expansion. I envisioned a new place to live that would encompass both what I desired in a home, combined with the things that would make my work life more productive and pleasurable. Honestly, once I was genuinely ready to leap, the house that I now live in was the first house I saw. Currently, I am typing this in a hotel room with an ocean view while my new home office is being painted.

Since that time in my 20s, I discovered that it is possible to create your world—like molding a piece of clay. Over 20 years later, I have accomplished many things professionally and financially. However, my dream of finding my soul mate/life partner has been somewhat elusive. I have had great epic loves and mind-blowing sacred sex. But as I sit here, I am in a personal inquiry into what may be in the way of bringing my final love affair into my life.

See, this trip was already planned months ago. Days before I left, a friend invited me to join this project. I live my life present for the moment, and if a potentially expansive opportunity is tossed in front of me, I check in and see if this is what spirit wants for me. So I said yes, not knowing where this journey would lead me. I knew this was a time for me to reflect and be introspective. I have recently ended a six-year love affair. Oh deep and sexy, this one was. But consistent and stable, it was not—but it did chisel and hone my desires for what's next. Writing this essay enabled me to acknowledge that I am a master of manifestation! I have done this in many ways in the most important methods and the little techniques. Here are the steps that have so well served me in the past that I will now direct towards manifesting this next dream.

## Get centered

Clear out quiet space and time. Come back to your center. This may look like going into nature, dancing naked, meditating, taking a run. Do what you need to do daily to keep coming back to center.

## Be clear

Create a picture of what you are desiring. As much detail as possible. When you create this visualization, you're looking for the feeling that it elicits in your body. Joy, comfort, warmth, strength, confidence. Keep going until you have created the feeling you would like.

## Remove resistance aka Raise your vibration

Often the visualization will lead you to where you are resisting this dream coming into fruition. This resistance will lower your vibration, and if you and what you desire are not a match, you will not draw it into your life.

## Follow your bliss—let your body be your guide

For some of us, bliss is right on the surface; we are crystal clear about what makes us happy. Others need to do work on self-love, acceptance, or healing to find our joy again. Go deeper or get professional help to assist you in shaking off that crust and uncovering what makes you happy. You know you are on your path if it brings you joy!

## Be inquisitive

Once you have removed the resistance and can feel the joyous feeling in your body, ask the universe questions about what the next steps are and be open to the answers.

## Pay attention to the sign

Be ready to accept what the universe is showing you—like bread crumbs on your journey. Big and small, they are there, but you have to listen to the whispers of spirit, and it will help you down the path to your dreams.

## Be flexible

Don't get locked into what it looks to be, even though you were extremely clear about what you desired. Allow miracles and divine inspiration to be able to create that feeling in ways that are beyond your imagination.

## Be patient

It is your soul's purpose, your life mission. It may take more time than you are comfortable. Find that place where you can enjoy the journey, not only the destination.

## Trust and believe

If I had to pick one to be the most important on this list, it's faith. You must return to this again and again. A belief that this shall be. Do not be dogmatic about this. It's not words, although affirmations are a step up the ladder from resignation. But statements are not enough to manifest; you must go deeper until you find that you *genuinely* believe.

## Acknowledge the process

Acknowledgment is twofold: one is giving credit to the progress, and the other is gratitude. Gratitude is sexy and creates more of those good feelings that ultimately will also guide you to your heart's desire, and when you know and feel your heart's desire, it shall be.

Manifesting is primarily an energetic game. A balance between intention, visualization, high vibrations, and listening to the sweet whisper of spirit. I hope you enjoy the journey.

# More Than Making Wishes
# By Marci Zeisel Rosenberg

This piece is related to my story, *Summer Sojourn—Sidelined*, published by As You Wish Publishing in the book titled: *Inspirations—101 Uplifting Stories for Daily Happiness*. Briefly, the intended messages from that story center on summoning courage, grace, and gratitude to survive when things get tough.

Initially, I felt reluctant and maybe a bit intimidated to share my experiences with this particular book topic, manifestation—bringing the imagined into reality, for fear of sounding a little "out there." To some, the idea that one can imagine something and make it real is magical thinking. That's not what this is. It isn't making wishes and blowing out candles, hoping that our wishes will come true.

No, it is about getting clear on what we want to manifest (make real) in our lives, and then getting the universal energy involved in co-creating what we have imagined. Neat trick? No trick, only a recognition of humans' ability to tap into the universal energy when we are clear-minded and open-hearted. Some call this praying, meditation, or intention-setting.

The first step in manifestation is to imagine, to conceive a clear image of what you want to make real. The next is to speak of that which you have imagined, to declare your manifesto. The third step is to recognize when opportunities, even coincidences, start showing up, and take appropriate action. Imagine, speak, act. When it all seems to be lining up, we are in our flow.

From the following three short personal stories, I hope to demonstrate my assertion that we have the ability to tap into the universal energy to bring the imagined into reality. If I don't convince you, I hope you're at least entertained.

### Story 1: Time To Imagine A New Job

My kids were aged five and eight, and I was miserable working a full-time job as a legal assistant in a busy law firm. It wasn't that I didn't enjoy the work, I did. But prior to starting at this firm, I had managed to land good jobs in law firms working only three days a week. I took this job because I needed one, but within a few short months, felt deeply unhappy and began to recognize that my life was troublingly unbalanced. It took nearly a year of powering through the discomfort to finally allow myself even to imagine something different. I finally began imaging what I wanted my daily life to look like: getting kids ready for school and going to work three days a week with more time for family, home, and for me. Within a week of getting clarity on what I wanted my life to look like, I received a phone call from an attorney I had worked with a few years before. His firm was looking for a legal assistant and he wondered what I was doing and if I might be interested. My first words were, "I might be if I can work part-time." He replied that would be fine, preferred even. Two weeks later, I began living what I had imagined.

## Story 2: Seeking More Consulting Work

Several years after the events in Story 1, I was working on contract with a different law firm, meaning that I was paid by the hour for whatever work was available. After a few weeks of little work, I called a public relations consultant with whom our firm had contracted for a few difficult rezoning cases. I was his primary contact at the firm and we had worked well together on these projects. In our friendly but brief phone call, I let him know that I was available to assist in any similar projects. He promised to keep me in mind and we hung up. Two hours later, I received a phone call from a partner in a large PR firm in California who was contracting with local consultants for a statewide public initiative campaign in Arizona, where I live. The Phoenix consultant had told him about me and he needed some additional help on this campaign. I was hired before the end of the phone call.

## Story 3 – Saying I Want To Write And Then Getting The Opportunity To Do It

Earlier this year, I attended the Second International Women's Summit here in Phoenix. It was an uplifting, refreshing, and empowering experience. A few weeks after the Summit, about twenty or so women from the Phoenix area gathered at a local resort for happy hour one workday evening. It was a reunion of sorts, reconnecting with women I had met at the Summit and finding easy conversation with other women I hadn't met until that afternoon. Sitting in comfortable, thick-cushioned patio chairs, I spoke with another woman about what we had gained from participating in the Summit. We shared writing ideas and she told me of her recently published book. To which I replied, "I've been thinking about writing, but I don't know about what." Only moments after those words left my lips, a friendly woman strolled into the area where we were sitting and asked, "Is anyone interested in sharing their personal story of inspiration for a book my company will be publishing?" Without hesitating, I said, "Yes, I'll write a story." And then, turned to the woman to whom I had just declared my desire to write and said, "Oh my God, is that synchronicity, or what?"

It could be seen as synchronicity, or as a step in the manifestation of a desire. Step 1 was my thinking about the desire to write, my imagining. Step 2 was saying out loud in conversation that I had the desire to write. Step 3 was seeing the opportunity knocking on my door and taking it.

The friendly woman inviting us to share a story was Kyra Schaefer, co-publisher at As You Wish Publishing. Thank you, Kyra, for showing up with the opportunity to manifest one of my desires.

# Author Information

**Rollie Allaire:** is an experienced holistic life and wellness coach who combines years of clinical psychotherapy skills with chakra work, Crystal Reiki, ThetaHealing, Akashic Records readings and clearings, meditation, Ho'oponopono, Qi Gong, moon medicine teachings, and looking at life through the medicine wheel in the form of life and wellness to facilitate her clients' journey to wellness. She has recently opened Bridging the Gap Wellness Center in her community, where she works with other practitioners to provide their services within their small Northeastern Ontario community. She is a proud and loving mother of two adult boys, a wife, and a daughter. Website: www.rollieallaire.ca
Email: info@rollieallaire.ca Phone number: 705-303-0248

**Linda Ballesteros**: Linda Ballesteros is a certified franchise broker, professional life coach, goal-setting coach, mindfulness coach, and law of attraction coach. She has a passion for assisting those who have a dream to be a franchise owner by identifying the brand that will leverage their skills and passion. Linda also provides coaching to her new franchise owners, helping them to create a solid foundation and build a successful business by using goal setting, mindset, and visualization. Contact Linda to make your dreams of being a business owner come true:
Linda@MpowerFranchiseConsulting.com;
www.mpowerfranchiseconsulting.com.

**Kim Balzan**: Kim is a holistic practitioner certified in numerous different modalities, with the most passion going into vibrational sound, working with her alchemy crystal bowls and gongs. She is a certified advanced Amrit Method Yoga Nidra facilitator, Reiki master teacher, 200-hour ERYT, and a Kundalini Yoga teacher, currently working on level 2. Sound completely changed and transformed her life in every way, and she now works with private clients and large groups throughout the country, using these tools of transformation to help others see their true connection to themselves and awaken. Contact Kim at kimbalzansound@gmail.com, kimbalzan.com, or 602-577-9408 (mobile).

**Kristi Blakeway**: is a school principal in Maple Ridge, British Columbia, where she lives with her husband and two sons. She is the founder of Beyond HELLO—a student-run initiative that helps the homeless in Canada's poorest neighborhood reconnect with family through greeting cards, phone calls, and reunions. She is the author of *Beyond Hello: Rekindling the Human Spirit One Conversation at a Time*, a TEDx Speaker, Olympic torchbearer, and winner of the YWCA Women of Distinction Award. Kristi encourages everyone to step outside their comfort zone, engage in soulful conversation, and connect with compassion. She blogs regularly at www.beyondhello.org.

**Gillian Campbell:** is a teacher in British Columbia who leads with her heart. She is passionate about bringing mindfulness practices to the students and adults she works with. Her purpose is to share her knowledge and experiences to give children the skills they need to navigate life's biggest challenges. You can reach Gillian at gill_glushyk@hotmail.com.

**Janet Carroll RN** has had an impressive triad career: 48 years in nursing, 35 years in massage therapy, and 5-1/2 years in laughter yoga. It has given her decades of experience on all levels—physically, mentally, and emotionally. It is from those experiences, and her passion for assisting others in healing, that her transformational programs, classes and presentations were birthed. Janet's mission is to assist professionals (education, healthcare, business), students, management and staff, and other groups in their healing of trauma, PTSD, mental and physical health diagnoses, and stress, and to restore joy, resilience, and teamwork. Contact Janet at www.JanetCarrollRN.com, Janet@JanetCarrollRN.com, www.facebook.com/janet.carroll, or 832-216-3713.

**Melissa Spears Casteel** is a wife to life mate Tony, Reiki master, certified master coach, a certified special education teacher, mom to two wonderful children, Sarah and Anthony, grandmother, business partner, e-Commerce seller, and an enthusiastic network marketer! Melissa currently lives in Lewisville, Texas, and is a firm believer in "bloom where you are planted!" Always the optimist, Melissa believes everything that happens to us, good and bad, builds us into the human we are now. She lives by the philosophy, "Create your great life!" Reach her at tonymelteach@gmail.com.

**Catherine Cates:** has helped thousands go from doubt to making their dreams come true. Primarily business-minded women find direction, focus, and success with her unique blend of intuition and twenty-five-plus years in the business world. As an intuitive visionary with her feet on the ground, Catherine gives you easy strategies on which low-hanging fruit to pick first—getting results faster, building confidence, and inspiring you to achieve even bigger successes. Fear kills more dreams than failure ever will. Transform your mindset. Turn your life and business from ordinary to extraordinary! Reach Catherine at www.catherinecates.com, me@catherinecates.com, or 469-850-2204.

**AJ Cavanagh**: is an intuitive channel, author, and Joy Practitioner™. He and his husband, Tom, are the founders of Camp Joy Ranch, a spiritual center in Phoenix, Arizona. Together they channel 'the Guides'—native elders, extraterrestrial beings, ascended masters, angels, and elementals. These divine beings share messages of source consciousness on the expansion of joy in body, mind, and spirit. Joy, they have expressed, is our natural divine state. Contact AJ directly or sign up for their newsletter at www.campjoyranch.com.

**Julie M. Clark:** lives with her husband, two children and dog, Rumi, on a small farm in Maple Ridge, British Columbia. She currently lives her values through her work as an elementary school vice principal. Julie can be reached at juliemclarke@gmail.com, or via Instagram at: @juliemclarke.

**Janice Dau:** spiritual growth coach and frequency alchemist, helps you solve your struggles and problems by identifying limiting beliefs. Accessing the intelligence of the universe, we can reprogram your brain to bring in more ease, joy, and grace. When told that her lack of boundaries was draining her vital energy, Janice began her journey into the metaphysical realm. She assists women who want to find that spark—to remember their purpose. Janice uses a variety of modalities and is a certified angelic master teacher, Akashic record librarian, and certified Anahata Code practitioner. Please contact Janice at dau5280@gmail.com.

**Dr. Saida Désilets:** is an author, counter-culture creatrix, and advocate for women's sexual sovereignty. As a psychologist specializing in women's psychosexual wellbeing, she supports women to embrace the messiness of the human experience while exploring their inborn erotic genius for pleasure, vitality, and freedom. Her passion is to call women to dare into their desire and to live life on their terms. When she's isn't leading Wild Women in the Wilderness Safaris in Africa, you can find her dancing to her individual rhythm or writing deliciously sensual poetry. You can reach Dr. Saida at DareYourDesire.com or TheJadeEgg.com

**Katie Elliott:** is a contributing author in *Inspirations: 101 Uplifting Stories For Daily Happiness*. She is also an academic tutor, providing individual and small group instruction to help students improve their educational performance, while uplifting their self-esteem. She has been a teacher for over 30 years, including college, high school, and elementary students.

**Kathryn Eriksen:** is an Empowered Way Coach, meditation and mindfulness teacher, author, and speaker. She shows women how to connect to the feminine side of money and peacefully create abundant wealth. Her passion is to raise the abundance vibration for women, so they step into their power and change the world. Learn more about Kathryn at www.EmpoweredWay.com. Join her email list and receive the Money Mindset Meditation that helps you connect to your creative manifestation power.

**Rina Escalante**: is a first-generation Salvadorian-American. Her first language was Spanish, and she is proud to be from the San Francisco Mission District. Rina is a grandmother of five and a multiple stroke and cancer survivor. She had an accomplished professional life and was an involved community volunteer. She coached youth soccer, was a catechist, a Lector, created a mentorship program at an at-risk high school that gave teens the inspiration to go to college, donated time at the Boys and Girls Club, and used to speak to women re-entering the workforce. She loves her San Francisco Giants and is a first-time author. Contact: rinaesca@gmail.com

**Corey Feist:** is a DJ, musician, and producer who has performed all over the Pacific Northwest. His vision for the world is to have everyone on the dance floor with no one and nothing left out. You can find out about Corey or contact him at: www.CoreyFeist.com.

**Beverly Fells Jones**: "The Silver Fox of Consciousness™," is an internationally-known author, speaker, and hypnotist on the topics of memory, empowerment, leadership, and success. Beverly gets to the cause of issues quickly, which enables her clients to realize real change. As a master of peeling away the layers of limiting thoughts that keep a person in mental poverty, Beverly's clients experience more abundance, create magnificent relationships, and live with a lot less stress. If you've wanted to live your dream easily and effortlessly, or to request Ms. Jones as a speaker, email her at: beverly@CommandingYourLife.com or call 484-809-9017.

**Kelly Fisher-Brubacher**: is a core French teacher in northern Ontario. She has spent 20 years in the education system, with a focus on inspiring children to love learning to speak French. She is also an avid equestrian with a passion for all research that is equine-related. Kelly enjoys playing ukulele and singing, as well as regularly attending church. She lives by the premise that God is always listening—all we have to do is trust and ask. You can reach Kelly at: jkbrub@gmail.com.

**Anne Foster Angelou**: lover of life, singer, and performer, lover of cats and the earth, curious woman always open to learning and new experiences, quick thinker, always enjoying laughter as a healer. Born in Atlantic City, NJ, 1943. Sacred Heart Academy, class of 1960. University of South Florida member of the Charter Class at age 16. Enrolled 1960-1963. B.A. University of Washington in "The Art of Performance," 1973. Daytime employment 48 years before retirement; professional chorister at Seattle Opera at night for 20 years. Professional paid singer until 2012. Still singing! fosterangelou@comcast.net

**Crystal Frame**: In addition to driving monster trucks, Crystal Frame is an LA-based writer, a triple-blind tested LWISSD certified advanced psychic medium, and a transformational healer whose vision is to awaken people to their infinite nature so they can manifest the life of their dreams. Whether you are seeking compassionate life coaching or would like to connect with a loved one in spirit, Crystal is here as your personal growth advocate. When she isn't empowering others, you can find this empathic soul salsa dancing or spending quality time with Dudley, the wonder beagle. To find out more, visit her official website at: www.mediumcrystalframe.com.

**Jami Fuller:** is an advanced angelic healer, Reiki master/teacher, medium, and intuitive coach. She helps people to heal themselves and realize their true potential through Emotional Mastery and law of attraction (LOA) principles. Her passion is helping others heal themselves. You can reach Jami at: visionsoflightsoulhealing@gmail.com.

**Karen Gabler**: is an attorney, intuitive coach, and psychic medium. She is also a published author and inspirational speaker. Karen is passionate about encouraging others to live their best lives. She provides clients with intuitive guidance regarding personal and business questions, facilitates connections with their loved ones in spirit, and conducts workshops on a variety of spiritual and personal development topics. Karen earned her Bachelor of Science in psychology and her Juris Doctorate from the University of Hawaii. She enjoys reading, horseback riding, and spending time with her husband and two children. You can find Karen at www.karengabler.com.

**Sarah Gabler:** is 13 years old and is in the eighth grade. She loves playing with her family and traveling to new places. She enjoys acting, singing, dancing, and horseback riding. When she grows up, she intends to be a motivational speaker or work in fashion design. She loves empowering people, even if they don't reciprocate! She began exploring spiritual teachings and soul empowerment concepts when she was ten years old and believes it has made her a better person today. It also has motivated her to find ways to help others on their journey to live their best lives.

**Jaime Lee Garcia:** has been a certified law of attraction practitioner, through the Global Sciences Foundation, since 2015. She loves to inspire others through inspirational blogs and writing, has a passion for seeing people truly happy, and aspires to teach others the law of attraction principles, which helped manifest great things into her life. You can reach Jaime by email at: secretwayoflife@yahoo.com or on Facebook @secretwayoflife.

**Roxane Gaudet:** is a life-long student of anything spiritual, natural, and/or out of the ordinary. Lessons learned have mostly been used for self and family up until now. Roxy is working hard to bring her healing modalities to everyone, so they too may experience self-love. Indian head massage, rejuvenating facial massage, Reiki II, crystal use, precious stone jewelry, essential oils, and soon to come, reflexology! Reach her at roxane.gauds@outlook.com or 705-498-7539.

**Jae Hart:** lives in Scottsdale, Arizona, with her two sons. She earned her certification in hypnotherapy from the Southwest Institute of Healing Arts in 2001. Since then, she continues taking classes and attending seminars to further her education. Jae currently uses hypnosis, EFT, and Reiki to help her clients achieve their personal goals. Her main focus is to encourage people to embrace compassion and forgiveness for themselves and others so they may ultimately love themselves fully. To receive a free gift, visit Jae's website, RisingHart.com, and email her with the code "101 Manifestations."

**Rev. Dr. Debbie Helsel, DDMS**: is a Heart 2 Heart Healing and Heart 2 Heart Connections practitioner. While additionally trained in Reiki, reconnective healing, SRT, and rose alchemy, crystals, flower essences, and essential oils additionally compliment her work with her guides and angels. She holds a DDMS through the ADL Ministry and studies with the Center for Healing in Orlando. Debbie is the executive director at Back to Nature Wildlife Refuge in Orlando, Florida. Since 1990, Debbie has dedicated her life as a federal and state licensed wildlife rehabilitator educating and caring for injured and orphaned wildlife. BTNdebbie@gmail.com. www.BTNwildlife.org

**Dr. Vicki L. High:** is an international, multiple best-selling author, life coach, counselor, speaker, founder of Heart 2 Heart Healing, Reiki Master Teacher, and former mayor. Her books include *Heart 2 Heart Connections: Miracles All Around Us,* and is a contributing author to *When I Rise, I Thrive, Healer, Life Coach, Inspirations, When Angels Speak,* and *Holistic.* Dr. High boldly journeys into frontiers of healing, counseling, empowerment, and spirituality. Dr. High connects ideas and concepts, creating patterns for coaching and healing. She encourages people to live their purpose authentically and courageously. You can contact Dr. High at Vhigh4444@aol.com; www.heart2heartconnections.us; www.empowereddreams.com; and on Facebook at @heart2heartprograms; @ce2oinc; @stoptraumadrama; @kalmingkids; and @empowereddreams.

**Lisa Holm:** As an intuitive guide, spiritual life coach, medium, teacher, and author, Lisa has been empowering clients across the U.S. and internationally through classes, clairvoyant counseling, intuitive readings, mediumship, animal communication, and spiritual healing since 2002. Lisa has studied with medical intuitive, Tina Zion, Hay House author and psychic medium, John Holland, and the Church of Religious Science. Lisa also teaches intuitive development, animal communication, and mediumship mentoring. It is her joy to help clients get clarity and find their joy as well. Phone: 360-786-8617. Website: lisaholm-psychic.com. Email: lisa@lisaholm-psychic.com.

**Caitlin Hurley-Jenkins:** is a Virginian, currently living in Arizona with her two sons and a dog named Miracle.

**Rosemary Hurwitz:** is passionate about an inner-directed life, and she found the focus for it in the Enneagram. The Enneagram is a personality-to-higher-consciousness paradigm trusted worldwide. Since 2002 she has taught, coached, and written for emotional wellness and deeper spiritual connection internationally. Rosemary has certifications in the Enneagram, intuition, and angel card reading, and uses these wisdom traditions in her work. For twenty-five years, along with her husband, Dale, she gave Discovery Weekends for engaged couples, patterned after Marriage Encounter. An accredited professional of the International Enneagram Association, Rosemary's 2019 bestseller, *Who You Are Meant To Be, The Enneagram Effect*, and nine inspirational books, including *When Angels Speak* and *Manifestations* are available on Amazon. www.spiritdrivenliving.com

**Foxye Jackson:** is a forensic nurse, Reiki master, transitions coach, intuitive reader, and community advocate. With Foxye's *I Speak*, she helps individuals heal from the traumas of sexual assault, domestic violence, and mental abuse, through a monthly support group, Butterfly Warriors Retreat, and Chrysalis Day Camp. She also uses Reiki and her gift as an intuitive reader to assist others going through various life transitions, relationships, and healing. This all fulfills her purpose as a healer of souls. You can reach Foxye at peacewithfoxye@gmail.com, on Facebook at: facebook.com/groups/ispeakfoxye, or Instagram @ispeakfoxye.

**Carmen Jelly Weiss:** is a registered psychotherapist with a master's degree in counseling psychology. She works with people to heal complex trauma, depression, anxiety, grief, addictions, and many other life wounds. She brings over 25 years of experience to her private practice: New Perceptions. In collaboration with Natalie Lebel and Suzanne Rochon, Imagine New Perceptions on Being Human creates WER3 podcasts and therapeutic groups experiences. Connect with Carmen at carmen.jelly@newperceptions.ca or www.newperceptions.ca.

**Debra Kahnen:** is a registered nurse and naturopath. In recent years, she has done research to help chronic pain patients and nurses deal with stress using mindfulness. She has presented her research nationally and internationally. As a column editor for a professional nursing journal, she wrote about healthy practice environments and resilience. She is the author of *The Power of Clarity: What to do Today to Create Tomorrows You Love*, available on Kindle. As a Theta Healing practitioner, she assists individuals in healing. She can be reached at debrakahnen.com.

**Susan Marie Kelley:** a freelance writer, began a spiritual journey twenty years ago when her spirit guides began speaking audibly to her through her husband, Dave. Her first book, *Spirits in the Living Room*, is a humorous and heartfelt memoir. Her second book, *Ravens in the Back Yard*, explains how Susan learned to use the magnificent universal laws to create and manifest her heart's desires. Susan has also contributed to *Inspirations*—a compilation of 101 articles that guide the reader through personal stories to overcome the challenges we all face. Susan holds metaphysical workshops and blogs regularly to help others on their journey. You can reach Susan at https://susanmariekelley.com.

**Donna Kiel:** Donna Kiel has dedicated her life to helping others live their lives with truth and courage. As a school counselor, principal, professor, life coach, and author, Donna has inspired hundreds to find their purpose and live without fear and within their truth. Donna shares her deep gratitude to those who have ignited her own unique purpose and passion and who are her consistently her source of inspiration, most especially her granddaughter Charlotte, daughter, Courtney, son Karl, and all her students, colleagues, and clients. In her words, "In all our lives there are moments when we feel hopeless. It is a connection with a loving and open heart that turns hopelessness to triumphant truth and love. I thank all those who have invited me to transform their hopelessness and I especially thank those who have given me the same." Donna offers all those in search of a confident and purposeful life and a successful career the practical tools through her workshops and individual coaching. Donna can be reached at drdonnakiel@gmail.com.

**Amy King:** is a certified life coach and owner of Your Phenomenal Life, LLC. Amy's greatest joy is using her experience as a teacher and the personal challenges that she has overcome to help people move past their personal blocks to becoming empowered to live the phenomenal life of their dreams. You can reach Amy King by text or phone at (916) 975-3017.

**Becki Koon:** is a heart-based intuitive life coach, HeartMath coach, Reiki master, author, and speaker. Through her business, Step Stone, Becki empowers people to activate, energize, and catalyze healing energy, reduce stress and take charge of their life through remembering their divine essence. Because she raised a uniquely gifted yet challenging and labeled child, Becki explored alternative healing practices. She is a multi-faceted holistic healing practitioner with a passion for sharing energy awareness with those seeking a new way to experience their realities. Reach Becki at www.facebook.com/becki.koon.consulting, or www.beckikoon.com stepstone2you@gmail.com,

**Barbara Larrabee**: has had success in several fields, and has also founded a multi-million-dollar direct sales company. She has a diploma in personal nutrition from Shaw Academy, is certified as a longevity wellness specialist, and is an ambassador for the Dallas Holistic Chamber of Commerce. Always wanting to uplift others, Barbara is a global sales leader in the network marketing profession. She is passionate about educating people on wellness solutions that may be outside the box of traditional western medicine thought. This includes ways to influence genes, DNA, and how we age. You can reach Barbara at Your-Longevity-Coach.com, barbara@your-longevity-coach.com, Facebook.com/barbaralarrabee.5.

**Christina Lawler:** is a licensed professional counselor, writer, lover, mother, friend, compass. She lives in Connecticut with her wife and three teenagers, with baby and foster children on the way. She specializes in attachment, blending family, trauma work, vulnerable open processing, the art of story, and radical acceptance for who/where we are, and working with the LGBT+ population. She wants to thank her children, her wife Courtney, and Elizabeth Gilbert for being her spirit animals and making her a consistently better human. Her mission is simple: she wants to give to others the nurturing and care she always wanted to receive. Koenigfamilytherapy@gmail.com, 203-623-4373. www.theemotionalalchemist.org, www.koenigfamilytherapy.com,

**Kenneth I Laws II:** has been on a spiritual path after a series of life-altering events in 2013. Kenneth has spent his time trying to understand the unexplainable, his awakening. Through his search for answers, he has come to understand the true meaning of "oneness," as well as divine events designed to elevate the mind above the ego-driven, fear-based life. Kenneth has come to accept that part of his mission is to write about love, forgiveness, and kindness. His first book, *365 Goodness Abounds*, in which he is a contributing author, was only the beginning. His newest contribution can be found in the book, *Inspirations, 101 Uplifting Stories for Daily Happiness*.

**Natalie Lebel**: is a registered psychotherapist in Ontario, Canada. Natalie has been providing psychotherapeutic interventions to individuals, couples, and families for ten years. Her passion is helping individuals learn to increase their ability to balance acceptance with change in their journey from wounds to wellness. Natalie is also part of WeR3, creators of the podcast series *Stories From Within*. Learn more and contact Natalie at: www.beinghumanpsychotherapy.ca, 705-471-2056 natalielebel@beinghumanpsychotherapy

**Rhonda Lee, MAEd**: is the creator of Spirit Mist Smokeless Smudge, a Reiki master, and a Laughter Yoga leader. As a keynote speaker, she has delivered programs concentrating on stress release, healthy living concepts, and the power of laughter as a healing tool from NYC to LA. One of Rhonda's many passions is teaching others to feel empowered by taking control of their personal and surrounding energies through various modalities. She enjoys deep laughter, too many gemstones, endless adventure with family, and is completely owned by her 3 spoiled rotten fur children Buddha, Scarlett, and Oliver. Find out more: www.infusionoflife.com

**Stephanie Levy:** is a writer and artist who creates porcelain jewelry and sculpture. She and her husband became innkeepers when they bought a bed and breakfast across the street from their house in upstate New York. The stories of their struggles and their interesting guests just "fell into her lap," and she's finishing a memoir of the eight years they operated the bed and breakfast. She now lives in Santa Fe, New Mexico. Stephanie can be reached at www.cestlevy.com.

**Donna Lipman**: is a master certified presentation skills trainer. She works with individuals and groups in the corporate, education, and non-profit sectors who are ready to step into the spotlight as a powerful speaker. Regardless of your vision for growth as a student, community leader, technologist, teacher, or business manager, Donna's coaching techniques help you find that passion, clarity, and confidence to bring your best forward. Her mission is to create a safe space in which you can boldly step into the full self-expression of yourself. You can reach Donna at www.donnalipman.com, donna@donnalipman.com, or 512 784-4519.

**Amanda Long**: is an educator who has taught public school and university. She recently completed her master's in educational leadership through Simon Fraser University in Vancouver, B.C. She loves teaching, mentoring, and collaborating with others. Her passion is education, and she hopes to engage and inspire people to keep learning and pursue their dreams no matter how difficult they seem. You can find Amanda on twitter @MsAmandaLong or email her at msamandalong@gmail.com.

**Kit Cabaniss-Macy**: is a holistic healer, with a master's degree in acupuncture and Oriental medicine. She works with individuals who seek a better quality of life for themselves and their environment. Her passion is vibrational healing and energy medicine.
Her mission is to 'cure the incurables.' You can email Kit at: dancingdoctor13@gmail.com, or leave a voicemail at 480-251-2800.

**Stef Mann:** is an image coach who specializes in shifting mindsets around self-image, branding, and photography. She loves working with spiritually curious entrepreneurs who want to make a positive impact with their business and in their lives. Her life mantra is "Love Wins," and she spends her days with her husband and Dachshund, showering the world with a little more purple, wandering the forest and the seaside, and living life to the fullest. She is currently writing a novel about love. Learn more at www.violetenergetics.com or find Stef on Facebook and Instagram under Violet Energetics.

**Maria McGonigal**: is a Soul Coaching® master practitioner and trainer, advanced yoga and meditation teacher, sound healer, and international speaker. Maria is a teacher of inter-connectedness, who focuses on bringing different, yet integrated systems together to help you create deep, lasting transformation in your life. Praised for her keen intuition and profound wisdom, she assists you in finding missing pieces, energetic or physical, to connect you with your soul. Maria is a jewel of a teacher, offering profound pearls of wisdom to adorn the crown of your consciousness. You can reach Maria at www.mariamcgonigal.com.

**Rian McGonigal**: is a sound healer, therapist, and trainer. Rian has been developing highly effective methods of administering acoustic sound therapies since 1987. He has worked in public, private, and clinical settings and directed sound therapy departments for major cancer centers. Rian loves getting people started in the field of sound service and healing. He offers a sound healing certification program, available to anyone with a sincere interest, with or without musical training. Rian also enjoys assisting medical and holistic practitioners in incorporating sound therapy into their practices. He can be reached at rian108@cableone.net

**Paula Meyer:** recently retired from a position as events director for a *New York Times* bestselling author. She has more than 30 years' experience as an event/workshop/meeting planner and as a procurement/contracting specialist, and 12 years in author/speaker management. After recently becoming a widow at 54, Paula's goal is to help other widows get back in the game of life and realize there is still so much to learn and love with the time we have left. Paula travels internationally and lives in Washington, Colorado, and Florida. For information on her travels, events, and grief retreats, go to www.gpeventworx.com.

**Kardiia Milan:** represents living in the best interest of our planet + humanity. Our mission is to make our expressions of love and joy become our freedoms through enhancing the love of others. Learn more at kardiia.co. Love + Joy + Freedom

**Meaghan Miller Lopez:** is an artist, best-selling author, and creative advisor who works with art and energetic healing modalities to help people align with who they are and what they are here for. You can find her in the Touchstone Studio, a virtual space in which all are invited to practice living life as a work of art. TouchstoneStudioArt.com | IG @meaghan.miller.lopez. hello@touchstonestudioart.com

**Claudio Morelli:** is an educational leader, consultant, and writer. For over forty years, Claudio has activated his servant heart to teach, mentor, and influence individuals, school districts, organizations, and communities in Canada, China, and in Central East Africa. In the second half of life, Claudio believes that we all have a responsibility to continue to use our God-given gifts to serve. He is using his giftings to exhort and encourage all elders to march boldly in faith and not shy away from their commission to influence, inspire, and lead all generations. You can reach Claudio at www.leadershipisheart.com, dclaudio.morelli@gmail.com, or +1604.366.1155.

**Aerin Morgan:** is an artist, designer, avid world traveler, and animal lover. When she's not working, she can be found climbing Mt. Kilimanjaro, strolling through the markets of Bangkok, or photographing the street dogs of Istanbul. Aerin is currently writing her first full-length book and mapping out her next great adventure. You can join her at www.aerinmorgan.com.

**Dr. Fred Moss:** is a physician committed to altering the conversation about mental health and mental illness. He has been practicing in the mental health industry for 40 years, and has now evolved to being a non-diagnosing psychiatrist/mental health restorative coach. Each and every person shall know that who they are and what they do matters and that their voice is heard. Seeing life from a vantage point that emphasizes that each person is whole and complete, we can then see life's many uncomfortable moments and experiences are simply manifestations of the entire infra-structure of simply being a human being.

**Astrid Navarrete:** is an independent dance choreographer, film writer, and a mental health social media influencer. As a visual artist, she shares her healing journey through short videos and films in hopes to inspire others who relate to her personal story.

**Janet Grace Nelson**: is an award-winning spiritual life coach, inspirational speaker, teacher, and author who inspires people worldwide to listen to their heart's deepest desires, to live with more passion and purpose, and to prosper doing what they love. Janet shares her dynamic and powerful processes to bring about real change as you follow your heart and empower yourself to create a life you love—*now*—this is not a dress rehearsal! You can reach Janet Grace at: www.JanetGraceNelson.com.

**Nicole Newsom-James**: is an educator, designer, and heart-centered realtor. Her studies include healing the body by studying the spirit. She combines both eastern and western philosophies and techniques to remove energetic blocks from her client's lives and environments. Nicole also works with real estate companies to shift the energies of the properties they want to sell. Her passion is to guide her clients through the storms of life via education, designing a supportive environment, and locating their dream home. You may reach Nicole at 918-443-0592 or via her website NewsomJames.com.

**Sophia Olivas:** is co-owner of a cryptocurrency hedge fund and is the co-founder of 1WorldNow Ventures, a non-profit whose focus is women's financial sovereignty. As the CEO of GreyThorn Marketing for over 20 years, Sophia developed a love and expertise for technology and its impact on humanity. She is a United Nations

Association member, a best-selling author, and a global speaker. She is also known as a butterfly chaser, tree climber, kite flyer that cart-wheels barefoot on soft grass, with an infectious wanderlust glow. Connect with Sophia: www.sophiaolivas.com
www.facebook.com/theSophiaOlivas
https://twitter.com/SophiaOlivas
www.linkedin.com/in/sophiaolivas/

**Karen Weigand Oschmann:** is a certified paralegal who lives in Phoenix, Arizona with her husband and their two dogs, Reilly and Ruby. Karen is an avid reader, and also loves horror and superhero movies and binge-watching television. This will be her first published work.

**Josef Peters**: is a novice writer, former carpenter, civil engineering student, and father of two. He has survived many health and life challenges and, through sharing his story, would like to display the benefits of perseverance and determination.

**Kim Purcell:** is a wellness workshop facilitator and self-love coach. Married for 18 years, they have three thriving, teenage children. Kim worked in publishing for 15 years, where she developed her passion for nutrition. Diagnosed with Crohn's/Colitis, Kim healed herself through food and nutrition. Her passion for healing her body is rivaled only by her passion for healing her whole soul self. For the past five years, Kim has been working with women and teen girls on their journeys toward mind, body, and spiritual wellness in Ponte Vedra Beach, Florida. She loves to help in any way she can. To reach her, find her at www.facebook.com/thrivetribekp, or email agehealthier@gmail.com.

**Grace Redman:** owns and manages one of the most successful employment agencies in the San Francisco Bay Area for the past 20 years. She is also a success and transformational coach who helps guide others to diminish their negative mental chatter and create the lives they have been dreaming of. If you are interested in learning more about Grace and scheduling a call to see how she can guide you to diminish your negative mental chatter and create a life you love, please visit her at www.daretoachieve.com and submit a request to connect with her. You can also reach her at grace@daretoachieve.com.

**Suzanne Rochon:** is the creator of Imagine Life Solutions Counseling and Psychotherapy. As a registered social worker, she is in awe of the resiliency of the human spirit. With a certificate in holistic health practices, she is able to blend eastern and western approaches in her practice. In collaboration with two psychotherapists, WeR3, *Stories from Within*, and Imagine New Perceptions on Being Human were created. Together, they offer groups, podcasts, and retreats using the therapeutic framework of raw, risky, and real. Follow Imagine New Perceptions on Being Human on Facebook and iTunes. You can reach Suzanne at www.imaginelifesolutions

**Julia Ross**: is a professional artist, inspired to create works of art that give back. Each art series is created for the purpose of inspiring others and providing a channel for the education of causes. You can reach Julia Ross at JuliaRossArt.com, and Artist@JuliaRossArt.com.

**GG Rush:** is a perpetual student and seeker of knowledge, experience, and enlightenment. She is a Wayfinder life coach in-training. She attended Martha Beck's African Star Program at Londolozi Game Reserve in South Africa. She is certified Reiki II, studies aromatherapy, and is learning the ancient art of pulse reading. She has traveled the world solo, and is currently working on a book about her journeys and self-discovery. GG, aka Gail Rush Gould, resides in Cary, North Carolina, with her cat Bella. ggrush1@gmail.com

**April Sanchez:** is an empowering life coach, Reiki master, and an inspirational speaker. She assists her clients by meeting them where they are on their journey, finding clarity with what is holding them back, and supporting them as they move forward into living their best lives. She has made it her life's mission to help others rediscover their truth, speak their truth, and live every day in the expression of who they truly are. You can reach April Sanchez at www.Innercompasslifecoaching.com, call or text (480) 888-4784, and via email at april@innercompasslifecoaching.com.

**Dr. Carra S. Sergeant, LPC-S** is a Licensed Professional Counselor and a Certified Clinical Hypnotherapist. Events in life can leave you shattered and scattered, and Dr. Sergeant is dedicated to helping individuals reclaim and reframe their life. She is particularly passionate about trauma work and anxiety disorders. She works with teens, adults, couples, and families. Her private practice, Peace from Pieces Counseling Center, is located in Lake Charles, Louisiana. For details on all the services provided by Dr. Sergeant, check out her website at peacefrompieces.net. You can reach out to her at peacefrmpieces@gmail.com.

**Felicia Shaviri**: is a former correctional deputy turned trans-formational coach, inspirational speaker, and best-selling author. Felicia believes every person can turn their life around regardless of the circumstances, "I stand fast with an unbending belief that there is always an opportunity to learn and grow with every experience." Felicia has an incredible ability to connect with troubled teens and women, and has helped countless clients through her one-on-one, group coaching, and wellness retreats. Contact Felicia at: feliciashaviri.com.

**YuSon Shin**: is a master healer, psychic medium, author, and international teacher of the healing and intuitive arts. She helps animals and people heal themselves using the Bengston Energy Healing Method. She also uses past life, karma, and ancestral clearing techniques utilizing the Akashic records and Chinese energy healing. In addition, she is also a practitioner of Reiki (Usui,

Archangel & Kundalini), Integrated Energy Therapy, 5th Dimensional Quantum Healing, Quantum Touch, DNA Theta, and Access Bars. Her passion is helping people awaken their spiritual gifts and superpowers. You can reach YuSon at: YuSon@ShinHealingArts.com and get more information at www.ShinHealingArts.com.

**Terry Om:** lives with her daughter in Phoenix, Arizona, and her sons attend college out of state. She is currently a high school teacher at a public, all-girls, Title 1 charter school in downtown Phoenix. Terry finds it rewarding to help her students cope with living in poverty, along with other struggles. She enjoys singing, playing piano and guitar, and hiking. Her spirituality is an extremely important part of her life, and she has merged music with manifestation for the majority of her life. Her Buddhist, Korean mother and her astrology-loving father gave Terry her spiritual foundation.

**Josie Smith:** refers to herself as the unapologetic girlfriend everyone should have! She is a thought leader who coaches and trains people to live courageously curious and bold, while having fun living a life they love. Josie has been affectionately referred to as a miracle worker/ manifestation queen! She lives up to this title by constantly becoming a student of self-transformation herself. Josie has been involved in self-transformation for the past ten years, and she dedicates her life to constant growth to be of better use to her community. You can reach Josie at JosieSSmith@gmail.com.

**Alica Souza:** is the mother of four children Makayla, Izaya, Mason, and Uriah. She is currently a bank employee. Her passion is to share her story with others to help find hope and inspiration in their lives. She is in the process of utilizing her intuitive gifts to share with the world. You can reach Alica at alica0911@icloud.com.

**David Stevens:** is an intuitive energy healer and teacher, as well as the founder of Yoga of the Mind. He helps people deeply explore heartfelt desires through stretching, strengthening, and balancing all aspects of their inner being, aka, the Mind. Applying these discoveries results in clients enjoying life more, as well as improving their relationships, career, finances, and health. He can be reached at ww.YogaoftheMind.com.

**Janice Story:** brings over thirty years of expert horsemanship into her work as an equine coach. She is a gifted certified Reiki master/teacher, mind/body/spirit practitioner, and a published author and speaker. Janice's compassionate and gentle spirit provides safety for others. She has a strong connection with her team of horses, who have always been a big part of her healing. With the presence and unspoken language of her horses, together, they help create an opening for healing and transformation to occur in ways beyond that of human contact alone. Connect with Janice at: janicestory.com or janice.story@me.com.

**Erin Talbot:** is an Aboriginal resource teacher in British Columbia, Canada. She assists teachers with incorporating indigenous content and perspectives into their curriculum. She is a passionate advocate for youth in care and aging out of the foster care system. You can reach Erin Talbot at talbote812@gmail.com. Dedicated to my social worker Jeff Kizuk, and to my chosen mama, Cheryl Vatne.

**Dr. Lisa Thompson, Ph.D.:** is a scientist, award-winning interior designer, and life/love/soul coach specializing in past life regression therapy and human design. She works with clients to create environments that support them physically, emotionally, and spiritually, to release limitations, and to access self-love, worthiness, and inner wisdom. She is the bestselling author of *Sacred Soul Love: Manifesting True Love and Happiness by Revealing and Healing Blockages and Limitations* and *Sacred Soul Spaces: Designing Your Personal Oasis*. She is a contributing author of the international bestseller *Inspirations: 101 Uplifting Stories for Daily Happiness.* You can reach Lisa via her website at www.MysticManta.com.

**Katie Tryba:** is a graduate student finishing her master's to be a mental health counselor. Her background includes teaching special education and facilitating at a day treatment for children and adolescents with severe mental illness. She is passionate about helping others heal. You can reach Katie at: tryba.katie+book@gmail.com.

**Chantalle Ullett:** is a licensed massage therapist who specializes in treating the body, mind, and spirit utilizing a variety of modalities that include Linking Awareness, which creates heart-to-heart connections with other sentient beings, and the Bodytalk System, which addresses the whole person. She has traveled the world working with sentient beings of all kinds and has experienced deep, transformational healings with animals such as horses, cats, dogs, orangutans, elephants, and dolphins to name a few. Chantalle is a French Canadian residing in McHenry, Illinois, with her husband Jim and two daughters, where she practices her therapy and continues her lifelong healing journey. She can be reached at chantalleullett@gmail.com.

**JamieLynn** is a three-time best-selling author, a public speaker, mother of two, and CEO of Arise Empowered, LLC. Having endured sexual assault as a child, JamieLynn spent over ten years working on personal development and leadership training, transforming her life from survivor to thriver. JamieLynn delivered a talk on thriving after sexual abuse at DEBx Tempe. JamieLynn hosts Awareness Talks, the Empowerment Program, and the Breakthrough & Thrive Summit. JamieLynn makes a difference for others and has chosen to lead others in finding their path to healing. To book her for speaking engagements: 715-600-1926 or JamieLynn.AriseEmpowered@gmail.com .

**Breyen Wee:** is a French Immersion Kindergarten teacher, blogger, and loungewear enthusiast. She lives in Pitt Meadows, British Columbia, with her husband, Jeremy, and daughters, Layla and Madison. Breyen is passionate about helping other moms and teachers find balance in their lives through self-care practices and embracing imperfection. You can read more of her work at www.breyenwee.com and reach her at hello@breyenwee.com.

**Dorothy Welty:** is a community college administrator and teacher. She holds an MS in psychology from Illinois State University. She is passionate about the power of education to change individual lives and the world in which we live. In her free time, Dorothy enjoys meditation, hiking, kayaking, writing, baking, and a variety of other creative pursuits. You can reach Dorothy at dwelty50@gmail.com.

**Blyss Young**: is a mother of three, midwife, entrepreneur, podcaster, yoga instructor, and energy healer from Los Angeles. Most often, you will find her guiding families to utilize the fertile ground for growth and transformation that pregnancy and natural births bring. However, her other passion is empowering individuals to discover and joyously give their gifts in the same way she feels blessed to do every day. Contact Blyss at birthingblyss.com or on social media at Birthingblyssmidwifery.

**Marci Zeisel Rosenberg** is an urban planning consultant. She helps property owners and their design consultants prepare plans, negotiate solutions with local neighborhoods, and navigate the land development approval process. Her mission is to promote public policies and programs that reduce homelessness, facilitate the creation of affordable housing, strong neighborhoods, and healthy communities. Marci can be reached
at MarciZRosenberg@gmail.com.

Final Thoughts From The Publisher

It has been a true honor to work with the authors in this and all our other incredible books. At As You Wish we help authors avoid recjection, your words are our passion.

**Visit us at**

www.asyouwishpublishing.com

We are always looking for new and seasoned authors to be part of our collaborative books as well as solo books.

If you would like to write your own book please reach out to Kyra Schaefer at kyra@asyouwishpublishing.

**Recently Released**

Happy Thoughts Playbook

When I Rise, I Thrive

Healer: 22 Expert Healers Share Their Wisdom To Help You Transform

Life Coach: 22 Expert Coaches Help You Navigate Life Challenges To Achieve Your Goals

Selling Emotionally Transformative Services By Todd Schaefer

The Nudge: Life Is Calling, Wake Up by Felicia Shaviri

**Upcoming Projects**

Holistic: 22 Expert Holistic Pracitioners Help You Heal In A New Way

When Angels Speak: 22 Angel Practitioners Help Connect You To The Wisdom Of The Angels

Made in the USA
Coppell, TX
17 January 2020